THE GREAT DECEPTION

A **FALLEN NATION**, AND A **WEEPING PROPHET**

MICHAEL CHOREY

The Great Deception
Author: Michael Chorey

Publication Date: September 2023 January 2024 Update
ISBN: 978-1-945423-59-8
Published by Five Stones Publishing, a division of
The International Localization Network.

© 2023/2024 by Michael Chorey. All rights reserved. No part of this publication may be reproduced, distributed, or transmitted in any form or by any means, including photocopying, recording, or other electronic or mechanical methods, without the prior written permission of the author or the publisher, except in the case of brief quotations embodied in critical reviews and certain other noncommercial uses permitted by copyright law.

All Scripture quotations in this book are taken from the King James Version of the Bible.

Publisher Contact:
Randall Johnson
Email: randyjohnson@ilncenter.com

For the Author:
JOSHUA REVOLUTION
PO Box 923
Grand Island, New York 14072
Phone: 716.229.8000 / 1.888.444.2920
Email: info@joshuarevolution.org
Website: www.joshuarevolution.org

Contents

A SPECIAL THANK YOU 4

A FALLEN NATION AND A WEEPING PROPHET 5

2020 VISION 8

AMERICA THE MODERN ANCIENT ISRAEL 17

BABYLON IS ALIVE AND WELL 33

THE DOWNFALL OF AMERICA 54

IT'S TIME TO CONNECT THE DOTS 79

FALSE PROPHETS IN THE LAND 92

THE APOSTATE CHURCH 103

WOLVES IN SHEEP'S CLOTHING 143

FIGHTING THE WRONG BATTLE 153

GOD IS OUR ONLY HOPE 175

THE REMOVAL OF THE HEDGE 188

THE WEEPING PROPHET 205

BARABBAS OR JESUS...WHOM DO YOU WANT? 215

ISRAEL'S GLORIOUS FUTURE 230

A SPECIAL THANK YOU

I want to offer a special thank you to the School of Joshua (SOJ), which is the Bible School of Joshua Revolution. To all the students who attended our classes on the book of Jeremiah, thank you for providing me a platform to teach on one of the greatest prophets who ever lived.

Back in 2020, during all the confusion regarding the epidemic of COVID 19, I believe the Lord spoke to my heart and told me to read and study the book of Jeremiah. As I did, I believe the Holy Spirit began to show me the similarities between ancient Israel and America today.

On the last night of our class on the book of Jeremiah I was pulling into the parking lot of our church, when I noticed a huge rainbow over our church. It was an amazing sight and I believe it was a confirmation from God that what I had been studying and teaching on for several months in our church needed to be shown to a bigger audience.

Also, on that same night one of the students encouraged me to consider putting the key revelations from our class into a book for many more to read. I felt that the dear sister's encouragement was in fact from the Holy Spirit; thus, **"The Great Deception"** was written.

So, I want to thank our whole church, CrossRiver Tabernacle, and my personal editors who worked so hard at no pay, to help bring this project to completion. I also want to thank my dear family, particularly my wife Kathy for assisting and allowing me to write this manuscript which took us over three years to complete.

Most of all I want to thank God the Father, my personal Lord and Savior Jesus Christ, and the Holy Spirit for opening my eyes, guiding my heart, and inspiriting my pen to write **THE GREAT DECEPTION!** All the Glory is His for He is the Teacher, and the revealer of Truth.

As this book is distributed it is **MY PRAYER** that what is revealed in this book with help many. However, if it helps only one person and brings them out of deception and into the glorious light of the Gospel then all the hours of study and writing has been worth it, if it is only for ONE.

INTRODUCTION

A FALLEN NATION AND A WEEPING PROPHET

The book of Jeremiah contains one of the most scathing rebukes of the nation of Israel found anywhere in the Word of God. In 629 B.C., God raised up a prophet by the name of Jeremiah to warn and rebuke Israel. The name Jeremiah means "Jehovah is high, Jehovah raises up or launches out." Jeremiah, inspired by the Holy Spirit, is the author of both this book that bears his name and the book of Lamentations.

Jeremiah is respected as one of the greatest prophets who ever lived. When Jesus asked His disciples, *"Whom do men say that I the Son of Man am? And they said, Some, say that You are John the Baptist: some, Elijah; and others, Jeremiah, or one of the Prophets"* (Matthew 16:13-14).

Notice that the people compared Jesus to three great prophets, which by the way is the greatest compliment these men could ever receive. It also reveals the three major aspects of Jesus' ministry:

- Repentance: Just like John the Baptist's message, Jesus' message was one of "repentance."

- Miracles: Jesus performed great miracles as did Elijah the prophet.

- Prophetic Warnings: Jeremiah's warning that judgement was coming to the people if they did not repent, and Jesus' message contained prophetic warnings as well.

Every true ministry led by God should contain these 3 components: (1) repentance (2) miracles, and (3) prophetic warnings.

As a prophet, Jeremiah announced that judgment would come to the people of Israel unless they repented and turned back to God. Unfortunately, no record exists that Jeremiah ever converted a single soul from their sinful waywardness within his 40-year ministry. In fact, Jeremiah's message was not only rejected by the nation of Israel, but he was put in a dungeon and left to die. The truth is Israel tried to shut up this great prophet of God and remove him from society. But God was with this prophet and his message still rings true today, almost 2,600 years later.

What makes the book of Jeremiah so compelling for us today is that the United States of America appears to be a mirror image of ancient Israel. In this book entitled, **"The Great Deception,"** the compelling question is being asked, is America about to experience the same judgment that Israel experienced 2,600 years ago? I personally believe that God has showed me that the book of Jeremiah offers a clear and sobering parallel between ancient Israel and America today. In other words, it looks like history is about to repeat itself and if this is true, then what you are about to read is a dire warning for our nation and the people who live in it.

The LORD called Jeremiah and said, "*I ordained you a prophet unto the nations*" (Jeremiah 1:5). He was not to be just a prophet to Israel, but also to the other nations around Israel. However, Jeremiah is also a prophet who is giving a warning today for America and the nations of the world.

As you read **The Great Deception**, get ready to discover sobering realities, convicting truths, and a spiritual challenge that I believe is from the Spirit of God that must be taken seriously by us all. What you currently know about the events that started in 2020 may look very different after you read this book. I believe there is a message found in the pages of this book that God is sending to you today that Satan, the great deceiver, is trying to keep from you. In my 35 years of ministry, God has never given me anything more challenging, heartbreaking, and confronting to teach or write about than the warnings that are in the book of Jeremiah.

Back in Jeremiah's day, sin was rampant, judgement was immanent, and a holy fear of a sovereign God was non-existent. The message God gave Jeremiah to proclaim was not easy for him to deliver back then nor is it easy for one to deliver today. What you are about to read is not a feel-good message. This is not a message you will hear listening to Joel Osteen and other ear tickling preachers. This is not a feel-good book called "your best life now." Instead, it is a warning, and I believe it is from God who loves us and calls us to return to Him while there is still time left. The Apostle Paul said it this way:

> "*For do I now persuade men, or God? Or do I seek to please men? For if I yet please men, I should not be the Servant of Christ*" (Galatians 1:10).

As you begin to read this book, my prayer is that the Lord will give you His "2020 vision." In the world of ophthalmology 20/20 is considered "perfect vision." May God's gift of discernment replace the deception found in many people in society and churches today. May the warnings of Jeremiah echo in your hearts loud and clear and bring you to your knees as we plead with God to heal our land (II Chronicles 7:14).

Jeremiah was a weeping prophet because his heart was broken for the sins that was in his nation and he knew utter destruction and death was coming to his nation because the people refused to listen to his warnings and repent. Here are the words of the weeping prophet that display his true heart for his nation.

> *"For these things I weep; my eye, my eye runs down with water, because the comforter that should relieve my soul is far from me: my children are desolate, because the enemy prevailed"*
(Lamentations 1:16).

CHAPTER 1

2020 VISION

The Bible warns that in the last days, just before Jesus returns, there will be a great apostasy. The word apostasy is defined as, "a departure from the faith." How does an apostasy happen? By listening to and following seducing spirits and doctrines (teachings) of devils.

According to recent research, today in America (2023) only 20 percent of people attend church weekly, 10 percent almost every week, and 11 percent once a month. The rest of America does not attend church at all or very seldom.
(https://www.statista.com/statistics/245491/church-attendance-of-americans/)

The fact is most of our nation sees no need to worship God, at least not in a local church. This means that they are not hearing the Word of God preached on a Sunday morning unless they find it from other sources, which may not be sound biblical doctrine. Instead of looking to the Bible for answers, most people run to man through media outlets such as television or the internet. They do not see the importance nor understand how to have a personal relationship with Jesus. They in fact look for other things to meet their spiritual or human needs. The results are devastating to them personally and to the moral fiber of our nation.

For those who do attend church, most attend watered-down churches, where they are not hearing the warnings of the Bible. They are not learning the truths of what is going to happen in the last days, which are the literal days we are now in. Sadly, most are hearing modern pastors who don't warn them about the Great Tribulation or teach them about the coming Rapture of the Church. Most people today are ignorant of what the Rapture even is. They don't know that the Lord Jesus is going to descend from heaven very soon and will appear in the sky, that He will lift His true church off the earth before He begins to pour out His wrath on the world.

The result of this watered-down preaching in America has caused many people to look through a tainted biblical lens. They blame and condemn each other instead of praying, seeking God and repenting from their wicked ways. For example, they continually blame liberals and globalists for the COVID-19 virus and the violence that plagues America's cities, but do not realize that what the world and our nation is experiencing is a result of their own sin and rebellion.

The COVID-19 pandemic was a major problem in America and the world, and there are those who are still sick and dying from this virus. For the most part, churches have not recognized that this world-wide pandemic is a result of sin and a biblical end-time pestilence. Why? Because most people in the world and in most churches today are spiritually deceived.

The reported American death toll from COVID-19 as of 2023 is over 900,000 with over six million worldwide. Before the 2020 presidential election, there was a belief that COVID-19 was just a political ploy to remove President Trump from office. Remember that? We were told as soon as the election was over, the virus would go away. When that didn't happen, they blamed it on China, and they even tried to explain it away as an exaggerated hoax. Even though there may have been some validity in what they were saying, the truth of this end-time plague was that it was very real, and it was due to the evil that continued to be sown in our nation and around the world. The Bible tells us that *"God is not mocked: for whatsoever a man sows, that shall he also reap"* (Galatians 6:7).

When you stop and look at where all this illogical and exaggerated thinking comes from, we find that it is from two main sources: the internet and the mainstream media. The internet is filled with conspiracies that come in all shapes and sizes. Most of it is filled with some truth but exaggerated with lies. The truth is, the enemy uses the internet to flood us with lies day after day, and millions of Americans believe these falsehoods. The source of much of this false information is from unsaved people and unsanctified outlets, surprisingly believed by many in the church. These untruths bring fear and confusion to many Christians, not to mention much dread to the world.

During 2020, a bizarre report spread that the Chinese Army was surrounding America and ready to invade our country. Although, this could happen in the not-too-distant future, it was a false report that many believed. There were other false reports that said the U.S. government was preparing to transfer unvaccinated people to concentration camps. For those who believed these lies, fear and anger erupted. Like always, the devil tried to stir people up, and even succeeded with some of those in the Church.

Satan's tactic is to distract the Church and move it away from its true mission.

One way he accomplishes this is by redirecting the Church to fight for its political rights and freedoms instead of concentrating on reaching lost souls for Jesus.

As a preacher once said: "He wouldn't be such a bad devil if he wasn't such a good devil." In other words, Satan is a master at deception. The word devil literally means "deceiver," as his craft is to lie and cause people to be deceived and become blind to the truth of the Gospel. The Bible says, *"In whom the god of this world has blinded the minds of them which believe not, lest the light of the Glorious Gospel of Christ, Who is the Image of God, should shine unto them"* (II Corinthians 4:4).

THE KNOWLEDGE OF GOOD AND EVIL

Today there is a mixture of truth and lies. This is exactly what the devil knows will work as he presents a little bit of truth with a little bit of lies, persuading people to swallow his poisonous deceptions. Remember back in the Garden of Eden, the serpent tempted Adam and Eve to eat from the tree of *"the Knowledge of Good and Evil."* So that tree did not just contain the knowledge of evil, but good as well. It is the mixture of good and evil that deceives us. In fact, the Bible says the tree looked appealing to the eyes of Adam and Eve.

Think about the irony of how most people get information from their "Apple" phones today and eat up everything they learn from it. I believe our Apple phones have become the modern-day Tree of the knowledge of Good and Evil and the serpent is still the one behind tempting us into believing the lies that bring forth sin and death.

My family owns a cute little white Maltese dog named, "Johnny." He is adorable to look at. Unfortunately, Johnny suffers from allergies. The veterinarian prescribed him medicine to help alleviate his itchiness. However, he did not like the prescribed pill and refused to eat it. So, to get The medicine he needed, my wife imbedded the pill into his food and then Johnny ate it. He did not know that he was eating the pill that he hates. This is the same tactic the devil uses to deceive humanity. He disguises the lies by imbedding them into a little bit of truth so there is a mixture of truth and errors. This is the art of counterfeiting.

The year 2020 was a very deceptive year. Many people were led astray with the spread of diabolical thoughts and ideas as COVID-19 contributed to a shutdown of schools, factories, churches, etc. This provided people with more available time at home to surf the internet and tap into very evil and deceiving material. On the internet today, false prophets are a dime-a-dozen as they operate by deceiving spirits and taking aim at many in the church who are biblically illiterate. Instead of people turning to the Bible and the Lord for answers, most run to social media, fake news outlets, and the internet. This is where the Great Deception has gained momentum across our nation.

Daniel the prophet was told by God that in the last days knowledge would increase at a rapid pace. God said to Daniel, *"But you, O Daniel, shut up the words, and seal the Book even to the time of the end: many shall run to and fro, and knowledge shall be increased"* (Daniel 12:4). The truth is that knowledge is at our fingertips and the question must be asked, "what is good and what is evil in the knowledge we are receiving today?" In the chaos of COVID-19 and the conspiracies circulating within and outside the church, I knew that as a pastor of a local church, I needed to provide my congregation and community with truthful answers to the question, "what in the world is going on?"

At the start of the pandemic, I received overwhelming information from people in and out of my church who were surfing the internet daily and finding things that were considered "classified" information. To be honest, it was getting so confusing to me that I wanted to throw my hands up and just scream. I finally went to the Lord and cried out to Him for answers. It was in prayer that God led me to an ancient prophet known as "the weeping prophet." His name was Jeremiah, and he wrote on a scroll about 600 years before Christ, revealing what was about to happen to Israel for their many abominations. Today, that scroll is known as the book of Jeremiah (the 24th book of the Bible) and as I read and studied the book of Jeremiah, I believe the Lord gave me the knowledge and discernment of what was really happening in America.

During the pandemic God began to open my eyes to the racial unrest and political turmoil that was increasing in our nation. I began to receive an understanding and wisdom as to what was really going on in our nation. This is why I am writing this book, to share it with all of you. I believe the Lord gave me His discernment not only for my family and our church family, but also for you and the greater Body of Christ. God said in Jeremiah 33:3, *"Call unto Me, and I will answer you, and show you great and mighty things, which you know not."*

It is here that I want to begin to offer what I believe God revealed to me. It is my prayer that the Lord will show you the truth that can keep you from the great deception that is happening in America and around the world today. By the way, the deception is only going to get greater from here on out.

MY SOURCES TELL ME

During the COVID-19 crisis I kept hearing from a close friend in the Lord say to me, "my sources tell me." In fact, before the 2020 election, this person insisted that their "sources" are never wrong, and that Donald Trump would be re-elected based on what the "elites" wanted. This person said that these "elites," whomever they may be, determine who becomes President of the United States of America and who is not. In other words, they believe every election is rigged.

> *However, there is a verse in Daniel that contradicts this belief. It reads: "Blessed be the Name of God for ever and ever: for wisdom and might are His. And He changes the times and the seasons: He removes kings, and sets up kings: He gives wisdom unto the wise, and knowledge to them who know understanding"*
> (Daniel 2:20-21).

In the above passages, we are given the truth that it is God Himself Who has absolute rulership and control of His creation. He allows and He changes Empires. I personally do not believe the 2020 election was stolen, however if it was stolen, it was by divine providence because God was removing Donald Trump as President. I know this makes some people mad to hear this but if you believe the Word of God than you cannot disagree because God's Word clearly says, *"He removes kings, and sets up kings."*

Obviously, my friend's supposed "never-wrong source" got the election results of 2020 completely wrong. I said to that person after the election, "So, I guess your sources, which you said are never wrong, were in fact wrong this time." I also could not refuse the temptation to point out that "my sources" were telling me something different than their sources and my sources are never wrong. Being surprised with my statement, the person asked me abruptly, "who are your sources?" I said very boldly, "Jeremiah, Ezekiel, Daniel, John, and JESUS to name a few!" The person looked at me with a smile on their face and said, "Those are pretty good sources." Glory to God, yes, they are! Hallelujah and Amen! In fact, you cannot get any better sources than the Bible and Jesus Himself!

PERFECT VISION

Never in my lifetime, nor since the Civil War in 1861, have we seen anything like what happened in America in the year 2020. It was as though God took His hand of protection off this nation and decided that this would become the beginning of the end of our nation as we have known it. Could it be possible that God was starting to open up the eyes of His Bride to show her how close He is to taking away His children from this world and from the Apocalypse? I believe so!

Ophthalmologists specialize in the medical and surgical care of the eyes, and they say that perfect vision is measured as 20/20. I find it intriguing how many prophetic ideologies were swirling around during the year 2020; and in hindsight, we now see that many of these prophesies were lies right from the evil one. However, during that year when such false prophetic ideas were being spewed out left and right, God was also revealing His truth.

I believe the Lord started to open the eyes of His Church in the year 2020 to reveal just how close we are to the Rapture of the Church and the beginning of the Apocalypse. However, it was also in that year when the devil brought in his lies spewing even greater deceptions to the Church and the world. For those who study their Bibles and seek God about what He is doing in these last days, I believe you will see a clearer vision of what in the world is going on and for those who don't, you are going to get caught up believing in the "fake news" and you are going to be deceived. But ultimately one day soon the faithful will see Jesus face-to-face, and then and only then will we truly have perfect vision.

"For now we see through a glass, darkly; but then face to face: now I know in part; but then shall I know even as also I am known" (I Corinthians 13:12).

GOD'S REVELATION

In the book of Amos, a remarkable and interesting verse reads: *"Surely the LORD GOD will do nothing, but He reveals His secret unto His servants the prophets"* (Amos 3:7). This one verse tells us that God first reveals things to His prophetic servants who walk close to Him, so they understand and hear what He is saying and what He is about to do. The Bible says that He reveals **"His secrets to His servants the prophets"** just as we have seen throughout the Old Testament and throughout history. There have been prophets like Isaiah, Jeremiah, Ezekiel, Daniel, Jonah, etc., who warned their nation of the coming judgment before it occurred; giving the people of their day an opportunity to repent before it was too late. God always gives man time to repent before He sends His judgment.

Likewise in the New Testament, we also read about prophets such as John the Baptist, the Apostle Paul, Peter, John the Revelator, and of course the greatest prophet of all, the Lord Jesus Christ. It was Jesus who warned Israel that the Temple would be destroyed and "*There shall not be left here one stone upon another, that shall not be thrown down*" (Matthew 24:2). This prophecy was fulfilled almost 40 years to the day after Jesus gave it.

Amos did not say that God would reveal some of His secrets before He did them, but he said, *"surely the LORD will do nothing"* without revealing it first to those He determines to be His prophets. Some think that the gift of prophecy was available only in Old Testament times or used only up to the time when the final book of the Revelation was given to John. However, I differ with this opinion and believe that the gift of prophecy is still active and current even today. The word prophecy means "a prediction, a miracle of knowledge, a declaration or description or representation of something future, beyond the power of human agency to foresee, discern, or conjecture."

The question is, can one know exactly when the Lord Jesus Christ is coming for His Church? Yes and no, not exactly! How is that for an answer? The truth is God chose to keep this truth a secret as Jesus said, *"But of that day and hour knows no man, not the Angels of Heaven, but My Father only"* (Matthew 24:36).

Several years ago, I realized world events were rapidly moving towards the Rapture of the Church and the beginning of the Great Tribulation. In 2017, I believed the Lord brought my attention to the spelling of President Donald "TRUMP." I felt in my spirit there was a meaning for our nation and the world. The message revealed was that the literal "TRUMP" of God was about to sound.

You may call it a coincidence that the 45th U.S. President's last name happens to be "Trump." But consider that the only time in the Bible when the word "Trumpet" is spelled "T-R-U-M-P" is when the Bible is talking about the Rapture. The Bible refers to the "Last Trump," when Jesus appears in the sky and removes His church and millions of people around the world show up missing (I Corinthians 15:51-52, I Thessalonians 4:13-18).

Also, what was very interesting is Donald Trump's choice for Vice President was a man by the name of Mike Pence. When both of their last names are joined together, it spells "Trumpence." When pronounced, it sounds like you are saying "trumpets." A coincidence? I met a Jewish man once who said "coincidence is the way God stays anonymous."

If you have not noticed (and I am sure you have), Donald Trump's name in the year 2023 has been all over the newspapers, internet, and television almost every day due to the many legal problems he is facing amid running for President again. It all is a little freaky when you stop and think about it.

The events that have transpired in America during the past few years look like a movie trailer of what is about to come to the whole world, that being the Great Apocalypse. Regarding this time in Biblical prophecy, Jesus said, *"For then shall be great tribulation, such as was not since the beginning of the world to this time, no, nor ever shall be"* (Matthew 24:21).

The prophet Ezekiel gave the following warning when the nation of Israel was about to be judged: *"An end is come, the end is come: it watches for you; behold, it is come"* (Ezekiel 7:6). God always shows His secrets to His prophets to warn the people and give them one last chance to repent of their sins and turn to God before it is too late. I believe this is what is happening in America and around the world today. I believe the year 2020 is when God began His final countdown. In appears by world events that God has turned over His hourglass of time and is trying to open the eyes of the spiritually blind before it is too late. Right now, friend, it is very late. In fact, I believe that it is only a few minutes before the strike of midnight.

Most have no vision for God nor any understanding of how soon Jesus will come back. Soon and very soon every man will have to give an account of how they lived their life on earth. Most people have no revelation or belief in a Judgment Day, and therefore they have no fear of God, nor any restraint from living a sinful and rebellious life.

The Apostle John was given the vision of a Great White Throne Judgment, when he saw God sitting on the throne. He then saw the final Judgment, as stated in the book of Revelation: *"And I saw the dead and great, stand before God; and the Books were opened: and another Book was opened, which is the Book of Life: and the dead were Judged out of those things which were written in the Books, according to their works"* (Revelation 20:12).

Many in the church today do not even want to hear what the Bible says about what is to come. Why? Because they love this world more than they love the One that is to come. Through the Prophet Hosea, God said: *"My People are destroyed for lack of knowledge: because you have rejected knowledge, I will reject you, that you shall be no Priest to Me: seeing you have forgotten the Law of your God, I will also forget your children"* (Hosea 4:6).

God wants every child of His to have their eyes opened so that they can see what is really going on. He wants us to have "perfect vision," knowing and understanding His Word. The year 2020 was the year that God wanted to heal the church of its spiritual blindness so that every believer could see how close we are to the Rapture of the Church. The all-important question is, have your eyes been opened? Jesus said, "anoint your eyes with eye salve, that you may see" (Revelation 3:18). The Word of God is the "eye salve" that heals spiritual blindness from THE GREAT DECEPTION!

CHAPTER 2

AMERICA THE MODERN ANCIENT ISRAEL

We are living in the most deceptive time in human history. There is evil all around us and the enemy of our soul is roaming about like a roaring lion seeking to devour whosoever he can capture and pull into his diabolical schemes. Many people are searching for answers and truth, but most are looking for them in all the wrong places.

One of the great blessings and curses of the 21st Century is that we have excessive knowledge at our fingertips. So long ago, the prophet Daniel was told by the Lord that in the last days *"knowledge shall be increased."* Those days are the exact days in which we are living right now, and although it is a blessing to receive knowledge so easily, the unfortunate reality is that most people receive knowledge from the wrong sources. Therefore, their wisdom is skewed because it is built on a foundation of lies.

Most people receive their so-called information and suppose evidence from sources that do not speak truth. They do not seek it from the Person of the Holy Spirit whom the Bible calls the Teacher and the only One Who can lead you into all truth (John 16:13). Even in the church many people spend hours each day searching the internet for information deemed as "classified" evidence from sources that say the media and the government does not want you to know. They say that the mainstream media is "fake news," and their news is the "real news." The truth is most of it if not all of it is "slanted news" or "mixed news." Remember that it is the devil's tactic to CONFUSE you. The truth is the only news that can be counted on as 100 percent factual is the Word of God. Anything that does not line up with the Bible is definitely "fake news."

In the Gospel of Matthew, Jesus said, *"Hear and understand. Not that which goes into the mouth defiles a man; but that which comes out of the mouth, this defiles a man"* (Matthew 15:10-11). Jesus is teaching us that words really do matter and what you hear coming out of a man's mouth will show you where HIS heart is. So, when someone is quick to assault another person's character, beware because that man's heart is not right before God.

Jesus also said:

> *"That which comes out of the man, that defiles the man. For from within, out of the heart of men proceed evil thoughts, adulteries, fornications, murders, thefts, covetousness, wickedness, deceit, lasciviousness, an evil eye, blasphemy, pride, foolishness: All these evil things come from within, and defile the man"*
> (Mark 7:20-23).

In other words, you will know what kind of a person you are dealing with by the fruits in their life. The first step to finding truth is to consider the source of where your knowledge or information is coming from. If you are looking to sinful man to give you the truth of what is happening behind the closed doors in our nation, be ready to be deceived. Stop and ask yourself the question of how a spiritually blind undiscerning person can lead you to the truth? How can someone who does not possess the very foundation of Truth, that being Jesus Christ and Him crucified, lead you into truth?

The answer is, they can't.

Even so-called religious leaders will lead you astray if they are not filled with the Holy Spirit. Jesus said of the religious leaders of His day: "they be blind leaders of the blind," and He said if you follow them, *"both shall fall into the ditch"* (Matthew 15:14).

One must be careful about getting information from sources without knowing the person's heart. I am not saying that you should never listen and receive news from secular outlets, but be careful that you do not get pulled into a spirit that is vicious, controlling, multiplicative, judgmental, deceptive, and angry. Also, do not take what they say as gospel truth unless you have what is referred to as first-hand knowledge, meaning you were there to see it with your own eyes and ears.

A new American pastime is now ripping into the other side, those who don't agree with their ideologies. Throughout our country, we have a hard time discussing our differences with respect and honor. Most people demean and attack people who do not believe what they believe. Every night, our television news networks battle each other as they try to convince viewers of their way of thinking. It is a daily battle for ratings and political advancement. Have you noticed this approach is not working? It only makes the divisions in our nation wider and full of more strife.

SALT & LIGHT

Most Christians today do not realize that God never called the Church to save our society but only to preserve it by being salt and light in a dark world. God has called His church to save people out of this perverse world. As the Bible tells us, evil men and seducers shall wax worse and worse in the last days (II Tim. 3:13). So, it is not going to get better friend, it is only going to get worse as we approach the end of the church age. So, our number-one mission should always be to save souls out from this evil and perverse world.

Ask yourself the question, how can you reach someone for Christ when you call them evil and despicable every day? Hate never leads to love; it just leads to more hate. To reach a sinner, you must love them despite their sinful ways. The apostle Paul said, *"To the weak became I as weak, that I might gain the weak: I am made all things to all men, that I might by all means saved some"* (I Corinthians 9:22). The balancing act is to love those who commit the sin but to not condone the sin. Like the old saying goes, "Hate the sin, but love the sinner."

If I were to teach a course on evangelism, I would use CNN, Fox News, and other networks as the way "not" to reach people. Why do I say this?

Because these networks violate two main principles. Number one they speak with condemnation, ridicule, and mockery towards people who do not believe the same way they do. What we see in America today is a mean spirit behind the news reporting. Number two they harshly disregard and do not consider the opinions of the person who disagrees with their ideals. This shuts the door for any civil dialog that could lead to a change in the heart of the one they differ with.

Remember a person can say the right thing but with the wrong spirit. The Bible tells us to speak the truth in love (Ephesians 4:15) and *"a soft answer turns away wrath: but grievous words stir up anger"* (Proverbs 15:1).

Consider a litmus test on Proverbs 15:1, which was written by the wisest man who ever lived (i.e., King Solomon). Compare it against what you hear from mainstream media, television, social networks, and the internet. Do you ever hear any soft answers given as a response to those who they disagree with? Most often, if not all the time, you hear grievous words that only stir up more anger.

The word *"grievous"* used in Proverbs 15:1, means pain, hurt and toil. It also means the physical pain that a woman experiences in childbirth or the emotional pain caused by inappropriate words. The bottom line is that it matters how something is said to another person. God's truth must be spoken strongly sometimes, even with a strong rebuke that is sharp, but it always must be in love to try to correct a wrong. There should be no intention to hurt or bring pain, but instead to assist a person in being set free from deception.

THE WICKEDNESS OF ISRAEL

The wickedness that occurred across Israel during the time of Jeremiah cost the people everything they owned, their possessions, their freedom, and even their very lives. I fear that if our nation does not come back to God's truth very soon, starting with the Church, the same demise that happened to ancient Israel will also happen to America, which means God will judge our nation. God told Jeremiah to go out and cry into the ears of Jerusalem and say, *"Thus saith the LORD, I remember you, the kindness of your youth, the love of your espousals, when you went after Me in the wilderness, in a land that was not sown"* (Jeremiah 2:2). Israel was called to be holy and set apart unto God. In turn, this would have provided divine protection from their enemies. Every child of God needs to recognize this. If we obey the Lord and walk in holiness through faith in Jesus Christ and Him Crucified, we will be divinely protected.

Through the Prophet, God asked the question,

> *"What iniquity have your fathers found in me, that they are gone far from Me, and have walked after vanity, and are become more vain?"* (Jeremiah 2:5-7).

God is faithful. The mere fact that He wants a close relationship with sinful man is completely amazing. God was so faithful to bring His people into His plenteous land; that being the land of Canaan. However, Israel continued to be unfaithful as pointed out to Jeremiah by God, as the people defiled the land. The kings, priests, prophets, and the entire nation departed from Jehovah God to worship Baal, a false god, which did not spiritually profit them anything. God told Jeremiah that he was to plead with the people to repent and turn back to God.

Every generation and every nation need men of God who will plead with their nation to follow Him and to turn away from sin. In America and Canada today, we have very few preachers who plead with the people to repent and turn back to God. Most preachers do not want to rattle anyone's spiritual cage. Why? Because they don't want to offend the people and risk losing their tithe. They may sound blunt, but it is in most cases true.

THE NATION OF ISRAEL CHANGES THEIR GOD

God asked the question, *"has a nation changed their gods, which are yet no gods? But My people have changed their glory for that which does not profit"* (Jeremiah 2:11). I'm afraid the American Church is making the same mistake that ancient Israel made over 2600 years ago. In fact, in the past 50 years, the United States has been running parallel to ancient Israel. God said that Israel ought to be astonished at what Jeremiah was saying. They ought to be horribly afraid. However, it was business as usual just like it is now in the United States. Why? Because the fear of God is missing in the life of most people.

God told Jeremiah that the people had committed two main evils, *"they have forsaken Me, the fountain of living waters, and hewn themselves cisterns – broken cisterns that can hold no water"* (Jeremiah 2:13). The modern Church in America has done the same thing by denying the Holy Spirit. Because the Holy Spirit has been quenched, the true message of the Cross has been lost or misunderstood. We see very little conviction of sin anymore. Few churches even give altar calls on Sunday mornings anymore, so that people can come forward, repent, and get right with God. There are very few healing miracles seen in these churches. Most do not even receive prayer for healing in a Sunday morning service. Most of our churches have become *"broken cisterns that can hold no water."*

God asked Israel 3 questions: (1) Is Israel a servant? (2) Is he a homeborn slave? (3) Why is he spoiled? (Jeremiah 2:14). Israel was a son, not a slave; yet they were about to become slaves because of their sin and rebellion. They turned away from Jehovah and started worshiping heathenistic gods. Their punishment for this great sin was that they would soon become slaves to a foreign power (i.e., the Babylonians).

The second question God asked Israel was, *"Is he a home-born slave?"* This refers to how animals were created to be free; but if the animals were instead born in a zoo, they would be slaves to their masters. Such was Israel, and such are many of the churches in America and Canada. They have become slaves to sin instead of living free from the stronghold and bondage of sin.

God also asked the question, *"why is he spoiled?"* This refers to Judah, where the people had sinned so often and for so long that there was no longer a fear of God's judgment. The Holy Spirit gave Israel a picture of what was soon to come. Jeremiah said, *"young lions roared upon him, and yelled, and they made his land waste: his cities are burned without inhabitant"* (Jeremiah 2:15). This speaks of what the Babylonian army was going to do to Israel. They were going to burn Jerusalem and take most of the people captive.

Israel's main problem was that they had forsaken the way of the Lord and went the way of the world. I am afraid this same thing could be said of America today! Through the prophet, God said that their own wickedness would convict Israel and their backsliding would reprove them. He said, *"know therefore and see that it is an evil thing and bitter, that you have forsaken the LORD your God, and that My fear is not in you, saith the Lord GOD of Hosts"* (Jeremiah 2:19).

When a nation lacks the fear of God, it backslides, and the people lose their desire to repent from sin (Proverbs 1:7). Instead of fearing God, Israel forgot the Egyptian bondage that they were once in. Now they were about to be put into Babylonian bondage, and why? Because again, they no longer feared God nor the consequences of their sin.

It is always regretful when we fail to remember the hard lessons of life that we have learned from our past. Many of us make the same mistakes that once put us in the place of despair. This treadmill of life is so avoidable, yet our wicked minds somehow think that God will look the other way and not hold us accountable for our sins. We think God is too busy to notice what we are doing or He will just let us slide.

The United States would do well to remember what happened to ancient Israel. God said He planted Israel as a noble vine. This means that their beginning was right and good. But they turned this noble vine into a degenerate plant of a strange vine unto God (Jeremiah 2:21). Please understand that it is not how you begin that matters, but how you finish.

Israel was moving away from where it once was with God, and this was going to prove to be the demise of the nation. Jesus said, *"to whom much is given, much is required"* (Luke 12:48). Simply put, the more God blesses a nation, the more He expects from that nation.

THE GUILT CANNOT BE WASHED AWAY

No matter what Israel tried to do to erase their iniquity, nothing would wash it away. Only the blood of Jesus takes away sin (Isaiah 1:18). Man tries to clean himself up through all sorts of programs and schemes, but nothing will work. The Government will throw millions and millions of dollars into programs of man to try to solve man's problems, but the problem only gets worse. We must understand that there is only one answer for sin, and it is the Cross of Jesus Christ.

Israel was blinded by the spiritual pollution that had been created in their nation. The Prophet Jeremiah pointed to the Valley of Hinnom, which was filled with idolatrous altars. Judah's problem was not that it stopped the worship of Jehovah, but that it added false gods to their true worship. They accepted other types of worship and became a nation of many gods. For the last 50 years or more, this is exactly what has been happening in America.

Former President Barack Obama, while in office declared in a speech that the United States is no longer a Christian nation. Listen to the words of our former president spoken in 2012:

> "Whatever we once were, we are no longer a Christian nation at least, not just. We are also a Jewish nation, a Muslim nation, and a Buddhist nation, and a Hindu nation and a nation of non-believers. And even if we did have only Christians in our midst, if we expelled every non-Christian from the United States of America, whose Christianity would we teach in the schools? Would it be James Dobson's or Al Sharpton's? Which passages of scriptures should guide our public policies? Should we go with Leviticus which suggest slavery is ok and eating shellfish is an abomination? Or we could go with Deuteronomy which suggests stoning your child if he strays from the faith or should we just stick with the Sermon on the Mount? A passage that is so radical that it's doubtful our own defense department could survive its application. (https://www.youtube.com/watch?v=35sGJrWKcmY)

Now if these were the words from some secular professor at a university in America, they would be shocking enough, but these were the words spoken by the 44th President of the United States. President Obama's words are laced with unbelief, doubt, mockery, absolute deception, ignorance, and blasphemy. However, it sums up the type of leadership the people in our country have not only elected but have been following for a long time.

America has not necessarily rejected Christianity but allowed false religions to come alongside our Christian faith. We give false religions and false gods legitimacy, treating them as if they are equal with the Bible. However, they are not equal and the sin of idolatry and the worship to these false religions are straight from the pit of hell and embracing them is exactly what ancient Israel did. God said to Israel long ago that they were *"playing the harlot"* (Ezekiel 16:15) and make no mistake that is the same thing God is saying to America today.

On her nationally syndicated television program, Oprah Winfrey once said that "all roads of religion lead to the same God." This statement could not be any further from the truth.

The Bible declares that:

> "Neither is there salvation in any other: for there is none other name under heaven given among men, whereby we must be saved" but by the Name of Jesus Christ of Nazareth (Acts 4:10, 12). The Bible also says, "For there is one God, and one Mediator between God and men, the Man Christ Jesus" (I Timothy 2:5).

God held Israel to a higher standard compared to the rest of the world, just as He now holds America to a higher standard and Why? Because God gave both nations the responsibility of being light bearers to the world of His Salvation plan. If Israel failed to be faithful to their calling, the world would have no knowledge of the one true God.

Starting with the American Church, if there is an unfaithfulness to God's call and His Word and we play the harlot and worship other gods like Israel did, then inevitably the same judgement that fell on Israel of old will eventually fall on us. If that wasn't true, then God would have to apologize to ancient Israel, and listen friend, God is not about to do that.

God compared Judah to a camel and an ass in mating season, referring to how they run from mate to mate. Likewise, the nation of Israel ran from idol to idol, loving strange gods more than they loved the One True God. How true this is in our nation today. We worship celebrities, sport figures, political leaders, our jobs, our possessions, etc. In essence, we worship created things instead of worshipping the One Who created all things (Romans 1:21-23).

ISRAEL'S IDOLATRY

The blame of Israel's fall must land at the feet of their spiritual leaders. There is a truth that says, "as the church goes, so goes the nation." In the time of Jeremiah, God placed the blame and shame on the leaders in the land of Israel, the Kings, Princes, Priests, and Prophets.

In America today, the blame of our country should be placed first on our leaders who have become the same type of leaders Israel had; they just go by different titles. The titles today are President, Governors, Senators, and Pastors. The leaders of ancient Israel turned their backs on God, and it could be said today that most of the leaders in America have turned their back on the Bible and on God Himself. God said to Israel that when the time of trouble comes, and they cry out to Me and say, "Arise, and save us." But then God said He will say to them, *"But where are your gods that you made for yourself? Let them arise, if they can save you in the time of trouble"* (Jeremiah 2:28).

One of Israel's gods that the people adored and worshiped was their prosperity. They loved their money more than they loved Jehovah. The Bible says, *"For the love of money is the root of all evil"* (I Timothy 6:10). This scripture does not say "some evil," but it says the love of money is the root of "all evil." John the Revelator wrote these words about the last church age: *"Because you say, I am rich, and increased with goods, and have need of nothing; and knowest not that you are wretched, and miserable, and poor, and blind, and naked"* (John 3:17).

The truth is money can never fix the sinful condition of man's soul, but in fact riches most of the time makes man even more wretched. Look at the United States of America, we have been blessed financially more than any other nation of the world, but our nation has become a decadent society for the most part.

PUNISHEMENT IS COMING

The nation of Israel tried to justify themselves before God, but it did not work. God said: *"Wherefore will you plead with Me? You all have transgressed against Me, says the LORD."* (Jeremiah 2:30).

The Lord sent corrective discipline to Judah but to no avail. God said, *"they received no correction,"* meaning that despite Judah's chastisements, they would not be corrected. They killed the prophets who tried to warn them. Their pride would not allow them to be corrected, and God called them a *"destroying lion."* This means that they were out of control and would not repent of their anger. Eventually, their arrogant anger murdered their own Messiah.

In America today, both political parties are like *"destroying lions,"* wanting to devour one another. The anger and hatred across our country's party lines is the worst it has been in 150 years. Most are not willing to be corrected. Their main desire is party dominance. Why? The love of money is at the root of most, except for a few good men. There are only a few today who care about what is best for America, but instead most only care more about what is good for their political party. In essence it is a war between two lions, each striving to be "king of the jungle."

God asked the people of Israel the question, *"O generation, see you the Word of the LORD, Have I been a wilderness unto Israel? a land of darkness?"* In other words, God was asking them, "did I lead you into misery and emptiness?" No, He blessed them with a beautiful, spacious, and prosperous land. But what did they say in return? They said, *"We are lords; we will come no more unto you?"* (Jeremiah 2:31).

Israel's great sin was her independence and the same could be said of America today. It could be said that both nations, then and now, believe that they were and are their own masters and do not need nor want to follow the God Who created them and blessed them.

It could be said that trouble is in store for any nation or people who reach the point of saying, "I got this, I don't need God anymore." Leaders may never openly admit this, but their actions speak louder than their words in that they live a lifestyle that screams, we do not need God, nor do we need to follow His Word or His ways.

Have you noticed that the modern American church rarely has a prayer meeting anymore and has become mostly a prayerless church. The great missionary George Muller once said, "prayerlessness is the church's greatest sin." Why? Because when the church fails to pray, they are in essence saying to God "we got this, and we don't need your help."

Today, most do not attend a prayer meeting except for a few steadfast saints. Most Christians do not see the importance of participating in weekly corporate prayer meetings. They say they are just too busy to attend. Most church folks only attend prayer meetings when they are personally going through troubled times themselves. God said to ancient Israel, *"but in the time of their trouble they will say, Arise, and save us"* (Jeremiah 2:27).

Most Christians today don't understand the power of corporate prayer. Jesus said: *"Again I say unto you, That if two of you shall agree on earth as touching any things that they shall ask, it shall be done for them of My Father which is in Heaven. For where two or three are gathered together in My Name, there am I in the midst of them"* (Matthew 18:20). There indeed is a supernatural power that comes over the church when the saints gather to pray and agree together.

When Peter was put in prison and was about to be executed for his faith the next day, the church called for an all-night prayer meeting for Peter. The Bible says:

> *"Peter therefore was kept in prison: but prayer was made without ceasing of the Church unto God for him. And when Herod would have brought him forth, the same night Peter was sleeping between two soldiers, bound with two chains: and the keepers before the door kept the prison.*
>
> *And, Behold, the Angel of the Lord came upon him, and a light shined in the prison: and he smote Peter on the side, and raised him up, saying, Arise up quickly. And his chains fell off from his hand.*

And the Angel said unto him, Gird yourself, and bind on your sandals, and so he did. And he said unto him, cast your garment about you, and follow me. And he went out, followed him; and wist not that it was true which was done by the Angel; but thought he saw a vision. When they were past the first and the second ward, they came unto the iron gate that leads unto the city; which opened to them of his own accord: and they went out, and passed on through one street; and forthwith the Angel departed from him" (Acts 12:5-10).

Peter was supernaturally freed by the angel because the Church prayed all-night for him. The question should be asked what would have happened if the church didn't call for a corporate prayer meeting for their brother and friend? I think the answer is obvious, Peter's life would have ended. If you ever doubted the power of corporate prayer let the above story encourage you, and revive you to start attending your churches weekly prayer meeting, and if there isn't a weekly prayer meeting at your church, then start one.

A STRIKING PICTURE OF REBUKE

"Can a maid forget her ornaments (i.e., decorations of the house), or a bride her attire (her wedding dress)? Yet my people have forgotten Me days without number" (Jeremiah 2:32).

God created Israel to worship Him. It was to be the number one purpose of who she was and why she was created in the first place. When Israel was in Egyptian bondage, Moses relayed God's message to the Pharoah and told him that God said, "Let My people go." Pharoah's curiosity grew of what Moses and the people would do once they arrived in the wilderness, so he asked him the question, "why should I let them go?" The Bible says: *"And afterward Moses and Aaron went in, and told the Pharoah, Thus says the LORD God of Israel, Let My People go, that they may hold a feast unto Me in the wilderness"* (Exodus 5:1). Jewish feasts were designed and commanded by God to be times of worship for the Jewish nation. So specifically, God wanted the Jews free from Egyptian bondage so that the people could worship and celebrate their God.

So, God delivered the children of Israel from Pharoah's strong hand so that Israel could freely worship Him. But when they received their freedom, they lost their way over time and became a people that they never intended to be. What was that? A nation who no longer worshipped Jehovah as the One True God.

This is exactly what has happened to the United States. We were created as a nation to freely worship the Lord, Jesus Christ. Our nation broke away from Great Britain's Church of England for that very reason; to have religious freedom. Our founding fathers believed in the Bible and wrote the Constitution based on the Word of God. They believed that Jesus was the One True God, and the founding fathers were unashamed to announce that great truth. But today, we allow idols and other gods to take the place of Jesus or to come alongside the one True God. The bottom line is that as a nation, we are no longer who we once were. We are a nation that has fallen from grace.

When former President Barak Obama declared that America was no longer a Christian nation by stating that we are a nation for all religions, he received some outrage from American Christians. However, his statement, although upsetting, had truth in it. Although the United States was not founded on Hinduism, Islam, Judaism, Roman Catholicism or any other false religion or faith for that matter, it had now allowed these false religions to receive equal respect with Christianity. We have forgotten that our country was founded on the truth of Jesus Christ of Nazareth, the One and only True God. The men who wrote our Declaration of Independence believed in the One True God, Jesus Christ. They believed in the Cross, His death, and His Resurrection; and they were not afraid to say so.

Listen to what our founding fathers believed and were willing to openly state:

Patrick Henry: Revolutionary General, Legislator, "The Voice of Liberty," Ratifier of the U.S. Constitution, Governor of Virginia.

> "Being a Christian… is a characteristic which I prize far above all this world has or can boast. The Bible… is a book worth more than all the other books that were ever printed. Righteousness alone can exalt [America] as a nation…Whoever thou art, remember this; and in thy sphere practice virtue thyself, and encourage it in others.

John Jay: President of Congress, Diplomat, Author of the Federalist Papers, Original Chief Justice of the U.S. Supreme Court, Governor of New York.

> Condescend, merciful Father! to grant as far as proper these imperfect petitions, to accept these inadequate thanksgivings, and to pardon whatever of sin hath mingled in them for the sake of Jesus Christ, our blessed Lord and Savior; unto Whom, with

Thee, and the blessed Spirit, ever one God, be rendered all honor and glory, now and forever.

Thomas Jefferson: Signer of the Declaration of Independence, Diplomat, Governor of Virginia, Secretary of State, Third President of the United States.

> The doctrines of Jesus are simple and tend all to the happiness of man. The practice of morality being necessary for the well-being of society, He [God] has taken care to impress its precepts so indelibly on our hearts that they shall not be effaced by the subtleties of our brain. We all agree in the obligation of the moral principles of Jesus and nowhere will they be found delivered in greater purity than in His discourses. I am a Christian in the only sense in which He wished anyone to be sincerely attached to His doctrines in preference to all others. I am a real Christian – that is to say, a disciple of the doctrines of Jesus Christ.

Francis Scott Key: U.S. Attorney for the District of Columbia, Author of the "Star Spangled Banner."

> May I always hear that you are following the guidance of that blessed Spirit that will lead you into all truth, leaning on that Almighty arm that has been extended to deliver you, trusting only in the only Savior, and going on in your way to Him rejoicing.

Benjamin Rush: Signer of the Declaration of Independence, Surgeon General of the Continental Army, Ratifier of the U.S. Constitution, "Father of American Medicine," Treasurer of the U.S. Mint, "Father of Public Schools under the Constitution."

> The Gospel of Jesus Christ prescribes the wisest rules for just conduct in every situation of life. Happy they who are enabled to obey them in all situations!. My only hope of salvation is in the infinite transcendent love of God manifested to the world by the death of His Son upon the Cross. Nothing but His blood will wash away my sins [Acts 22:16]. I rely exclusively upon it. Come, Lord Jesus! Come quickly! [Revelation 22:20]

Roger Sherman: Signer of the Declaration of Independence, Signer of the Constitution, "Master Builder of the Constitution," Judge, Framer of the Bill of Rights. U.S. Senator.

> I believe that there is only one living and true God, existing in three persons, the Father, the Son, and the Holy Ghost, the same in substance, equal in power and glory. That the Scriptures

of the Old and New Testaments are a revelation from God, and a complete rule to direct us how we may glorify and enjoy Him.

Zephaniah Swift: U.S. Congressman, Diplomat, Judge, Author of America's First Legal Text (1795).

Jesus Christ has in the clearest manner inculcated those duties which are productive of the highest moral felicity and consistent with all the innocent enjoyments, to which we are impelled by the dictates of nature. Religion, when fairly considered in its genuine simplicity and uncorrupted state, is the source of endless rapture and delight.

Noah Webster: Revolutionary Soldier, Judge, Legislator, Educator, "School Master to America."

The religion which has introduced civil liberty is the religion of Christ and His apostles... This is genuine Christianity and to this we owe our free constitutions of government. The moral principles and precepts found in the Scriptures ought to form the basis of all our civil constitutions and laws.

All the... evils which men suffer from vice, crime, ambition, injustice, oppression, slavery, and war, proceed from their despising or neglecting the precepts contained in the Bible.

The Christian religion is the most important and one of the first things in which all children under a free government ought to be instructed. No truth is more evident than that the Christian religion must be the basis of any government intended to secure the rights and privileges of a free people.

The Bible is the chief moral cause of all that is good and the best corrector of all that is evil in human society – the best book for regulating the temporal concerns of men.

George Washington: Judge, Member of the Continental Congress, Commander-in-Chief of the Continental Army, President of the Constitutional Convention, First President of the United States, "Father of His Country."

You do well to wish to learn our arts and ways of life, and above all, the religion of Jesus Christ. These will make you a greater and happier people than you are. While we are zealously performing the duties of good citizens and soldiers, we certainly ought not to be inattentive to the higher duties of religion. To the distinguished character of Patriot, it should be our highest glory to add the more distinguished character of Christian. The blessing and protection of Heaven are always necessary *but especially so in times of public distress and danger. The General hopes and trusts that every officer and man will endeavor to live and act as becomes a Christian soldier, defending the de*arest rights and liberties of his country.

Produced by WALLBUILDERS
(www.https://wallbuilders.com/founding-fathers-jesus-christianity-bible/)

HOW FAR AMERICA HAS FALLEN

Does it appear to you that the men who founded the United States were afraid to name Jesus Christ as the one True God and the Bible as being the book in which this nation must follow? The answer is NO! These men clearly knew and understood who formed this country, and they wanted the people to know that it was God, and God alone who blessed this nation.

Do these founding fathers seem open-minded to worship other gods or recognize other faiths as being equal to the True God of Creation when they founded America? The answer again is a definitive NO!

The United States is on the verge of suffering the same fate as Judah and ancient Israel, and its fate will be that our nation will experience the same Judgment arm of God just as Israel did. Why? Because we became an interfaith nation just like Israel of old; today, worshipping many gods.

Most governors of American states do not follow Jesus Christ or the Word of God anymore. Most American pastors are backslidden themselves and continue to give people soothing, watered down Sunday morning messages that make the people feel good. They want the people to feel comfortable as they come to church in casual clothes, even going so far as serving bagels and coffee during services. Few Churches give altar calls anymore providing time for people to repent and get right with God. Consequently, the people leave the same way they came to church; lost, disobedient, lukewarm, and defeated.

A message on the Cross is sparingly preached, possibly heard in a once-a-year Easter message. The rest of the year, sermon messages focus on self-help topics. We no longer preach Jesus, but we preach on the peoples felt needs. We are more interested in prosperity than holiness. Instead of picking up our cross, we pick up the false god of selfishness and follow our own path in life.

Today, most preachers don't teach the message of the Cross for holy living, nor do they call for the repentance of sins. There are few sermons that promote Jesus Christ as the Lord of every area of our lives. When I first got saved, I would frequently hear my pastor say, "if Jesus is not Lord of all, then He is not really Lord at all." This kind of preaching has been lost under the guise of being too judgmental and bringing too much of a "fire-and- brimstone" message. The major problem facing our nation today is compromise. Let me state that again so it sticks in your mind, one of the major problem facing our nation today is compromise.

The false teachers and prophets in our land today are running around and offering soothing words of blessings and saying they have heard from God when they have not. There is little talk about repentance as being the condition for those blessings. It is all being done in the Name of Jesus and these preachers are nothing more than soothsayers. During the days of Israel, there was only a few true prophets, Jeremiah being one, who was trying to call the nation back to God. However, he was ignored, rejected, and even imprisoned for speaking the truth. I guess not much has changed in the past 2,500 years of human history, has it? The Great Deception is on!

CHAPTER 3

BABYLON IS ALIVE AND WELL

From the moment Adam fell in the Garden of Eden until today, it has been Satan's plan for man to rebel against God. He wants the whole world to go against God and to worship him and one day soon to worship his Antichrist who is also referred to in the Bible as the "son of perdition" which means "the son of eternal damnation."

Satan attempted this diabolical plan shortly after the flood of Noah's day. It is stated in Chapter 11 of Genesis, *"And the whole Earth was one language, and of one speech."* With no language barrier, Satan attempted to start a one-world movement where men would join to build a city and a tower to implement false worship (i.e., the zodiac or stars-planetary bodies). This was done as an act of rebellion against God. It has always been Satan's number one goal, to redirect the worship of man from God to something else, mainly himself.

As described in the Bible, Babel was the city where Satan tempted man to build a tower. It was the location where the first organized nationwide rebellion against God took place. It occurred about 100 years following the flood of Noah's day. The city of Babel was ground zero for man to build something together without the help of God. This organized rebellion was the work of Satan, as he was the master planner behind it all back then, and is still the master planner behind what man does without God today.

The name Babylon means "the gates of gods" and can also mean confusion. Today, the ruins of ancient Babylon are in modern-day Iraq. At the very start of the year 2020, the world saw an American military strike that eliminated the number one terrorist who led the revolutionary guard in Iran. His name was General Qasem Soleimani. This strike took place at Baghdad International Airport on Friday, January 3, 2020, inside Iraq and only about 70 miles north of the ancient city of Babylon. I believe that this strike had prophetic overtones as the year 2020 advanced as one of the most revolutionary years of the 21st Century.

Since 2020, the world has witnessed more clearly the plans for a one-world government and one-world religion. This plan is in fact, unfolding faster than the powers behind it could have ever imagined or hoped for.

In the Bible, the prince of the city of Babel was a man named Nimrod and the Bible describes him as *"a mighty hunter"* (Genesis. 10:9). This title has nothing to do with hunting animals, but rather as being one in opposition to the Lord. Some Bible scholars believe that Nimrod literally hunted down and killed people who worshipped Jehovah.

In Bible typology, Nimrod and the city of Babel represents the coming of the Antichrist and the city he will rule. The nation of Babylon (modern day Iraq) has always stood for false religion and false doctrines against the Word of God. In the Book of Revelation, Mystical Babylon is described as the *"Great Whore"* (Revelation 17:1-5). This is all because it is the place of the original rebellion. In fact, the Garden of Eden is believed to have once sat in this vicinity and hell itself is thought to be located there in this same place, beneath the earth, where Adam and Eve first sinned and disobeyed God and sin entered the world. How profound is that if it is indeed true.

THE PLAN OF NIMROD

The plan of Nimrod and the people of that day was to build a great tower in the center of the city that would reach into the heavens (Genesis 11:4), and the project was driven by ego and human ingenuity. The tower was built as a tower of worship to the stars, and it was built out of pride, as stated in the Bible, *"and let us make us a name, lest we be scattered abroad upon the face of the whole Earth"* (Genesis 11:4).

The root of sin is always driven by ego and thoughts of making a name for oneself. Going back to the Garden of Eden, the pride of man is what the serpent used to tempt Adam and Eve. He lied to Adam and Eve and told them that when they ate from the tree that God had forbidden, *"you shall be as gods"* (Genesis 3:5). Satan's tool that he used to tempt them into disobedience against God was pride and this caused them to eat from the tree of the knowledge of good and evil (Genesis 3:5). Satan knew if they disobeyed God it would cause spiritual death and separation between man and God.

Both Adam and Eve took Satan's bait and ate from the forbidden tree, and they fell from God's Grace. When they fell, all of humanity fell with them. This has resulted in all the death, sickness and evil in the world. It can all be traced back to the Garden of Eden in ancient Babylon, or in what is known today as Iraq.

Led by Nimrod, the people of Babylon had evil hearts with no regard for God or His ways. They were rebellious against the true ways of Jehovah and bent on uniting the world together under a one-world system. Even though the people of that time were unaware of what they were being baited into, they worked diligently towards creating a united worship to one god, who would end up being Satan.

Remember that anything worshiped other than the LORD HIMSELF is idolatry. God told Moses, *"You shall have no other gods before Me"* (Exodus 20:3). If God had not intervened by confusing the languages, mankind would have continued in this direction and Satan's goal would have been achieved.

LUCIFER

Some may ask the question, "Where did Satan come from?" The Bible teaches that at an undetermined time, before the creation of man, God created an angel named Lucifer. Initially, Lucifer served the Lord but later fell from grace as stated in Isaiah 14:12, *"How are you fallen from Heaven, O Lucifer, son of the morning! How are you cut down to the ground, which did weaken the nations!"*

Lucifer was Satan's original name before he fell. When Lucifer fell, he led a revolt against God and approximately one-third of the angels threw in their lot and followed him. The Bible describes this fall in Revelation 12:4, *"And his tail drew the third part of the stars of Heaven and did cast them to the earth."*

The Bible calls Lucifer the *"old serpent, called the Devil and Satan"* (Revelation 12:9). Satan is called the great deceiver who *"deceives the whole world"* and deception is, in fact, his greatest weapon. He deceives others into believing what is false; he is a pathological liar as he believes his own lies.

All the pain, misery and suffering in this world can be traced back to the Garden of Eden. Yet, we must go back even farther to Lucifer's revolt against God that occurred in time past. The Bible says that he fell because of his pride, *"For you have said in your heart, I will ascend into Heaven, I will exalt my throne above the stars of God: I will sit also upon the mount of the congregation, in the sides of the north."*

I will ascend above the heights of the clouds; I will be like the Most High" (Isaiah 14:13-14).

Lucifer lost his place in heaven and one-third of the angles threw in their lot with him and fell as well. We now have "demon spirits" who oppose us and the work of God. Satan wanted to be worshiped as God and the Bible says that he was a beautiful angel: *"every precious stone was your covering"* (Ezekiel 28:13).

Evidence also exists that God gifted Lucifer in music: *"and of your pipes was prepared for you in the day that you were created"* (Ezekiel 28:13).

When the earth was first created, scripture says, *"when the morning stars sang together, and all the sons of God shouted for joy"* (Job 38:7). It is believed that Lucifer was the angel created to lead choruses of songs to worship God. This gives one even more discernment when one understands how the music of the world has become so deceptive and used by Satan to corrupt the minds of the youth and the entire culture, no matter what the age.

THE DECEPTION OF ROCK MUSIC

So many of America's youth have been corrupted by "rock" music and it has been used to shape the culture like nothing else. Joseph Stalin, one of the architects of communism, once said, *"if we can enslave just one generation in any country, that country will fall to Soviet communism and the way to enslave that generation is by means of immorality, music, and drugs."* (Joseph Stalin, 1935, Rape of a Nation, 1985 Jimmy Swaggart Ministries, 1985, page 173).

The music industry over the past 70 to 80 years has served as our nation's *"preachers of unrighteousness,"* indoctrinating our youth with smut, garbage, and utter blasphemy against God. Meanwhile, our political leaders, educators, parents, coaches, etc. today, allow this blasphemous music into our culture under the guise of the first amendment.

The style and sound of music began to change in the 1950's and has spiraled deeper into what it is today, saturated with overt obscenities, sexual perversions, and prideful rebellion against what is right, pure, and Godly.

Our public schools' pipe in this music throughout their buildings before, during, and after sporting events, at proms, and during class time as our nation also blares it over our airways. Vulgarity of the grossest nature is played in the automobiles of our youth and adults all the while its content is protected under the banner of "free speech." The reality is that the use of free speech has been highjacked to promote evil and corrupt the minds of our youth. All of which has been used by Satan to change the mindset of our children and our culture, just as Joseph Stalin said it would do.

For the past 50 to 60 years, the deception of rock music has made it into the church where even well-known pastors are fans of secular rock music. Some even post on the walls of their pastoral office pictures of secular band such as the Beatles and wear T-shirts of these bands who have been responsible for leading so many away from God.

I recently watched an interview of a pastors interviewing one of the most popular Christian recording artists who has 1.3 million followers on his social media platform. This musical artist is all tattooed up (which are not tattoos from before he got saved), clearly violating Leviticus 19:28 which says: *"You shall not make any cuttings in your flesh for the dead, nor print any marks upon you, I am the LORD."* Yet today in the church this commandment is completely ignored and is another sign of the ignorance and rebellion towards the Word of God.

The musical artist was wearing a Pink Floyd t-shirt and the pastor interviewing was wearing a Beatles t-shirt. Now let me ask you why would they be wearing these bands shirts who are not even around anymore, but are responsible for the degradation of the lives of so many. The Beatles and Pink Floyd bands represent drugs, rebellion and an antichrist mindset. They might as well have been wearing a Satan t-shirt because that is who the Beatles and Pink Floyd were working for.

However, most Christians see no problems with this due to the fact they love Rock n' Roll music. This all stinks in the nostrils of God. One must remember Lucifer was a worship leader before he became the Devil.

To book one of the most popular Christian recording artists today can cost anywhere from $75,000 to a $150,000. When these artists tour on their own they charge their audience anywhere from $25 to $40 for the nosebleed seats in a large arena to over $200 for good seats. If I wanted to take my family of six to one of their concerts and I wanted to sit up close in the "good seats" it would cost me anywhere from $1300- $1500 to go and worship the Lord.

But my friend, Jesus when sending out His disciples said:

> *"And as you go, preach, saying the Kingdom of Heaven is at hand. Heal the sick, cleanse the lepers, raise the dead, cast our devils: freely you have received, freely give"* (Matthew 6:6-8).

The Apostle Paul wrote the church at Corinth something that every national speaker and musical artists needs to read. He said: "I speak not by Commandment, but by occasion of the forwardness of others, and to prove the sincerity of your love. For we know the Grace of our Lord Jesus Christ, that, though He was rich, yet for your sakes He became poor, that you through His poverty might be rich" (II Corinthians 8:8-9).

The ministry of Jesus Christ is not a ministry to make a lot of money that is a worldly mindset. Jesus gave up the riches of Heaven to be poor to be an example of a servant and He was the greatest example of servanthood who ever lived.

The Apostle Paul continue to write, he said:

"But this I say, he which sows sparingly shall reap also sparingly; and he which sows bountifully shall reap bountifully. Every man according as he purposes in his heart, so let him give; not grudgingly, or of necessity: for God loves a cheerful giver. And God is able to make all Grace abound toward you; that you, always having all sufficiency in all things, may abound to every good work" (II Corinthians 9:6-8).

Now let me ask you does that sound like one is to get rich off the gospel. To make over a million dollars a year or more preaching or leading worship concerts? Yet in the modern church we see today many are getting rich through charging high costs in speaking events and music concerts.

Paul was very clear with his ministry. He said:

"What is my reward then? Verily that, when I Preach the Gospel, I may make the Gospel of Christ without charge, that I abuse not my power in the Gospel" (I Corinthians 9:18).

Paul is saying that a price should never be put on the Gospel. The Preacher and the recording Artist who does nothing more than preach the Gospel to rhythm, must be ever careful not to exploit the people.

I am afraid many today are abusing the power of the Gospel as they rake in millions of dollars at their concerts at the expense of Christians who want to worship God. The only way this sin will be stopped is when Christians say ENOUGH, I am not going to support or be a part of a secular business model in the church.

I should point out here that I believe strongly in the minister and the musicians and worship teams being blessed for their work in the Gospel, but based on the above scriptures, it should be done on a free-will offering basis so that there is not a reproach on the Gospel presentation. It should be the churches conviction that no matter who you are rich or poor all can come to hear the Gospel and worship the Lord together.

"LENNON, DYLAN, ALICE AND JESUS"

The deception in the modern church regarding music is shocking. Many today see nothing wrong with rock music, be it secular rock or "Christian" rock, and all that comes with it. They have lost the reason why the instruments of music, and our voices were created by God. It was all primarily created and meant to worship a Trice Holy God.

In an interview in 2019, Pastor Greg Laurie who pastors a very large church in Orange County, Riverside, California agreed with Alice Cooper that although he has made a profession of faith, he does not have to stop being the demonic, rebellious, perverted Alice Cooper when performing on stage. Listen to Pastor Laurie's words from one of his latest books "Lennon, Dylan, Alice and Jesus":

"Quick: what do you think of when I say the name "Alice Cooper"? The guy with a woman's name wearing extreme eye makeup? The rocker who killed a chicken on stage during a concert. (or did he bite the head off a bat?) Rock and roll's boogeyman? A guy who belts out loud music with a huge boa constrictor draped around his neck. The godfather of shock rock? A cultural icon? Would it surprise you to learn that this Rock & Roll Hall of Famer is a Christian? Let me correct myself; he's a shameless, outspoken, and strong Christian. He is also a nice and down to earth person."

Now, what Pastor Greg Laurie is saying is shocking. I will not debate the one-time conversion of Alice Cooper, or that he is a nice human being, because I don't know that man, I hope he is all that Pastor Laurie says he is, but I will earnestly object to the performances that Alice Cooper is still preforming after making a public confession that he is now a follower of Jesus.

For my research has concluded that Alice Cooper's stage performance is still the same as it always way. His concert songs are still the same and most of his demonic antics in concert are mainly the same as well.

The fact that Grep Laurie who has written over 70 Christian books and pastors a very large church in California and leads very large "Harvest Crusades" sees nothing wrong with Alice Cooper's music and demonic performance that continues to poison the minds of thousands and thousands of people across our nation and the world is not only shocking, but is repulsive, and can I say blasphemous. Once one comes to Christ he lays down his old life, for now he is a new creature, and the Bible says old things has past away (II Corinthians 5:17).

In this book that pastor Laurie co-authored with Marshal Terrill, he makes the following statement right in the first sentence of the introduction of the book. He boldly writes: "It's time I admitted it…..to quote the great theologian, Joan Jett, "I love Rock 'n Roll."

Here is the root of the problem with many modern church pastors today. They are still holding on to the world, be it their music, style, or greed for money and fame. The truth is the Bible tells us to come out of the world and to not love the world or the things of the world because if we do than the scripture says that the love of the father is not in us (II Corinthains 6:17, I John 2:15).

Laurie goes on to write in his book: "Starting with Elvis Presley, my love for rock really took off when I heard the first words of "I Wanna Hold Your Hand" for four young lads who came from a place I had never heard of before a port city in England name Liverpool. They were called the Beatles and they literally impacted the world." (my words- they have literally impacted the world with evil Pastor Greg)

Greg Laurie continues: "Many musicians have acknowledged that they decided to start a band after first seeing The Fab Four" in 1964 on a Sunday evening variety program called "The Ed Sullivan Show." Frankly, I wonder where all the rock bands have gone of late. (my words- most have gone to hell unless they repented before they died) I have had the privilege of personally meeting and getting to know a lot of rock icons over the years, and I have such great admiration for their talent (my words- yes talent that was corrupted and used by the devil) So, yes, I admit it. I'm a fan."

I want to respectfully say that this is one of the most ridiculous, stupid ignorant, shameful spiritually ridiculous statements I think I have ever heard come out of a pastor's mouth of Greg Laurie's stature. In his own words he is confessing to loving something that has been used of the devil to destroy millions and millions of lives. The garbage that comes out of most of the bands that Laurie like such as the Beatles, Alice Cooper, John Lennon, etc., is filled with anti-God, anti-Christ, and anti-respect for biblical truths.

In general Rock music's beat, rhythm, lyrics, lifestyle, and overall presentation is a bold representation of a rebellious spirit that opposes all that is holy, righteous, pure and good.

In a Crusade in Boise, Idaho in 2022, Greg Laurie's son Jonathan, who is on the pastoral staff at Harvest Church in Orange County, Riverside,

California which is pastored by his father, he said the following words as the MC of that crusade:

"He (speaking of his father) grew up in the 50's which I considered one of the greatest decades ever for music, right. This was the 1960's and 70's with classic rock icons. You know we got Led Zeppelin, the Beatles, the Doors, Jimmy Hendricks, Janice Joplin, Beachboys, come on there is so much good music there. The saying back then was it was the devil's music' right. O that's the devil's music. Well, the joke is on them because we know today that God can use anybody, anywhere for His Glory and we have seen so much of this music and so many of these musicians use their lives and their platforms to glorify God now."

So, according to asociate Pastor, Jonathan Laurie, the joke is on the ministers, parents, and church leaders whom back in the 60's and 70's tried to warn us that Rock n' Roll music would destroy the youth culture of our nation. Now looking back at our nation 50 years later and the state of our youth and the rebellion we are seeing in the streets of America, I want to ask Jonathon who is the joke really on?

As far as Rock music being used to glorify God, that is in my estimation blasphemy. If one has ever step foot in one of the concerts named by Johnathan and if you have one ounce of spiritual discernment, I think you would completely agree with me that music is and its presentation is 100 percent opposed to the way of Christ.

There are rock stars like Elvis Presley, Michael Jackson, Whitney Houston and I could name so many more whose lives were shortened because of working an industry that is filled with lewd and licentious behavior, drugs and alcohol abuse, which is all filled with demon activity. The Bible warns us Christians: *"Avoid all appearances of evil"* (I Thessalonians 4:22), *"but put ye on the Lord Jesus Christ and make not provision for the flesh, to fulfill the lusts thereof"* (Romans 13:14).

The Bible teaches us not to look like the world, acts like the world, sound like the world, but simply to come out of the world. But Jonathon Laurie like his dad, is enamored by the worldly music of Rock n' Roll. I guess the apple doesn't fall too far from the tree.

In the Bible we read of a time when the King of Babylon used music as a means for the people to worship his golden image that he created. Daniel 3:4-6 reads: *"Then an herald cried aloud, To you it is commanded, O people, nations, and languages, that at what time you hear the sound of the cornet, flute, harp, sackbut, psaltery, dulcimer, and all kinds of music, you fall down and worship the golden image that Nebuchadnezzar, the king has set up.*

And when whoso falls not down and worships shall the same hour be cast into the midst of a burning fiery furnace."

Just as Nebuchadnezzar demanded worship of his idol of himself, the devil demands worship of himself, which he uses secular music to do so. He is trying to turn worship away from Jehovah God to other idols but ultimately to himself. That is why Rock music is called the "devils music" because it redirects music away from the One in Whom it was created for, God alone.

The very name "rock" music should tell you something, in the Bible Jesus is called the "Rock" (Matthew 16:18). Botton line Rock Music industry is an assault on the Rock of Ages.

THE LAST GENERATION

The Apostle Peter wrote about a generation who completely and totally parallels this generation, he stated,

> *"But chiefly them who walk after the flesh in the lust of uncleanness and despise government. Presumptuous are they, self-willed, they are not afraid to speak evil of dignities. Whereas angels, which are greater in power and might, bring not railing accusation against them before the Lord. But these, as natural brute beasts, made to be taken and destroyed, speak evil of the things that they understand not; and shall utterly perish in their own corruption; And shall receive the reward of unrighteousness, as they who count it pleasure to riot in the daytime. Spots they are and blemishes, sporting themselves with their own deceivings while they feast with you; Having eyes full of adultery, and that cannot cease from sin; beguiling unstable souls: an heart they have exercised with covetous practices; cursed children"*
> (II Peter 2:10-14).

The generation labeled the "Z" generation should instead be called the *"cursed children"* generation, which describes anyone who goes in their own way of life rather than following the Way of Jesus. The leaders of this end time revolutionary movement manifested in the streets of America back in 2020. Make no mistake, the rioting in our streets that is seen all too often today, is being led by none other than Satan himself. You can rest assured that what we see happening in America right now is an "antichrist revolution." This is moving our nation and the world towards a one-world government that will place the Antichrist, the Son of Perdition, as its ruling leader with Satan thrown down upon the earth.

Jesus said, *"I beheld Satan as lightning fall from Heaven"* (Luke 10:18). This will literally happen at the mid-point of the Great Tribulation (Revelation 12:9). When this occurs, Satan will know that he has only a short time and he will throw his subtle and deceptive means aside. At that time, he will reveal himself as who he really is. In other words, the Great Deception will be revealed in plain view, but for now the GREAT DECEPTION ROLLS ON IN MANY AMERICAN CHURCHES!

THE TOWER

The tower that Nimrod and the people constructed was a one-world project. This city of Babel was a political, civil, and religious union of the earth's inhabitants at that time. David Hunt, in his book *A Woman Rides the Beast,* says the following of the Tower of Babel:

> "The tower was clearly a religious project created by man to reach heaven. Babel thus represented the unity of state and church, involving the entire world to elevate man to God's level. That this would be accomplished through a tower built by human genius and energy, obviously represents man's religion of self-effort" (Woman Rides the Beast, Dave Hunt, page 56).

During the time of Nimrod, the whole world joined together as one. They were unified in their obsession to build a one-world tower under a one-world government and a one-world religion that would reach God. In Revelation 17, we see the *"Great Whore"* who represents all the false religions of the world being judged as God will bring it all down.

The unity movement of churches today in most places is a great deception devised by man, which is a substitution for the true way of Jesus Christ and Him being crucified. The Bible says that the *"Great Whore"* sits on many waters (Revelation 17:1) which is symbolic of multitudes of people. In the Great Tribulation, there will be a false prophet who will unite all the religions of the world together. I believe that this false prophet will be none other than the Pope, the leader of the Roman Catholic church. Why do I say that? Roman Catholicism is one of the biggest counterfeits Satan has ever come with and Pope Francis has already begun to unite other religions of the world together even though these other religions deny Jesus as the One True Messiah.

Just as Nimrod's Tower of Babel stood in stark contrast to the true way of salvation, today's one-world religious movement of unity also stands in contrast to true salvation. In 1994, evangelical leaders along with leaders from the Catholic Church signed a document that encouraged bridging the division between these two major religious groups.

These two religious groups were at odds ever since the Protestant Reformation. This document called "Evangelicals and Catholics to Come Together" was signed by prominent leaders on the Evangelical side and declared unity between the Roman Catholic Church and the Evangelical Church. The document emphasized the supposed commonality of both faiths and allowed for doctrinal differences, while stating a common mission. I should point out that the issue of "justification by faith alone" for salvation is not upheld by Roman Catholic teaching and was never addressed or solved between the Catholic and Evangelical leaders.

On March 29, 1994, this document was signed by leaders from both sides and considered the most significant development in Protestant-Catholic relations since the Reformation. However, the truth is that nothing that divided the two sides for hundreds of years had really changed at all. The document called for unity according to Jesus' prayer in John 17:21, which says, "That they all may be One; as You, Father, are in Me, and I in You, that they may believe that You have sent Me."

The fatal flaw of the drafters assumed that Jesus was talking about anyone who calls on the Name of Jesus shall be considered "One." That could not be further from the truth. In fact, Jesus said, "Take heed that no man deceives you. For many shall come in My Name, saying, I am Christ; and shall deceive many" (Matthew 24:5). The Apostle Paul wrote, "But though we, or an Angel from Heaven, preach any other gospel unto you than that which we have preached unto you, let him be accursed" (Galatians 1:8).

The reality is the Gospel that the Catholic Church preaches is not the same Gospel that Jesus or Paul preached. The call for unity with different faiths is not consistent with the Bible. Jesus prayed for unity within His True Church and said, *"I pray for them: I pray not for the world, but for them which you have given Me, for they are Thine"* (John 17:9). Those who are truly "born again" by the Spirit of the living God belong to the true Church of the Lord Jesus Christ. You cannot or should not try to merge the religious world and the true Church together. To do so is condemned by the scriptures (Galatians 1:6-9).

AN UNHOLY MIXTURE

To unite Roman Catholicism with true Christianity is in fact a unholy mixture. You cannot mix Law and Grace together. The Bible says: *"a little leaven leavens the whole lump"* (Galatians 5:9). It should be quite clear that the true Christian Church cannot unite with such non-biblical teachings like the Roman Catholic eucharist, their devotion and worship of Mary, praying to saints, the seven sacraments, infant baptism, praying for the dead, indulgences, purgatory, saying the rosary, etc.

Although the Roman Catholic Church and the Bible-believing Christian Church do share some common moral convictions, such as abortion being murder, moral education, anti-obscenity laws, human equality, pro-family legislation, etc. However, there is in fact too many opposing doctrines and spiritual differences that prohibit the unification of these two religions coming together, at least for those who hold to the true integrity of the scriptures.

Another dangerous compromise of this evangelical document was the call to halt the proselytizing of active Roman Catholics. This was labeled as "sheep stealing" and the document signers believed that attempts to win converts from each other's fold undermines the Christian mission. The designers of this unity document failed to recognize that those who hold to true Catholic doctrine are not "true sheep." This doesn't mean that a Catholic cannot be born again and on their way to heaven. However, it is very important to understand that if one holds firm to the teachings of Catholic doctrines for salvation, they are following a perverted Gospel and cannot be saved (Galatians 1:6).

The following statement in this document should cause the most concern:

> "In view of the large number of non-Christians in the world and the enormous challenge of our common evangelistic task, it is neither theologically legitimate nor a prudent use of resources for one Christian community to proselytize among active adherents of another Christian community."

The fatal flaw in this statement is that most Catholics believe that the salvation experience occurs by being baptized as an infant or because they are a member of the Roman Catholic Church. In fact, they are even told by some priests if they leave the Roman Catholic Church they will lose their salvation. However, Jesus said you must be "born again" (John 3:3) to enter the Kingdom God. Most concerning is that the document stated that the

Roman Catholic Church members must be given full freedom and respect to remain Catholic. In other words, all evangelism efforts to convince a Catholic to be saved should not be the mission of evangelical churches.

What is being ignored in this unity movement is the fact that millions of Catholics are not saved and all across the world and down through the ages millions or Roman Catholics have been trapped in superstitions and religious rituals not found in the Bible. What makes this so alarming is the vast approval it gained from such organizations like Christianity Today, the Southern Baptist Convention, and church leaders such as Kenneth Copeland who met with Pope Francis regarding church unity. Leaders like Louie Giglio, Joel Osteen, Rick Warren, etc., embrace the Pope as a legitimate religious leader. The truth is that Pope Francis is a globalist, endlessly working to unite all the major religions of the world. It is actually his personal mission to merge the State (i.e., government) and religion together as one.

Dave Hunt stated in his book:

> "The city and Tower of Babel set the pattern of the unholy alliance between civil government and a religion of self-effort and rituals which continued for thousands of years. These were exemplified both in pagan Rome and in "Christian" Romans following Constantine's "conversion." The "separation of church and state" is a concept of recent origin, largely since the Protestant Reformation, and one which the Roman Catholic Church, as the religious continuation of the Roman Empire, has consistently and even viciously opposed" (A Woman Rides the Beast, David Hunt page 54).

CONSEQUENCES OF A STATE RELIGION

A state religion is what Nimrod wanted and it is what many others wanted after him. Nimrod formed the first World Empire whereby church and state were one. Such is the idea that Roman Catholicism has always strived for. They want to control the world spiritually, and in order to that there must be a unification of all religions.

The Catholic Vatican I reads as follows:

> "While the state has some rights, she has them only in virtue and by permission of the superior authority (of) the Church."

In the mind of Catholic supremacy, the state must bow down in submission to the church. The word Catholic means "Universal" and the Roman Catholic Church sees themselves as the One and only true church.

They insist that anyone who is not in their church is not truly saved. Many catholic children are being raised by parents who embrace the conviction that if you leave the Catholic Church, you will lose your soul.

Mussolini, the fascist dictator of Italy, aligned himself with Adolf Hitler during World War II, and made Roman Catholicism the official state religion. He stated that any criticism against the Catholic Church would be considered a penal offense. Roman Catholicism, like all false religions, promotes "self-effort" as the means to reach God, and was exactly what the Tower of Babel was all about. It taught that men could reach God by building a tower with their own hands. When the United States was formed, the founding fathers made sure to prevent the formation of a state church. The writers of the First Amendment of the Bill of Rights wrote: "Congress shall make no law respecting an establishment of religion or prohibiting the free exercise thereof." They wrote this to protect the church from the state establishing its own religion.

ONE-WORLD RELIGION

The people created a city and a tower with a plan to worship the stars (i.e., Zodiac) or, in other words, to worship Lucifer the "morning star." From the very beginning, it was Satan's plan for man to worship him as God. The Bible says, *"And they said, Go, let us build a city and a tower, whose top may reach unto heaven; and let us make us a name, lest we be scattered abroad upon the face of the whole Earth."* (Genesis 11:4). In this one verse, we see the word "us" used three times. This speaks of a unity throughout the whole world at that time, where mankind would be under a world system. To the minds of the nation, a world-wide government bringing about world unity sounded good to their ears. There was only one problem with that idea, it was being done without God, and inspired by Satan who wants the world to worship him.

In the above (Genesis 11:4), we find the seedbed, the root, or the bedrock of man's rebellion, that is inspired by Satan, he wants us to worship other gods. The plan under Nimrod was the same plan that is now beginning to take place in America and around the world. It has been going on for a long time. But in the year 2020, this plan became much more visible than in previous years. In other words, the Great Deception is more obvious than it has ever been since the time of Nimrod, but most can't see it.

What can man do about this one-world global plan? In Psalms 11:3, it says *"If the foundations be destroyed, what can the righteous do?"* The truth is that once the "Nimrods" of this world remove the foundation on which

America was built, that being Jesus Christ and the Cross and the Word of God, there won't be many people who will be able to stop the onslaught of evil as it spreads across our nation.

So, the better question is "what will God do?" The Bible says,

> *"The LORD is in His Holy Temple, the LORD's Throne is in Heaven: His eyes behold, His eyelids try, the children of men. The LORD tries the righteous: but the wicked and him who loves violence His soul hates. Upon the wicked He shall rain snares, fire and brimstone, and a horrible tempest: this shall be the portion of their cup. For the righteous LORD loves Righteousness, His Countenance does behold the upright"* (Psalms 11:4-7).

These verses say that God is watching everything that man is doing and the children of men and those who are righteous, believers in Christ, will be tried. But He will rescue the righteous. However, the wicked and all who love violence will be judged. The LORD was watching Nimrod and the wicked intention of the people who tried to form a one-world government and one-world worship to a false god. God said,

> *"Behold, the people is one, and they have all one language; and this they will begin to do (i.e., rebel against God): and now nothing will be restrained from them, which they have imagined to do"* (Genesis 11:6).

This is exactly where we are right now. The global elites who hold much of the wealth and power in this world are attempting to unite the world under a one-world global system. They plan to create a global currency that will one day lead to implementing a mark on the forehand or forehead to ensure that people who refuse the mark will not be able to buy or sell. (Revelation 13:16-17).

Right now, they are tampering with DNA and want to inject superhuman cells into people that will affect their genetic makeup. Some fear that the COVID-19 global vaccination is the beginning of this creation to make a "new man." The way God prevented the first one-world global rebellion was by breaking up the people's unity by confusing their language. It is believed that God introduced over 100 different languages during the time of Nimrod (Genesis 11:7). However, there are much more than that now.

In other words, God did not sit back and allow man to form a one-world global plan and one-world global worship to false gods. He intervened back then, and He is about to intervene again in these last days. God scattered the people back in Nimrod's day, stated in the Bible as, *"So the LORD scattered them abroad from thence upon the face of all the Earth: and they left off to build the city"* (Genesis 11:9).

THE SPIRIT OF BABYLON

Some 1600 years after Nimrod attempted to build the Tower of Babel, a man named Nebuchadnezzar became the ruler of the Babylonians. Nebuchadnezzar built a city around the ruins of the Tower of Babel, making the false religion of self-effort the center of this new and vast empire.

The European Union (EU) today has 27 countries, mostly united in Europe. Incredibly, the EU used the Tower of Babel as their official poster with the caption that reads "Many Tongues, One Voice." This caption seems to point towards the New World Order. In addition, EU displays a woman riding a beast on its currency. Today the world is on a fast track to unite all nations into a one-world order. God confused the languages back in Nimrod's Day, but modern technology is aimed at breaking down language barriers.

In the Book of Revelation, John shows us that Babylon will be very much alive in end times. "And he cried mightily with a strong voice, saying, *"Babylon the great is fallen, and is become the inhabitation of devils, and the hold of every foul spirit, and a cage of every unclean and hateful bird. For all nations have drunk of the wine of the wrath of her fornication, and the kings of the earth have committed fornication with her"* (Revelation 18:2-3).

In Revelation 17 and 18, the word Babylon is used to describe two different things. The first one references mystical Babylon, which represents all the false religions of the world with its headquarters based in Rome today. The claim is that Roman Catholicism, which is headquartered in Rome, is supposedly Christian. However, its roots come from the historical and mystical Babylon where men were deceived into building a tower. The Book of Revelation describes her as:

> *"MYSTERY, BABYLON THE GREAT, THE MOTHER OF HARLOTS AND ABOMINATIONS OF THE EARTH"*
> (Revelation 17:5).

Then there is the literal Babylon, the location of the headquarters of the Antichrist. In the Great Tribulation, both the mystical and the literal Babylon will be judged and will both fall. This clearly describes the future of the global elites and all their diabolical plans. The big question asked by many biblical scholars is, "Who is the literal Babylon of today?" Revelation 17:9 says, "And here is the mind which has wisdom. The seven heads are seven mountains, on which the women sits." In history there have been six empires controlled by false religions, all took aim at attacking the nation of Israel.

A seventh one, with an eighth forming out of the seventh, is still to come. They are as follows:

- Egyptian Empire
- Assyrian Empire
- Babylonian Empire
- Medo/Persian Empire
- Grecian Empire
- Roman Empire
- Revised Roman Empire
- Antichrist Kingdom

Although literal Babylon is not in place yet, spiritual Babylon is. The spirit of the world and this move towards a one-world government is the Babylonian spirit of old and gaining momentum fast in America and around the world.

COVID 19

The definition of globalism is the operation or planning of economic and foreign policy on a global basis and a plan to bring the whole world together. Sounds good to men's natural ears, but it is an evil plan that will try to put the world under the control of government and one day under a one-world leader (i.e., Anti-Christ).

When the Apostle John was shown that a one-world government would mandate the placement of a "mark" on the people's wrist and/or forehead, he saw what our world is now rushing towards. The COVID-19 virus changed the world and most likely was used to set up the beginning of this one-government control. Mandatory vaccines, which limited access to public places, and the installation of tracking devices (called vaccination passports) point towards limiting people from being in certain places and countries.

When Donald Trump was president, he launched what he called "Operation Warp Speed" where millions of dollars were given to companies to quickly develop a COVID-19 vaccine. Three separate companies (Moderna, Pfizer, and Johnson and Johnson) created a vaccine in record speed. Former President Trump was so proud of this accomplishment that he suggested giving himself credit by saying it should be called the "Trumpcine." He said that people should picture his face in their minds as the shot was going into their arms.

The effectiveness of the vaccine is still being considered and highly debated. Some contribute the vaccine to long-term health issues and even death due to the vaccine. At the time of this writing (April 2023) really no one knows for sure the long-term negative effects of the vaccine. However, what we do know is that this vaccine is an avenue to put greater government restrictions on people who refuse to get the shot.

In Buffalo, New York, the Erie County executive announced (April 16, 2021) that anyone who is not vaccinated will not be allowed access into a Buffalo Bills football game or the Buffalo Sabres hockey game and other public indoor events. There was some push back of this violation of our freedoms, however the restrictions continued for some time. Perhaps this was a test to see how people would react to such governmental control. There were countries calling for "vaccine passports" to identify if a person was vaccinated. If not implemented, one could be refused entrance into that country. I believe this is all a preliminary sign of what is coming.

Very soon, these types of controlling governmental laws implemented by world leaders will bring many nations under a one-world system led by none other than the Antichrist. Although he will not cause all nations to join in, he will get many. He will receive his inspiration and miraculous powers from Satan himself. The Bible predicts that after the Rapture of the Church, a great deception will immediately take over the world. This occurs after the Lord takes His bride (i.e., His Church) off the earth. Paul, writing under the inspiration of the Holy Spirit, penned these words almost 2,000 years ago:

> *"Don't you remember, that, when I was yet with you, I told you these things? And now you know what withholds that he might be revealed in his time. For the mystery of iniquity does already work: only he who now lets will let, until he be taken out of the way"* (II Thessalonians 2:5-7).

What the Lord reveals here is that the Church, Christ in us, holds back the Antichrist from being revealed. Although the global system that Satan leads is being put in place right now, it will not be fully in place until after the Rapture of the Church. The Body of Christ (those who have Christ living in them) is preventing the Antichrist from being revealed at this time. There should be no doubt that he is alive today. He is waiting, and when the church is *"taken out of the way,"* the Antichrist will take up his earthly reign immediately. This will happen only when God wills, at His appointed time, not the devils or man's.

The Apostle Paul wrote,:

> *"And then shall that wicked be revealed, whom the Lord shall consume with the spirit of His Mouth, and shall destroy with the brightness of His Coming. Even Him, whose coming is after the working of Satan with all power and signs and lying wonders, and with all deceivableness of unrighteousness in them who perish; because they received not the love of the Truth, that they might be saved"* (II Thessalonians 2:8-10).

When Satan is allowed to reveal his Antichrist, the world will enter the final Great Deception. The world will be completely evil and there will be great tribulations on the earth, so awful that Jesus said, *"And except those days should be shortened, there should no flesh be saved: but for the elect's sake those days shall be shortened"* (Matthew 24:22).

In the nations where the mark of the beast is legislated, the people who are left on earth who do not know the Word of God, will most likely take the mark of the beast. That will be a decision they make, which will have eternal consequences and leave them with no hope to be saved. In other words, all those who take the mark will be damned forever, this is what the Bible teaches us.

For those who do not take the mark, they will lose their rights and ability to buy food or conduct any kind of business. The truth is the people who do not accept Jesus Christ as their Lord and Savior before the Rapture will be left on earth during the time of the Antichrist. They will be in between a rock and a hard place and remain on earth during the time of the Antichrist. Many will be given the choice to either take the mark of the beast and survive here on earth or refuse the mark and suffer persecution and likely death. Those who resist the mark and put their trust in Christ will be saved for all eternity.

Listen to these sobering words found in the Bible:

> *"If any man worship the beast and his image, and receive his mark in his forehead, or in his hand, the same shall drink of the wine of the Wrath of God, which is poured out without mixture into the cup of His indignation; and he shall be tormented with fire and*

brimstone in the presence of the Holy Angels, and in the Presence of the Lamb and the smoke of their torment ascendeth up forever and ever: and they have no rest day nor night, who worship the beast and his image, whosoever receives the mark of his name" (Revelation 14:9-11).

The biblical truth is if one takes the mark of the beast on their forehead or hand, there will be no chance for them to be saved. There is the likelihood that a computer chip or a tattoo could be used as such a mark to be placed under or on a person's skin. This technology is in place, ready, and even being implemented in countries and places in the world today including America.

5G TECHNOLOGY

The United States has began using 5G Technology, an internet speed 100 times faster than 4G, which is currently used in our cell phones. This new technology permits a car to drive automatically without a driver. To wit, the computer will drive the vehicle. These new developments are moving at speeds unlike anything we have ever seen or imagined.

This 5G technology also can track a person's whereabouts. There is also an app that can be uploaded onto a phone to identify if someone close to them has tested positive for COVID-19. No doubt, this tracking system was developed to have greater governmental control of the world. Once the chip (or tattoo) is implemented into humans worldwide, privacy will be a thing of the past. There is a popular song that I used to listen to during my BC days (before Christ) that had the words in it: "Private Eyes, They're Watching You." This is exactly what is happening to us today.

So, when the Antichrist rolls out his mark of the beast, there will already be a tracking devise in place (e.g., 5G or 6G), making it easy to know who does and does not have the mark of the beast. The scriptures give us an indication that not only will you be banned from buying and selling if you don't take this mark, but your very life will also be in danger. Revelation 13:15 reveals, *"and cause that as many as would not worship the image of the beast should be killed."*

Wake up Church! The Antichrist system is being set up right now. The all-important question that must be asked is, "how close are we to the coming of the Lord?" The answer is NOT LONG AT ALL!

CHAPTER 4

THE DOWNFALL OF AMERICA

Through the weeping prophet Jeremiah, God spoke to the nation of Israel and says these words:

"For thus saith the LORD to the men of Judah, and Jerusalem, Break up your fallow ground, and sow not among thorns. Circumcise yourselves to the LORD, and take away the foreskins of your heart, you men of Judah and inhabitants of Jerusalem: lest My fury come forth like fire, and burn that none can quench it, because of the evil of your doings" (Jeremiah 4:3-4).

God sends a clear and concise warning. He makes it clear that He will no longer tolerate Israel's abominations in His land. This is the nation that He called to be the light bearer of truth to the world. If they falter, then the whole world falters.

I believe that what God said to the nation of Israel so long ago He is also speaking to America today, starting with the church. God is saying that your heart must turn back to Him. The fallow ground has not been broken up; it is land that is laying empty and only weeds can be found. This means that there is no spiritual life and growth. Israel and Judah's hearts became empty, lacking a passion and love for God. The call was to break up their idols and remove them from their lives. This was God's condition for forgiveness and deliverance. For the sin nature to be dethroned in the heart of man, the sinner must first have his heart broken for God. With God, it is always about the heart and not about religious ceremonies. This was God's condition for forgiveness; get your heart right!

The Bible says that it is the anointing that breaks the yoke (Isaiah 10:27). It is only God, working through the Holy Spirit, that the sinful heart of man can be changed. Man needs to have a wretched-man moment. When he comes to the end of himself and his heart is broken because of his sin, he then cries out to God for help and deliverance (Romans 7:24-25, Psalms 105).

God said through the prophet Jeremiah:

> *"Declare ye in Judah, and publish in Jerusalem and say, Blow ye the trumpet in the land, cry, gather together, and say, assemble yourselves, and let us go into the defensed cities. Set up the standard toward Zion: retire, stay not: for I will bring evil from the north, and a great destruction"* (Jeremiah 4:5-6).

It is believed that this prophecy was given by God in the year 612 B.C. and was carried out 15 years later in 597 B.C. So, God gave Israel a 15-year warning of the Babylonian invasion. God always warns through His prophets before He acts (Amos 3:7). He does this because He is a merciful God and He is long-suffering, not wanting any to perish, but all come to repentance (II Peter 3:8-9).

God gave Israel a chance to avoid this great destruction due to their sin. Sadly, they did not listen to the warnings of Jeremiah. I believe that right now, God is trying to warn America just as He warned Israel. However, like Judah and ancient Israel, I am afraid our nation is not listening to these warnings. Unfortunately, great destruction came to Israel and the streets of Jerusalem ran red with blood and the Temple was destroyed. How terrible to think that this could have all been avoided if only the nation of Israel would have listened to the prophet Jeremiah and repented. If only they had done what God told them to do.

The prophet Jeremiah gave a scathing warning. He said:

> *"The lion is come up from his thicket, and the destroyer of the Gentiles is on his way; he is gone forth from his place to make your land desolate; and your cities shall be laid waste, without an inhabitant"* (Jeremiah 4:7).

The warning does not get any clearer than that my friend. The question is why did the nation not take heed to the warning and repent? The answer can only be because of unbelief. The people did not believe what the prophet Jeremiah said to them. However, Jeremiah wasn't speaking out of his own intellect, but he was speaking for God about what was to come. The lion referred to the evil King Nebuchadnezzar and the Babylonian invasion that was coming.

Jeremiah also told the nation something that I believe every true prophet of God should tell Americans right now:

> *"For this gird you with sackcloth, lament and howl: for the fierce anger of the LORD is not turned back from us. And it shall come to pass at that day, saith the LORD, that the heart of the king shall perish, and the heart of the Princes; and the Priests shall be astonished, and the Prophets shall wonder"*
> (Jeremiah 4:8-9).

God told the nation of Israel that the time of repentance was now; for when the destruction begins it would be too late to call on God to rescue them. Keep in mind that as far as personal Salvation goes, it is never too late to repent until you take your last breath. However, if national repentance is delayed too long then judgment will ultimately come and when it begins, no one will be able to stop it.

When judging a people and a nation, God always starts with the leaders. As the leaders go, so goes the nation. Let me say it a little more boldly. America is on the brink of judgment because ever since I can remember, the Presidents of the United States have been more concerned with how to make America succeed economically or militarily, instead of being more concerned about our nation's moral and spiritual health.

Every president since I have been alive, except for maybe Ronald Reagan (in my humble opinion) has shown very little spiritual discernment. Instead of solving abortion, pornography, vulgarity, drugs, spiritual ignorance, and the apathy problems in our nation for human life, they instead focused their political campaigns mainly around the economy and financial prosperity. Why? Because this is what buys them votes. As the Scripture says, "the love of money is the root of all evil" (I Timothy 6:10). Our country's obsession with the economy has caused us to be blinded to a more serious issue, how we treat one another and how we should live our lives before a trice Holy God.

GEORGE FLOYD

On Memorial Day, May 25, 2020, the nation witnessed the hideous and demonic murder of an African American man named George Floyd. During an arrest, a very deranged police officer in Minneapolis, Minnesota, put his knee on George Floyd's neck for 8 minutes and 46 seconds. Bystanders heard Mr. Floyd crying out, "I can't breathe" "I can't breathe." However, the officer showed no mercy for this man's life and remained pressing his knee on his neck until he took George Floyd's life.

What was almost more shocking than this unnecessary murder was the three other police officers who stood by and watched. This incident was caught on film and when the nation saw it, people responded with outrage. The officer who kept his knee on Mr. Floyd's neck was white, and this hideous and evil incident ignited the beginning of the worst racial riots seen in our nation since the 1960's.

The nation wanted justice. Not only for the officer who murdered George Floyd, but also for the three officers who stood by and watched without doing a thing to help Mr. Floyd. This event served as a racial time bomb, bringing the racial divide in our nation to the forefront of American politics and civil liberties. After the death of George Floyd, our cities became sanctuaries for law-breaking Americans and criminal citizens.

SEATTLE, WASHINGTON

Seattle was the city where COVID-19 outbreaks began in our nation, and it is where the CHOP movement began. CHOP stands for Capitol Hill Organized Protest, which was formed to oppose police brutality. Riots and trained anarchists took over a six-block area of Seattle and kicked the police out, and then ran an autonomous nation of their own. For about six weeks, they controlled all activities within that six block area of the downtown Seattle.

It was hard to believe that people could openly break the law and get away with it. They pushed the police out, shut down a precinct and blocked off certain areas of the city. No one, not even the State's Governor or Seattle's Mayor, implemented resistance to what was happening. All of America watched as lawlessness ruled the streets of Seattle. One of the end time signs will be lawlessness. Jesus said, *"And because iniquity (i.e., lawlessness) shall abound, the love of many shall wax cold"* (Matthew 24:12).

Following the murder of two people, police finally moved in and dissolved CHOP. Law and order was finally restored to this part of downtown Seattle. However, this all could have been prevented if the Governor had supported the police and allowed them to arrest and remove the insurgents who had set up shop. Two deaths could have been prevented, not to mention the loss of businesses that had to close and move out.

The people in the streets of America marched for days calling for justice reform, stricter laws on police brutality and the need to defund the police force. Over 40 cities across America participated in daily marches, including thousands of Americans amid the COVID-19 pandemic, who took to the streets and violated social distancing rules.

The peaceful demonstrations soon turned violent as groups like Black Lives Matter (BLM) were fueled by an evil organization called Antifa. They were brought into cities to cause civil unrest through the burning of businesses, police stations, churches, and civilian vehicles. The protesters started looting and burning stores, causing millions of dollars of destruction. The looters used profane graffiti to defame American stores, monuments, and buildings to present their message of hatred, racism and demonic intent that caused further anarchy in our nation.

We saw people being injured and killed; both police officers and those who were standing in harm's way. Night after night, we watched American cities being taken over by these ruthless anarchists. What was even more shocking, was it appeared that the police allowed the looters to ransack American businesses right before their eyes. This all took place as we watched it on the evening news.

The looters were getting away with highway robbery. Store owners who were already hit hard by the COVID-19 pandemic had to shut down their businesses. Others were trying to defend their property from invaders who were breaking store windows and rushing in to steal everything they could get their hands on.

In Santa Monica, California business owners witnessed looters breaking into their music store and destroying their business. Lana Negrete, who co-owned the music store with her husband, said, "It was just like a horror movie, they took everything from us, and no one stopped them. It was so violating. We heard windows being smashed. I saw a woman wearing snakeskin pants with her face pressed up against the glass of our store. Then she called a group over, Negrete recalled, bringing to life every second of her ordeal. "I saw them trying to get in, and I just started screaming and honking the horn of my car."

She said that at first it started with groups of five, then groups of 10; most with backpacks on skateboards and carrying machetes and hammers in their hands. Soon, there were looters coming from every direction as hundreds of people were barreling toward her store. She depicted it all as pandemonium. There were cars speeding up to the music center, including brand new luxury Mercedes SUVs and Infiniti vehicles; with trunks popping open and ready to be filled with loot.

These were mostly young men of every ethnicity and age who assaulted the building before her eyes. "I saw 16-year-old girls in designer clothes stealing. I saw a woman with a small child in the back of her vehicle, drive up and push her 13-year-old son, who looked nervous, out of the car to go in and steal," Negrete said. "There were just many groups of people there who had nothing to do with the George Floyd protests. Parents there, stealing with their children." Calling 911 proved to be futile. According to the frightened music center owner, they were informed that police could not get to the scene and if they were registered gun owners, they could protect their private property. However, California has some of the strictest gun legislation in the country.

The violence only escalated as more and more looters descended. "There were gunshots fired, and those trying to help had guns pulled on them," Negrete tremored. "Tons of bricks were also used to smash windows in and around the area." Negrete observed that the bricks were typically placed underneath trash cans earlier in the day ahead of the scheduled protest.

When the looters arrived, they knew where they were and put them to use to terrorize and destroy. In the end, and over the course of many hours, criminals had a field day taking dozens of cellos, trumpets, bases, amplifiers, speakers, and random merchandise. But if that wasn't enough, the looters also went about destroying the cash registers, smashing display cases, and busting up furniture.

"It wasn't just about taking the stuff. It was absolute anarchy," Negrete noted. "They didn't know who they were stealing from; we don't make much money, we're low-income ourselves. We give back to charities every month even though we don't have much money ourselves." She said 80 percent of their business has been obliterated, and right now, it's a fight between the landlord and the insurance company over who is responsible for paying for what. I'm struggling, and I have a family to feed too. We don't qualify for any help from the government." she added. Her voice breaking into tears. "We are tax paying, hard-working people. This isn't 'stuff' to us. This was everything we had." (story taken from Hollie McKay Fox News https://www.foxnews.com/us/santa-monica-music-center-looters-armed)

The above is just one story of thousands that are just like it from all over the nation. It is so sad to see the United States of America becoming a nation that is being destroyed from within. Just like Rome of old, we are seeing our country crashing down into a lawless anti-God nation. This is all a culmination of a nation that it being led by a mind-set of whatever is right in your own eyes, is right. The philosophy of "If it feels good, do it," is what this generation has been brought up with. So now, we are seeing the results of taking God out of our schools and our society that began over 60 years ago.

The lack of God-fearing leadership in our country has led us to this moment in American history. The result is and always will be anarchy. The last verse in the Book of Judges is exactly what America has become today. It says, *"In those days there was no king in Israel: every man did that which was right in his own eyes"* (Judges 21:25).

POLITICALLY MOTIVATED

One must keep in mind that 2020 was an election year, and the political war in the country had reached a feverish pitch. It really began four years prior when Donald Trump became president. Many on the left took to the streets to protest after his inauguration, chanting in cities across the country, "He's not my President." The far-left democrats had been relentless from the moment that President Trump took office in trying to find a way to impeach him and prevent him from being re-elected.

Our nation has watched secular news agencies such as CNN, MSNBC, CBS, The Washington Post, the New York Times, etc., use their daily print, media, and television networks to criticize, ridicule, scrutinize, and scandalize every move President Trump made. The question must be asked why was there such hate there Number one, the liberal left in this country had become a radical far-left movement, and the one they wanted to lead them was Hilary Clinton. They were convinced that she was going to be the next president and lead this country in the way they want it to go.

The last-minute comeback by Donald Trump was shocking to the liberal left. They were convinced that their socialistic, new-world government was going to be rolled out; but then, suddenly, they had a president who they didn't see coming. President Trump called them out for who they were, promising the nation that he was going to "drain the swamp." The swamp included political hypocrites who mostly were in their positions for the money and political power rather than the betterment of our nation. The personality and makeup of Donald Trump made for the perfect political storm. Trump is a businessman, not a politician. He is a fighter from the Bronx and probably the only thing bigger than his wealth is his pride. His slogan, "Make American Great Again," was filled with aspirations to bring this country back to its glory days, as it is called.

The only problem was that President Trump did not mention Jesus, but only talked of financial prosperity and military supremacy. However, given the alternative, most Christians overlooked Donald Trump's checkered past and boastful statements; thankful that liberal Hillary Clinton did not win and become our president. For them, this was more about having anyone other than Hillary. They would rather criticize her liberal and corrupt ways than scrutinize Donald Trump's character and demeanor. However, I must admit that there was a lot to like about Donald Trump as he was a mover and shaker who promised great changes compared to the Barak Obama era of leadership.

However, something very troubling was when asked in an interview what was his favorite verse in the Bible, President Trump quoted a portion of Matthew 5:38 and said: *"Eye for an Eye."* However, the full statement that Jesus said was: *"You Have heard that it has been said, An eye for an eye, and a tooth for a tooth: But I say unto you, That you resist not evil: but whosoever shall smite you on the right cheek, turn to him the other also."* (Matthew 5:38-39) I think President Trump's favorite verse is very revealing as to how he leads his life in terms of how he treats others. If you criticize him, he will strongly attack back and even harder to the one who comes against him. I believe his style of leadership and his rough personality, when attacked, was the perfect temperament for the storm that we find our nation in right now.

The United States of America has never been more divided not since the days of the Civil War. We are seeing a complete divide in our nation between Republicans and Democrats. There is literal hate and animosity between the parties that is being seen openly like never before. Many Christians are being caught up in all the political waring.

The war between parties is about who will control the Whitehouse, the Senate and the House and who will take this nation sharply in their direction. It really has become more about a political party than what is best for America. The political party, particularly the left, has shown a complete all-out assault on the ideas of capitalism and freedom; wanting to take us into a socialistic new form of government. The Bernie Sanders' ideals of free education, free health care, free handouts, etc., has become very appealing to the young millennial generation who grew up without the knowledge of the Word of God.

In 2020, this nation began to have their eyes opened to who America really is; an evil and divided nation, sitting on the eve of destruction. Like Rome of old, our nation is being destroyed from within. The church is caught in the middle and does not know how to stop what is happening.

ABRAHAM LINCOLN

The year of 2020 was screaming at the people of America that God was beginning to lower the hedge of protection that was once around this nation and terrible times were just ahead. He gave us time to repent, but we refused to face our sin and turn from it. But what if this nation were to turn to God and repent of our terrible sin that has invaded our nation?

What if President Trump would have called for a national day of fasting and repentance like Abraham Lincoln did in 1863? In that year America was in the middle of the Civil War and many men were dying due to the war. In fact, more men died in America's Civil War than all the wars put together up to the time of the Vietnam War.

In 1863, the nation was divided right down the middle and it looked as though our country was not going to make it. But then, President Lincoln wrote a declaration and called for a day of humiliation, fasting and repentance. It was held on March 30, 1863, and President Lincoln wrote in his proclamation the following words:

> "Whereas, the Senate of the United States, devoutly recognizing the Supreme Authority and just Government of Almighty God, in all the affairs of men and of nations, has, by a resolution, requested the President to designate and set apart a day for National prayer and humiliation.
>
> And whereas it is the duty of nations as well as of men, to own their dependence upon the overruling power of God, to confess their sins and transgressions, in humble sorrow, yet with assured hope that genuine repentance will lead to mercy and pardon; and to recognize the sublime truth, announced in the Holy Scriptures and proven by all history, that those nations only are blessed whose God is the Lord.
>
> And, insomuch as we know that, by His divine law, nations like individuals are subjected to punishments and chastisements in this world, may we not justly fear that the awful calamity of civil war, which now desolates the land, may be but a punishment, inflicted upon us, for our presumptuous sins, to the needful end of our national reformation as a whole People? We have been the recipients of the choicest bounties of Heaven. We have been preserved, these many years, in peace and prosperity. We have grown in numbers, wealth, and power, as no other nation has ever grown. But we have forgotten God. We have forgotten the gracious hand which preserved us in peace and multiplied and enriched and strengthened us; and we have vainly imagined, in the deceitfulness of our hearts, that all these blessings were produced by some superior wisdom and virtue of our own. Intoxicated with unbroken success, we have become too self-sufficient to feel the necessity of redeeming and preserving

grace, too proud to pray to the God that made us! It behooves us then, to humble ourselves before the offended Power, to confess our national sins, and to pray for clemency and forgiveness."

What an amazing proclamation of truth and humility stated by the 16th President of the United States. The President and the nation were in a time of desperation and thank God that Abraham Lincoln knew there was only one place to go for healing; and it was to the Lord Himself. He knew the only way to touch God was through humble repentance of our national sins.

Two days after the National Day of Prayer and Fasting, something happened that turned the Civil War around. The Civil War was in full force with no foreseeable end in sight and many Americans were dying. A confederate army commander named Stonewall Jackson was accidentally shot by his own men and died a few days later. This happened two days after Lincoln called for a National Day of Repentance. Civil War historians speculate that had Jackson not died, the Battle of Gettysburg that occurred two months later would have resulted in a confederate victory, thereby changing the entire outcome of the Civil War.

The words of Lincoln in that proclamation ring loud, as he said, "It behooves us then, to humble ourselves before the offended Power, to confess our national sins, and to pray for clemency and forgiveness." It is clear to see that President Lincoln had connected the dots of our national sins and the pain and destruction of the Civil War. Even though he was living under the New Covenant, he still believed that God judges' sin.

May God open the eyes of the American people and most importantly the pastors of the churches in our country to connect the dots between our nation's sins and the terrible problems our nation is facing today. As President Abraham Lincoln did in 1863, may the pastors declare it from behind their pulpits and in the streets. It may be too late for America, as something tells me that God has already turned this nation over to a reprobate mind. However, we pray that God would give us one last great revival and just a few more years to bring in the harvest before the *"Last Trump"* sounds (I Corinthians 15:51-52) and the Apocalypse begins.

We can see America is on the verge of another Civil War. As in 1863, we have also become too proud to pray to the God who created us. We, like ancient Israel, are close to God's Almighty hand of wrath coming down. In fact, by the looks of it, God's hand may have already begun to come down. The New York Times would be correct to post the following headline:

"AMERICA HAS FORGOTTEN GOD, DAYS WITHOUT NUMBER"

This is exactly what Abraham Lincoln said in his proclamation during the Civil War, and it is exactly what God said to ancient Israel through the prophet Jeremiah.

In 2020, I personally sent a certified letter to the Whitehouse address to President Donald J. Trump with a copy of Abraham Lincoln's famous proclamation. I encouraged President Trump to do what Abraham Lincoln did in 1863 and call for a National Day of Repentance and Fasting, unfortunately my efforts were in vain.

Jeremiah said, *"Also in thy skirts is found the blood of the souls of the poor innocents"* (Jeremiah 2:34). In our nation today, we have seen the death of poor innocents just as Israel did. In America, there have been over 60 million babies aborted since 1973. Yet, just like the nation of Israel, we will not admit our guilt. In our self-righteous minds, we do not believe we have done anything wrong. Yet, the Bible calls murder sin, both outside of the womb and inside the womb.

If one does not think he has sinned when wrath and destruction is poured out by God, he does not connect the dots. Most men believe all calamities that are happening are just a coincidence or, if it is a storm, it's just "mother nature." Unfortunately, our nation never realizes or believes it is "Father God" who is sending judgment for our continuous sins that our nation commits without repentance.

Israel said, *"I have not sinned"* (Jeremiah 2:35). My friend, there can be no revival without the admittance of sin first and a true repentance of turning back to God. Israel, instead of repenting, would attempt confident schemes with other nations to bring about further prosperity and supposed security. But their schemes would not stop the wrath of God. Jeremiah said, *"For the Lord has rejected your confidences, (alliances of men) and you shall not prosper in them"* (Jeremiah 2:37).

1962

In the year 1962, which happens to be the year I was born, America began on a downward slide to basically becoming a pagan nation. In this year, the Supreme Court of America decided that it was unconstitutional for state officials to compose an official school prayer and encourage its use in the public schools. This all happened in the great state of New York where I have lived most of my life. Years before, this state approved legislation that encouraged students to start their school days with the Pledge of Allegiance and a prayer. This prayer read as follows, "Almighty God, we acknowledge our dependence upon Thee, and we beg Thy blessings upon us, our parents, our teachers, and our country. Amen" (Wikipedia, The Free Encyclopedia, wikipedia.org/wiki/Engel v. Vitale).

The case against this school prayer was brought to the court by a group of families who sued school board President, William J. Vitale, Jr. The families argued that the voluntary prayer written by the state board of regents to "Almighty God" contradicted their religious beliefs. Led by a man name Steven I. Engel, a Jewish man, the plaintiffs sought to challenge the constitutionality of the state's prayer in school policy. The acting parties were all atheists. However, one of the plaintiffs claimed being very religious but was not a "churchgoer." In this case, he said he was unsure of what prayer would accomplish. (Wikipedia, The Free Encyclopedia, wikipedia.org/wiki/Engel v. Vitale).

The court ruled six-to-one in favor of the plaintiff, declaring government-written prayers in the public schools as unconstitutional, violating the Establishment Cause of the First Amendment (Facts and Case Summary - Engel v. Vitale *Engel v. Vitale, 370 U.S. 421, 422 (1962) "Engel v. Vitale | law case"*. Encyclopedia Britannica. Retrieved 2018-11-28.)

The court rejected the defendant's arguments that students were not asked to observe any specific established religion and that the traditional heritage of the nation was religious, and that the prayer was voluntary. The Court held that the mere promotion of religion is sufficient to establish a violation, even if that promotion is not coercive. The Court further held that the fact that the prayer was vaguely-enough worded not to promote any religion is not a sufficient defense, as it still promotes a family of religions (those that recognize Almighty God), which still violates the Establishment Clause. (Facts and Case Summary - *Engel v. Vitale.* ^ *Engel v. Vitale, 370 U.S. 421, 422 (1962) "Engel v. Vitale | law case"*. Encyclopedia Britannica. Retrieved 2018-11-28.)

In his dissenting opinion, Justice Stewart contended that the Establishment Clause was originally written to abolish the idea of a state-sponsored church and not to stop a non-mandatory, brief, non-denominational prayer. Most of the Court did not agree. (Facts and Case Summary - *Engel v. Vitale.* US Courts. Retrieved February 16, 2019)

This landmark decision was the beginning of removing God from all forms of public-assisted, government-funded activities in America. What the New York Supreme Court failed to recognize in the Engel vs. Vitale case was that the founding fathers of the constitution put the Establishment Clause in to protect the Church from government telling Christian churches what they had to do or believe. These men never meant it to separate the State from any mention or activity of God. I believe, the prayer that was removed in the public schools of America lifted the hand of God's protection from our public schools and would prove to be the beginning of an onslaught of evil in American schools. The statistics of how the public schools changed after 1962 are enlightening and at the same time frightening.

In 1940, the top disciplinary problems in public school included things like chewing gum, writing on desks, and not throwing paper in the wastepaper basket. Today, we have school shootings, murders, rape, arson, assault, etc. There has been a dramatic change in American schools since 1962. It is now a worry on the minds of many American parents every time they drop their children off at public schools. I don't think we ever imagine that schools would need simulation games to learn defense tactics against possible shooters in buildings or have on-duty police officers on campus all day long as a normal occurrence.

Maybe the experts of education and safety should take a second look at the prayer that was taken out of the school system in 1962. As quoted above, the words of that prayer are profound. It is a great deception when educated people remove Almighty God from their lives and, in this case, the children's lives; thinking they know better than God. Our dependence on God is what is lacking today. We are now depending on science, government, military, and our own personal possessions to provide safety. But the Bible says, *"except the LORD keep the city, the watchmen wakes but in vain"* (Psalm 127:1).

1973

Just eleven years after the removal of prayer from the school system, America made another decision that would trump all Supreme Court decisions for all time. It was a landmark decision when the Court ruled that the Constitution of the United States protects a pregnant women's liberty to choose to have an abortion without excessive government restriction. It struck down many U.S. State and Federal abortion laws and prompted an ongoing national debate in the United States. (Wikipedia https://en.wikipedia.org/wiki/Roe v. Wade)

This Law prompted an ongoing national debate in the United States between religious and moral views in the political world, dividing much of the United States into two groups; Pro-life vs. Pro-choice. No law has ever divided our nation more than this one, and no law enacted by the Nation's

Supreme Court placed our country in more jeopardy of divine judgment than this one.

Norma McCorvey (Jane Roe) was the woman who wanted the abortion. The local District Attorney, Henry Wade of Texas, fought for the right of the unborn. However, the highest Court in the land ruled seven-to-two in favor of Roe, setting this nation at odds with a thrice Holy God who said in His Word, *"You shall not murder"* (Exodus 20:13) and against one of the seven things that are an abomination unto God, *"hands that shed innocent blood"* (Proverbs 6:16-17).

The court resolved a balancing test by tying State regulations of abortion to the three trimesters of pregnancy. During the first trimester, governments could not prohibit abortions at all. During the second trimester, governments could require reasonable health regulations. During the third trimester, abortions could be prohibited entirely as the laws contained exceptions for cases when it is necessary to save the life or health of the mother.

In 1992, the Court revisited and modified the 1973 Roe vs. Wade ruling in a case called Planned Parenthood vs. Casey. The court reaffirmed Roe's right to have an abortion as constitutionally protected, but abandoned Roe's trimester framework in favor of standard-based fetal viability. (Wikipedia- Roe vs Wade- The free Encyclopedia). Fetal viability was defined as the ability of the fetus (i.e., child) to live outside of the uterus. There is only one big problem with this rationale; God defines in His Word that life begins at conception (Psalms 51:5).

Whenever a nation goes beyond the Word of God, it is in trouble. Since 1973, America murdered over 60 million babies and, all the while, called it the constitutional right of the mother. This has been labeled America's holocaust, and rightfully so. Whenever the Constitution of America or any country goes against the Word of God, it brings only judgment to that nation. In the Bible, 40 is the number of probation, as many times, the Lord gives a people or a nation a probation period of 40 years (or 40 days) to repent from their sin before He harshly judges them. It appears that America's judgment in 2020 is 7 years overdue. However, based on what has happened in 2020, it looks like it has now begun. God said in the Book of Leviticus,

> *"And you shall not let any of your seed pass through the fire to Moloch, neither shall you profane the Name of your God: I am the LORD"* (Leviticus 18:21).

Molech was a so-called deity associated with the people of Ammon, who were neighbors of Israel. This idol was called *"the abomination of the Ammonites"* and was associated with the sacrifice of children in the fire (Leviticus 20:2-5, II Kings 17:31). (Expositors Study Bible page 229). In fact, it was this sin of offering their sons and daughters to pass through the fire unto Molech that brought the judgment of God. In the 777th chapter of the Bible, God gave some very strong words to Israel recorded in Jeremiah.

> *"Therefore, thus says the LORD; Behold I will give this city unto the hand of the Chaldeans, and into the hand of Nebuchadnezzar king of Babylon, and he shall take it. And the Chaldeans, who fight against this city, shall come and set fire on this city, and burn it with the houses, upon whose roofs they have offered incense unto Baal, and poured out drink offerings unto other gods, to provoke Me to anger. For the children of Israel and the children of Judah have only done evil before Me from their youth: for the children of Israel have only provoked Me to anger with the work of their hands, says the LORD"* (Jeremiah 32:28-30).

Israel was going to be judged by God for the sin of worshipping other gods. The people were doing evil in the eyes of God, and one of Israel's greatest sins was child sacrifice. Jeremiah went on to say, *"And they built the high places of Baal which are in the valley of the son of Hinnom, to cause their sons and their daughters to pass through the fire unto Molech; which I commanded them not, neither came it unto My mind, that they should do this abomination, to cause Judah to sin"* (Jeremiah 32:35). There could be no greater abomination in the eyes of God than to kill an innocent child. The Bible says, *"Then were there brought unto Him little children, that He should put His hands on them, and pray: and the Disciples rebuked them. But Jesus said, Suffer little children and forbid them not, to come unto Me: for as such is the Kingdom of Heaven."* (Matthew 19:13-14).

The Greek word for infants in this scripture is "brephos", which is a noun that means "infant child or the unborn; God has a special place in His heart for the little ones, born and unborn. When you legalize the killing of the unborn you place yourself under God's divine anger. At this writing, it has been 48 years since the first legalized abortion was performed in this nation. Now, after the destruction of 60 million babies, the judgment for this great sin and many others is beginning to be seen in America.

1980

    Just seven years later, after Roe v Wade came another landmark decision was made by the United States Supreme Court in a case titled Stone vs. Graham. The Court ruled that a Kentucky statute was unconstitutional and in violation of the Establishment Clause of the First Amendment because it lacked a non-religious legislative purpose. The statute required the posting of a copy of the Ten Commandments on the wall of each public classroom in the state. While copies of the Ten Commandments were purchased with private funding, the court ruled that because they were placed in public classrooms, they were in violation of the First Amendment. (Wikipedia https://en.wikipedia.org/wiki/Stone_v._Graham)

    The Court held that the Kentucky statute that required the Ten Commandments to be posted in school classrooms was in violation of the First Amendment. To interpret the First Amendment, the Court rested on the precedent established in Lemon vs. Kurtzman and the three-part "Lemon Test." The Court concluded that because «requiring the posting of the Ten Commandments in public school rooms has no secular legislative purpose, it is unconstitutional. (Wikipedia https://en.wikipedia.org/wiki/Stone_v._ Graham)

    The Court approached the case through the lens created in Lemon vs. Kurtzman. They agreed that if Kentucky's statute broke any of the three guidelines outlined in the Lemon Test, the statute would be in violation of the Establishment Clause. The majority voiced that the commandments convey a religious undertone because they concern "the religious duties of believers: worshipping the Lord God alone, avoiding idolatry, not using the Lord's name in vain, and observing the sabbath day." But since "the commandments are [not] integrated into the school curriculum, where the Bible may constitutionally be used in an appropriate study of history," they have no secular purpose and a definite religious purpose. (**Wikipedia** https://en.wikipedia.org/wiki/Stone_v._Graham)

    So, in just 18 years, America went from removing prayer from public schools to legalizing murder of the unborn to removing the Ten Commandments from our school walls. Obviously, it would be self-convicting for a nation to legalize abortion while having *"Thou shalt not kill"* on school walls, which is the sixth commandment. So, they decided to remove God's law completely from the school walls. There is an interesting statistic regarding homicide rates in America. From 1950 to 2017, the year in which America had the largest homicide rate was 1980. Notice this is the same year in which the Supreme Court ruled it unconstitutional to place the Ten Commandments in public schools. I don't think this is a coincidence.

2015

Thirty-five years after removing the Ten Commandments from public school walls, another unbelievable Supreme Court decision was made and signed into law. On June 26, 2015, the United States Supreme Court ruled in the case of Obergefell vs. Hodges that a fundamental right to marry is guaranteed to same-sex couples covered by the fourteenth amendment, which states that same-sex marriages must be allowed. (https://en.wikipedia.org/wiki/Same-sex_marriage_legislation_in_the_ United_States)

I believe that when this law was passed it was the beginning of when God would turn this nation over to a reprobate mind, which means this was the last straw. Where there is no chance of saving what has been already lost, we are indeed doomed to reap God's judgment.

The Same Sex Marriage Law was passed in our country during the presidency of Barak Obama who was the first sitting president in our nation's history to acknowledge that homosexual unions were acceptable and right in his eyes. He lobbied hard for same sex marriage and when the Law was passed, he had the Whitehouse lit up in rainbow colors the night of ruling to celebrate the decision. But he didn't stop there, President Obama had one of the largest rainbow flags ever seen draped around the US Embassy in Israel.

I believe we could say on June 26, 2015, our nation became an "Obama Nation" before the eyes of God. The word of God says: *"If a man also lie with mankind, as he lies with a woman, both of them have committed an abomination"* (Leviticus 20:13).

The Word of God says in Romans 1:24,

> *"Wherefore God also gave them up to uncleanness through the lusts of their own hearts, to dishonor their own bodies between themselves: Who changed the truth of God into a lie, and worshipped and served the creature more than the Creator, Who is blessed forever. Amen. For this cause God gave them up unto vile affections: for even their women did change the natural use into that which is against nature: and likewise, also the men, leaving the natural use of the women, burned in their lust one toward another."*

The Word of God further reads, *"And even as they did not like to retain God in their knowledge, God gave them over to a reprobate mind, to do those things which are not convenient"* (Romans 1:28). The word "reprobate" found in this scripture is "adokimos" in the Greek language and it means "rejected, worthless, castaway." This word means that God is referring to something being worthy of condemnation, worthless, useless and should be castaway.

This means that any individual or nation God labels as reprobate becomes a castaway. In other words, they have reached the limit of God's patience, they have been rejected by God and are left to themselves; they only become more and more evil. We could say it another way, which is whenever the sin of homosexuality becomes common place in a nation and considered normal behavior (that which God calls unnatural and an abomination in His eyes), then that nation is headed toward judgment.

LGBTQ

Whenever sin is allowed to continue with no repentance, things only get worse and worse. In other words, sin becomes even more sinful and escalates. When you study the laws of God, you see that unless repentance occurs the sins that are forbidden become more and more extreme. For example, notice the following progression of forbidden sins in the scriptures that are escalating in our nation:

- Adultery (Leviticus 20:10)
- Incest (Leviticus 20:11-12)
- Homosexuality (Leviticus 20:13)
- Bestiality (Leviticus 20:15-16)

In the Old Testament all the above sins were to be judged with a penalty of death. The human heart is so wicked that left to itself with no restrictions, it continues downward to levels that are beyond human understanding and comprehension. For example, sexual sin begins with adultery and can spiral down to something as abhorrent as having sexual relations with an animal. This is incomprehensible to the human mind. In other words, the sinner who continues to sin with no repentance or restraint ends up in a demonical orgy of sexual insanity.

One can see the same trend happening in America after homosexual marriages were made legal, we were then bombarded with the LGBTQ movement. It started with only LGB, which stands for Lesbian, Gay, and Bisexual and a T and Q was gradually added for Transgender and Queer or Questioning. When sin is left unchecked, it only gets more sinful. What started in our country in 1924 with The Society for Human Rights, soon grew into what we have today. This society was founded by Henry Gerber in Chicago and was the first documented gay-rights organization. By 1950, we saw the Mattachine Society formed by activist Harry Hay and was one of the first sustained gay rights groups in the United States. The Society focused on social acceptance and other types of support for homosexuals.

Then, in September of 1955, we saw the first known lesbian-rights organization in the United States form in San Francisco. The Daughters of Bilitis (DOB) hosted private social functions for their members who feared police raids, threats of violence and discrimination in otherwise mainstream bars and clubs. By 1961, Illinois became the first state to decriminalize homosexuality by repealing their sodomy laws. Until this date, homosexuality was a criminal offense in every American state. On September 11, 1961, the first documentary in the U.S. was aired on a local California station.

In June of 1969, police raided the Stonewall Inn in New York City. Protests and demonstrations began, and it later became known as the impetus for the gay civil rights movement in the United States. That same year, the Los Angeles Chronical was renamed "The Advocate." It is considered the oldest continuing LGBTQ publication that began as a newsletter and published by the activist group called Personal Rights in Defense and Education (PRIDE).

On June 28, 1973, an event known as the Christopher Street Liberation Day is considered to be the first gay pride parade where people marched through the streets of New York City. In that same year, Lambda Legal became the first legal organization to fight for the equal rights of gays and lesbians. Lambda also became their own first client after being denied a non-profit status; however, the New York Supreme Court eventually ruled that Lambda Legal can exist as a non-profit.

On December 15, 1973, by a vote of 5,854 to 3,810, the American Psychiatric Association removed homosexuality from its list of mental disorders in the DSM-II, Diagnostic and Statistical Manual of Mental Disorders. In 1974, Elaine Noble was the first openly gay candidate elected to a state office when she assumed a role in the Massachusetts State Legislature.

On January 9, 1978, Harvey Milk was inaugurated as San Francisco City Supervisor and became the first openly gay man to be elected to a political office in California. In November, Harvey Milk and Mayor George Moscone were murdered by Dan White, who had resigned from his San Francisco board position and wanted Moscone to reappoint him. White later served just over five years in prison for voluntary manslaughter.

In 1978, inspired by Milk to develop a symbol of pride and hope for the LGBTQ community, Gilbert Baker designed and stitched together the first rainbow flag.

On October 14, 1979, the first National march in Washington, D.C for Lesbian and Gay Rights took place. It drew an estimated 75,000 to 125,000 individuals marching for LGBTQ rights.

On March 2, 1982, Wisconsin became the first state to outlaw discrimination based on sexual orientation.

On December 3, 1996, Hawaii's Judge Chang ruled that the state does not have a legal right to deprive same-sex couples the right to marry. This made Hawaii the first state to recognize that gay and lesbian couples were entitled to the same privileges that heterosexual married couples have.

In April 1997, comedian Ellen DeGeneres came out as a lesbian on the cover of Time Magazine as the article stated "Yep, I'm Gay."

On April 1, 1998, Martin Luther King Jr.'s widow, Coretta Scott King asked the civil rights community to help in the effort to extinguish homophobia.

On May 17, 2004, the first legal same-sex marriage in the United States took place in Massachusetts.

On September 6, 2005, the California legislature became the first to pass a bill allowing marriage between same-sex couples. Governor Arnold Schwarzenegger vetoed the bill.

In September 2011, the "Don't Ask, Don't Tell" was repealed and ended a ban on gay men and lesbians from openly serving in the military.

On May 9, 2012, in an ABC interview, Barak Obama became the first sitting U.S. President to publicly support freedom for a LGBTQ couple to marry.

On September 4, 2012, the Democratic Party became the first major U.S. political party in history to publicly support same-sex marriage on a national platform at the Democratic National Convention.

On June 26, 2015, the Supreme Court ruled that states cannot ban same-sex marriage. The five-to-four ruling had Justice Anthony Kennedy writing for the majority. Each of the four conservative justices wrote their own dissent.

On June 30, 2016, Secretary of Defense Carter announced that the Pentagon was lifting the ban on transgender people and they could openly serve in the U.S. military.

On June 27, 2017, the District of Columbia residents could choose a gender-neutral option on their driver's license. D.C. residents became the first people in the United States to be able to choose X as their gender marker instead of male or female on driver's licenses and identification cards.

Similar policies exist in Canada, India, Bangladesh, Australia, New Zealand, and Nepal.

(CNN https://www.cnn.com/2015/06/19/us/lgbt-rights-milestones-fast-facts/index.html (List is abbreviated from the original).

As you look at the progressive advancement of the LGBTQ movement, notice that it only became more and more acceptable and demented as the movement went forward without restraint. God said in His Word that when He turns a people or a nation over to a reprobate mind, it becomes exceedingly sinful:

"Being filled with all unrighteousness, fornication, wickedness, covetousness, maliciousness; full of envy, murder, debate, deceit, malignity; whisperers, backbiters, haters of God, despiteful, proud, boasters, inventors of evil things, disobedient to parents, without understanding, covenant breakers, without natural affection, implacable, unmerciful: who knowing the judgment of God, that they which commit such things are worthy of death, not only do the same, but have pleasure in them who do them" (Romans 1:29-32).

The above verses describe America to a T. Just think about how homosexuality was once a forbidden lifestyle in 1776 but is now encouraged and no longer considered a sociopathic personality disorder in the DSM-V manual on mental disorders. Same-sex couples can now get legally married, and our courts defend their rights to have the same benefits offered to heterosexual couples. Even though marriages between a man and a woman for the purpose of populating the earth are God-ordained, America supports paying for gender-change surgery for incarcerated criminals and believes that children should have the right to choose their preferred gender regardless of their biological gender.

Under the Old Testament the Word of God says that those who do such things deserve the judgment of death. But their sin goes even further, as they take pleasure in promoting it to others and inviting others to engage in it as well. God clearly calls homosexuality a sin, as He said, *"If a man also lie with mankind, as he lies with a woman, both of them have committed an abomination: they shall surely be put to death; their blood shall be upon them"* (Leviticus 20:13).

The words that come to mind regarding a man having sexual relations with another man or a woman having sexual relations with another woman is "sick and perverted." These individuals are mentally, morally, and spiritually depraved. Most of them will take offense with me for saying this, but up until 50 years ago most people in America would have agree with me. What changed? God's Word did not change, but people have decided to reject God's Word and instead rely on their own moral or immoral standards. This is part of The "Great Deception."

Right now, our nation has fallen so far from the Word of God that after the Rapture of the Church, America and the world will be like Sodom and Gomorrah. America's goodness has shrunk under the deceptive mantle of progressive humanism, which is another name for "anything goes." The slogan, "if it feels good, do it" has become the mindset of many Americans.

The Bible says that *"The wages of sin is death."* A growing number of Americans are becoming angry at Christians who hang onto the Biblical standards related to this topic, which has been in effect for nearly 6,000 years. They are upset that Christians refuse to go along with their secular, demented and progressive way of thinking.

However, consider this:

It is a known fact that a homosexual lifestyle takes an average of 20 to 30 years off a person's life as compared to one living a heterosexual lifespan. Dr. J. Satinover documents that homosexuals lose twenty-five to thirty years of life as they suffer from various illnesses such as gonorrhea, chlamydia, syphilis, herpes, HIV/AIDS and many other sexually transmitted diseases. In addition to this list, homosexuals also battle enteric infectious diseases, cancer, alcoholism, and suicide; all of which contribute to premature deaths (Christian Medical and Dental Association).

Even with the dangers of the gay lifestyles that contribute to an early loss of life, President Joe Biden still declared to the LGBTQ community that "he's got their back." Advocates of this perverse and dangerous lifestyle are encouraging an early death for these poor souls who are trapped in destructive and deceptive lifestyles that the Bible warns against.

It's time to repent before it is too late. The judgment of God is coming unless America repents and turns back to God. It will not be long, that just as Rome of old, America will fold like a deck of cards. Many wonder why the U.S. is not found in end-time Bible prophecies, but maybe it is because America has been in Bible prophesy all along and many people just don't see our comparison to Rome, ancient Babylon, and Israel.

> *"And he cried mightily with a strong voice, saying, Babylon the great is fallen, And is become the habitation of devils, and the hold of every foul spirit, and a cage of every unclean and hateful bird. For all nations have drunk of the wine of the wrath of her fornication, and the kings of the earth have committed Fornication with her, and the merchants of the earth are waxed right through the abundance of her delicacies"* (Revelation 18:2-3).

Notice it says, *"Babylon the great is fallen"* and the scriptures also say, *"For all nations have drunk of the wine of the wrath of her fornication."* All means all the nations of the world including America will also fall during the Great Tribulation. If Rome of old, as strong as that empire was, could fall and Babylon the Great fell, then why do we doubt that America would not also fall?

No doubt, the Rapture of the church will play a huge role in weakening this nation to just a liberal, financial, and spiritually bankrupt nation. But maybe, just maybe, America is removed as a superpower even before the Rapture due to God judging this nation for its repeated abominations.

The only reason that I can find for why God has not already judged this nation is due to the Gospel of Jesus Christ and the remnant of churches and ministries in our nation who continue to preach the message of the cross. This, and this alone, is the only good left in this nation. We are pleading with God to send one more great revival that would bring in a great harvest just before the last judgment begins. I pray that that revival is coming, and when it begins, we will know that we are in the last great awakening just before Jesus comes again.

AMERICA'S ABOMINATIONS

You may ask what are the "great" sins of the United States of America? I will only list the major undeniable sins that I believe will cause the Judgment of God to be sent on our nation unless we repent quickly.

TOP 10 SINS IN OUR NATION
(AS I SEE IT, ALTHOUGH THERE ARE MANY MORE)

- The worship of other gods instead of worshipping only the One True God, The Lord Jesus Christ. America no longer stands for Jesus Christ as the One True God as our founding fathers did.

- We are the number one producer of pornography IN THE WORLD. Our nation is filled with sexual immorality and our government does little to nothing to protect our children from it.

- Sex trafficking is at an all-time high as young children are kidnapped and sold for sex. It is hard to even imagine this sin going on in our nation so repeatedly. Our children are not even safe to walk or ride their bike around their block anymore.

- We have accepted and promoted gay lifestyles as normal, which God says in His Word is an abomination.

- We have murdered over 60 million babies from inside their mother's womb, all in the name of freedom of choice. This is a direct violation of God's Commandment that says: "***Thou shall not murder.***"

- We have changed God's definition of marriage and made it lawfully accepted and we have even encouraged men to have sexual relations with men, and women with women. These abominable marriages have not only become legal, but same-sex couples can legally adopt children. The lifestyle of the Homosexual reduces a life expectancy on average 25 years to the lifestyle of a Heterosexual. Yet, our government from the Supreme Court to the President on down continues to support and encourage this dangerous lifestyle.

- As our leaders are sworn into office (i.e., President, Supreme Court, etc.) they place their right hand on the Holy Bible, and then they make a mockery of their oath by creating and promoting laws against the very Bible on which they laid their hand on. How is that for hypocrisy?

- We no longer allow the 10 Commandments to be posted on our public-school walls or Bibles to be handed out in our public schools, but instead are allowed to hand out condoms to the students to make it seem acceptable to engage in pre-marital sexual relations.

- We allow and even promote gender switching and provide free health care for sex re-assignment surgery. So, a perfectly healthy young person can be cut open on the operating table to remove their biological parts that they were born with to permit them to change their sex and the government allows the health care physician to do that all legally. If that isn't barbaric, I don't know what is.

- Our Presidents make peace deals with Israel and Arab nations that does not allow the Jewish people to create settlements on their own land, but instead pressures them to give up land in the name of "peace." Meanwhile, this giving away of land violates Genesis 12:3, which says, *"And I will bless those who bless you, and curse him who curses you."*

The year 2020 to 2021 saw great economic disaster due to COVID-19; the likes we haven't seen since the 1929 Great Depression. Some experts predict that what is coming to America is going to be even greater than the Great Depression. The question is whether America is connecting the dots?

Today in 2024 only 20 percent of Americans go to church regularly, and most American churches no longer teach on repentance. Most Christians don't even attend a weekly prayer meeting, or a Bible study and most churches have eliminated these types of meetings from their weekly church calendar due to poor attendance. All because most Americans are either too busy to attend church more than once a week, or they no longer value the Word of God or the Church more than attending a once-a-week service, if they go to church at all.

I have to say I have never seen the modern church more deceived in my lifetime. Let me say this without any fear of contradiction, the Judgment of God is coming to America just as sure as it came to Israel over 2,500 years ago and this judgement is going to be very severe.

Jeremiah said: *"We have heard the fame thereof: our hands wax feeble: anguish has taken hold of us, and pain, as a woman in travail. The sword of the enemy and fear is on every side"* (Jeremiah 6:24-25). God told Israel that they should do the following, *"O daughter of My People, gird you with sackcloth, and wallow yourself in ashes: make thee mourning, as for an only son, most bitter lamentation: For the spoiler shall suddenly come upon us"* (Jeremiah 6:26).

Ask yourself the question what are American churches doing since the COVID 19 pandemic began in March 2020? Have the pastors called the people to repentance, prayer and fasting? No, most were too caught up in the vision to "Make America Great Again" (MAGA), debating and working towards getting their president reelected. They did not call on King Jesus to come, but instead called for more prosperity to continue as money continues to be most people's god. It seems only when their wealth is threatened, do they even think about God or their sins. However, God said that a person cannot worship "God and Mammon" (i.e., money or possessions). Make no mistake friend, Judgment is coming to America! No, change that the Judgment of God is already here!

CHAPTER 5

IT'S TIME TO CONNECT THE DOTS

Jeremiah warned the people that destruction was coming to their land, and they should prepare for war. There was an evil siege coming into the land and it was clear that God was sending the opposition. God gave them plenty of opportunities before He removed them from the Promise Land. The coming invasion was going to bring incredible grief, wounds, destruction, and death. The saddest part of it was that it could have been all avoided if they only heeded to the warnings given by the prophet Jeremiah.

God says, *"To whom shall I speak, and give warning, that they may hear?"* But they could not hear because the Word of the LORD was a reproach in their minds, and they had no delight in the true Word of God (Jeremiah 6:10). Their disregard for the Word of God caused the fury of God to come, as God said He was weary of withholding His fury on the people. All were going to be affected, and they would lose not only their homes to the Babylonians, but also their fields and even more tragic their wives and families. In other words, they were going to lose everything. How terrible is the judgment of God! But how much more terrible is the sin of the wicked. God says from the greatest to the least, Israel was given over to covetousness; and the Prophet and the Priest was dealing falsely with the people (Jeremiah 6:13).

The fashionable prophets of that day were claiming "peace, peace" for the people of the land. But the very opposite was on its way. They were reassuring the people that no judgment was coming; but unfortunately, the people would find out that most of the prophets were wrong. God asked the question, *"Were they ashamed when they had committed abomination? He said "no, they were not all ashamed, neither could they blush"* (Jeremiah 6:15). Therefore, he said that the false prophets would fall at the time He visited them, and they would be cast down.

God called Israel to turn away from their false priests and prophets who gave the people a message that they wanted to hear instead of God's truth. They dished out a fresh new message that tickled the ears of the people, but God declared the following:

> *"Thus says the LORD, Stand you in the ways, and see, and ask for the old paths, where is the good way, and walk therein, and you shall find rest for your souls. But they said, We will not walk therein"* (Jeremiah 6:16).

How tremendously sad it is to consider this terrible time in Israel's history. God offers rest and healing in the old path, but the people were unwilling to walk in these old paths. The message of the Cross, Jesus Christ, and Him Crucified is the old path. The Bible says that the Lamb was slain before the foundation of the earth (Revelation 13:9). Now, it doesn't get any older than before the foundation of the earth. What this means is that before God created the earth and all that is in it, He knew that Adam and all of humanity would fall. Fortunately, God had a plan to save the people. He would send His Son, Jesus Christ, to die for the sons of Adam's fallen race. However, tragically Israel didn't want this message.

The old path is Christ coming into this world and going to the Cross to die for sin. The Cross makes man deal with his sin and repent. However, rebellious man doesn't want to admit that he has sinned or needs to repent. Today, the church wants a new message that emphasizes prosperity, purpose, destiny, fulfilling dreams and blessings. But the power of God, through the Holy Spirit, is only found in the ancient path, the good way, which is the message of the Cross (I Corinthians 1:18).

THE BLIND WATCHMAN

Most preachers today are offering lukewarm, self-centered messages that have no conviction of sin. Their messages are not Christ-centered. When it comes to spiritual prosperity, God abundantly blesses; however, not necessarily with bigger cars and fatter wallets. He blesses us with a deeper love for God, a richer peace of mind, unspeakable joy, and a heart for souls. This, and so much more, is the real prosperity that God wants to give us. The focus of the Church identified in the Book of Acts is a church focused on preaching Jesus Christ, Crucified and Resurrected. They had their eyes on the "old path," fixed on winning souls for God.

God said that He set watchmen over the people to warn them, but the people said, "We will not listen." The job of the watchman was to position himself on top of a watchtower to be a look out. When he saw the enemy approaching, he was to put his lips to the trumpet and blast a loud sound as a warning that danger was coming. This is exactly what Jeremiah was called to do by God, and he was doing it loud and clear. However, the people didn't want to listen to this Prophet of God.

The role of every true preacher of the Gospel, regardless of whether the people or nation will listen is to warn the people when they see danger coming due the consequences of sin because the people will not repent. The Bible teaches that if the shepherd does not warn the sheep that a wolf is approaching but instead leaves the sheep and flees, that shepherd is nothing more than a *"hireling"* (John 10:12). The definition of a hireling is a person who works purely for material reward. This kind of preacher only fleeces his sheep and refuses to protect them. Jesus said that this kind of a shepherd does not really care for his sheep (John 10:13). Unfortunately, these kinds of preachers come a-dime-a-dozen in today's modern church.

The problem in the modern church is that we have mostly "blind watchmen" who are afraid to warn the people because they don't want to offend their congregations, and why? Because they are more concerned with pleasing the people and keeping the tithes coming in and the numbers of people attending their churches going up.

The Word of God speaks of this kind of leader:

> *"His watchmen are blind: they are all ignorant, they are dumb dogs, they cannot bark: sleeping, laying down, loving to slumber. Yes, they are greedy dogs which can never have enough, and they are shepherds who cannot understand: they all look to their own way, every one for his gain, from his quarter"* (Isaiah 56:10-11).

DIVIDED WE STAND

In the beginning of 2020, the false prophets boasted of how prosperous the nation was under Presidency Trump. Everything looked like it was going so well, and yet our country had never been more divided.

Former President Trump gave an address to the Union on February 4, 2020, in the Capital building. That night was a visual exhibition of how divided we had become as a nation. With the Senate on the verge of an impeachment vote, partisanship was observable as most of the democratic woman representatives were dressed all in white as a sign of protest against the president.

House Speaker Nancy Pelosi, with whom President Trump had not spoken with in months, initially extended her hand to greet the President when he first came to the podium to speak; only to have him turn away from her. She smiled in an obviously uncomfortable way as she glanced over to her Democratic caucus and shrugged her shoulders as if to say, "I tried to be cordial."

President Trump began his address to the nation that night, during a time when his approval numbers had reached nearly 50 percent. Such things as new trade deals with China and other countries, the newly formed Space Force military branch, tougher border security, his laid-out peace plan for Israel and the Palestinians were the focus of his message.

In President Trump's speech, he proclaimed that unemployment was at a 45-year low. He also proudly spoke about how African American unemployment stood at the lowest percentage ever recorded and Hispanic American unemployment had reached the lowest levels in history as well. He noted that small businesses were at an all-time high and the stock market had smashed one record after another, gaining as much as eight trillion in value.

In the room, there was a tangible buzz of excitement by the republicans on the right as the democrats of Congress on the left sat silent most of the night. Their Republican colleagues stood and cheered as President Trump made many statements on the progress and advancement of the country under his leadership. It was more than the Democrats could stomach, as some were even seen walking out at various points during the President's address.

Throughout his speech, President Trump boasted about the economic accomplishments of his last three years in office and said, "In just three short years, we shattered the mentality of American decline and totally rejected the downsizing." President Trump boldly stated, *"We are moving forward at a pace that was unimaginable just a short time ago, and we are never, ever going back."* His Republican audience responded with chants of "four more years."

President Trump refuted the idealism of the left, which he believed would take the country into a socialistic nation. He said, *"To those watching at home tonight, I want you to know; we will never let socialism destroy American healthcare!"* He also stated that "Socialism destroys nations, but always remember freedom unifies the soul." At the conclusion of his address, Nancy Pelosi stood behind the President and was seen ripping up a printed copy of his speech in front of the entire nation and the world. President Trump's bold and boastful pronouncements seemed to further distance one side from the other. I am sure that President Trump had no idea how fast things were about to change in our nation after that night.

PEACE DEAL OF THE CENTURY

Just about one week before the President's national address President Trump and Prime Minister Benjamin Netanyahu stood together at a press conference in Washington D.C. with Arab leaders present, but no one from the Palestinian leadership in Israel attended the meeting. It was a press conference to announce a peace plan for Israel and the Palestinians entitled, "Peace to Prosperity: A Vision to Improve the Lives of the Palestinian and Israeli People."

On January 28, 2020, President Trump boldly called this the *"Peace Deal of the Century,"* which was authored by a team led by President Trump's son-in-law and senior advisor, Jared Kushner, who is Jewish himself. The Palestinian leadership immediately rejected the plan upon its announcement. At the press conference, President Trump reminded those present what he had done for Israel. After Trump spoke, Netanyahu gave his remarks and boasted about President Trump's achievement. He boldly proclaimed that this day would be remembered in the same breath as Israel's 1948 Day of Independence. He also said that this was one of the most important moments in his life.

President Trump spoke about finding a new way to make peace between Israel and the Palestinians. Israel would get the security it needed, and the Palestinians would get the state they craved. However, the Palestinians were not so impressed, calling the United State the big "Satan" and Israel the little "Satan" after the speech. They stressed that they would never agree to any deal made by President Trump.

Through all the applause, hand shaking, smiles, standing ovations, laughter and photos taken that day, there was one major flaw in President Trump's Peace Deal that was not considered. Like presidents before him, President Trump failed to consider and believe what God told Abraham (the father of the nation of Israel), *"Unto your seed have I given this land"* (Genesis 15:8). The seed is the Jewish people, and the land is the Promised Land (i.e., Israel).

Nearly 4,000 years ago, God promised the land of Israel to the Jewish people giving a declaration to Abraham that goes along with the land as follows:

> *"And I will bless them who bless you and curse him who curses you: and in you shall all families of the Earth be blessed"* (Genesis 12:3).

The curses are what President Trump and other President's before him do not understand. What does it mean to curse Israel? There are two words in Hebrew that are used for curses or to curse. The first one is "qalal" and it means to be "small, to lessen or considered worthless." God was saying that no one was to reduce or lessen the amount of land that God gave to Abraham and the Jewish people. Whoever did so, they would be cursed by God. The second Hebrew word for curse is "arar" and means "to bind, to hem in with obstacles." It literally means "divine bondage that renders one powerless."

In essence, when President Trump announced his "Peace Deal of the Century," he was binding and narrowing Israel inside their borders by attempting to create a two-state solution. It was this day I believe President Trump's presidency began to change. Through this "Peace Deal" he was putting our nation under a curse, and he was doing it either through ignorance, neglect, deception or unbelief of God's Word. I want to ask the question where was his Evangelical Advisory Board and his Pastor Paula White to warn him biblically against this? Or did they warn him?

If you are in doubt, that this day was the beginning of the end of President Trump's presidency let me connect the dots for you. After the announcement of the Peace Deal of the Century on January 28, 2020, the following events occurred that same year.

- March 13, 2020 (just 17 days later)—Trump declared a National Emergency from COVID 19. From this day forward the economy began to crash.

- May 7, 2020 President Trump leads an interfaith prayer gathering in Rose Garden on the National Day of Prayer.

- May 25, 2020 George Floyd dies in police custody in Minnesota, sparking nationwide protests and riots. Over 40 cities experience civil unrest in their streets.

- Oct. 2, 2020 Trump says he is infected with coronavirus, hospitalized for three nights.

- Nov. 3, 2020 U.S. presidential election held.

- Nov. 7, 2020 Biden defeats Trump, according to U.S. media projections. Trump and key supporters declare the election was stolen.

- Jan. 6, 2021 Capital building is seized by thousands of Trump supporters after a pro-Trump rally. Five people died from it and many injured.

- 2023- A whirlwind of arrests of Trump followers as Former President Trump faces 4 Indictments and 91 different charges.

THE CURSE IS REAL

In his book entitled "Eye to Eye" author William Koenig writes: "In February 1993, President Clinton, with Secretary Warren Christopher traveled to the Middle East and met with Israeli officials to announce plans to promote peace that will serve the interests of Israel, the Arab States, the Palestinians, and the entire community. Clinton said that a passive American role was not enough. What was called for was an active role and positive efforts that will take advantage of what many believe to be a historic moment in that region."

In other words, just as President Trump did on January 28, 2020, President Clinton did the same things by trying to be a mediator and divide the land of Israel in hopes of bringing about peace.

Koenig continues:

> "In God's eyes, this is cursing Israel. The result was catastrophe and two days after Secretary Christopher made the above statements, the storm (called the "Storm of the Century") began to batter the Eastern U.S. for four days with tornado's, high winds, record low pressures and heavy snow. The storm affected 26 states, impacting the lives of nearly 100 million people. At one point, the storm covered one-third of the U.S. and damage was recorded from Texas to the Ohio Valley and Maine. Damages were estimated between $3 and $6 billion dollars."

(Eye to Eye, page 47).

William Koenig connected the dots. When America gets involved with dividing the land of Israel it always pays a great price. In January of 1994, President Clinton met with Syrian President Al-Assad, and they made the following statements at a joint news conference: "During our meeting, I told Assad that I was personally committed to the objective of a comprehensive and secure peace that would produce genuine reconciliation among the people of the Middle East. Accordingly, we pledge today to work together to bring the negotiations that started in Madrid over two years ago to a prompt and successful conclusion. Critical issues remain to be resolved, especially the questions relating to withdrawals, to peace and security."

Less than 24-hours later, on January 17, 1994, a powerful 6.9 earthquake rocked southern California. This $15 billion earthquake was centered in Northridge, about 25 miles from Los Angeles. The quake was the second most destructive natural disaster ever to hit the United States and second only to Hurricane Andrew. This also was the ground zero location of the U.S. pornography industrial site.

THE GAZA STRIP

From August 26 to October 24, 2005, Texas, Louisiana, Mississippi, Alabama, and Florida experienced the fury of three to six of the most intense and costly hurricanes in Atlantic Basin history. This happened as Israel's land was being negotiated and divided. Once again, as the land and people of Israel were being pressured into a divide by the U.S. leaders, our land was almost simultaneously being devastated.

On August 15, thousands of Israeli Defense Force (IDF) soldiers began to deliver eviction notices to Israeli settlers who were living in the land of Gaza and Northern Samaria for 35 years. They were given 48 hours to leave. The notification process also began in four Northern Samaria settlements. Settlers were given the option to leave voluntarily or be removed by force. Aerial Sharon, the former prime minister of Israel, committed 55,000 soldiers and 8,000 police to the effort. Soldiers who refused to carry out the orders faced a court-martial.

On August 17, despite some resistance, authorities said Israel's historic withdrawal from Gaza was rapidly progressing, predicting that 10 out of 21 Jewish settlements would be cleared by the end of the day. Unarmed Israeli troops and police went door-to-door, appealing to settlers to leave and threatening to move them by force if they did not follow the governmental orders. Some soldiers convinced protesters to leave after embracing them and joining them in song and prayer.

After a painstakingly slow start, Israeli officials said soldiers evacuated 583 homes, synagogues, and other buildings in the Gaza settlement. Soldiers loaded the evacuees onto dozens of rented tour buses, sending them out of the territory as part of a withdrawal that the Bush administration hoped would revive the Israeli-Palestinian peace process.

Ariel Sharon was the chief architect of the settlement movement. He said he was evacuating Gaza to give Israel more defensible borders and protect the viability of its Jewish majority from a fast-growing Arab population between the Mediterranean Sea and the Jordan River.

On August 17, 2005, U.S. Secretary of State, Condoleezza Rice, said that while she feels for evacuated settlers, Israel will be expected to make further concessions that would ultimately lead to an independent Palestinian state. She said, "Everyone empathizes with what the Israelis are facing, but it cannot be Gaza only."

On August 18, at Neve Dekalim, troops wrestled for hours against some 1,500 people making their last stand inside Gaza's largest settlement. Protesters lay on the synagogue floor with their arms linked, and kicked the Israeli forces while supporters held their shoulders in a tug-of-war.

After breaking the human chain, troops dragged the Jewish protesters out of the synagogue, holding them by their arms and legs as they twisted and squirmed. Other protesters chanted "blasphemy, blasphemy." On Friday, August 19, Neve Dekalim was virtually empty by morning with security forces, journalists, a few Rabbis, and a small number of pull-out resisters being the only remaining inhabitants. "It is terribly sad to see the empty streets," said Eitan Ben-Mor, who came from his home in the Golan Heights a week prior to lend support to the pull-out resistance. He planned to leave after the morning prayer. "The children are missing. The parents are missing," he said. The simplest things of day-to-day life were taken away cruelly, and by force.

On August 19, U.S. Assistant Secretary of State, David Welch, said the Gaza pull-out will re-energize the U.S.-sponsored "Road Map" peace plan, while giving Israelis and Palestinians more security and prosperity.

August 23, 2005, President Bush said, "First of all, I want to congratulate Prime Minister Sharon for having made a very tough decision. As I said in my remarks yesterday in Salt Lake City, the Prime Minister made a courageous decision to withdrawal from the Gaza. We have Jim Wolfensohn; the former head of the World Bank, on the ground helping President Abbas develop a government that responds to the will of the folks in Gaza. In other words, this is step one in the development of a democracy."

President Bush further went on to say, "This is a very hopeful period. Again, I applaud Prime Minister Sharon for making a decision that has really changed the dynamics on the ground and has really provided hope for the Palestinian people. My vision, my hope, is that one day we'll see two states- two democratic states - living side-by-side in peace."

The problem with this is that a two-state solution is not God's will for the Jewish people and for Israel. What President Bush failed to recognize was the same thing that President Clinton also failed to understand which is that any time you try to divide the land of Israel and give it to the Palestinians, you are in essence going against God's Word and cursing Israel and that in turns invokes a curse on our own nation. (Historical data taken from the book "Eye to Eye" written by William Koenig)

HURRICANE KATRINA

On August 23, 2005, the same afternoon on which the final Jews were driven from their homes in Northern Samaria, a tropical depression formed near the Bahamas. By 11 a.m. on August 24, the newly formed tropical depression was upgraded to Tropical Storm Katrina; and by 5 p.m. on August 25, Katrina became a hurricane.

On Friday, August 26, Hurricane Katrina hit Southeast Florida. By August 29, Katrina became a fierce and enormous Category 3 hurricane that pummeled Louisiana, Mississippi, and Alabama: devastating New Orleans. Katrina became the largest disaster in U.S. history. The storm forced one million people from their homes. Over 225,000 homes in Louisiana, Mississippi and Alabama were destroyed. There was over 473,000 people who were without work due to the devastation of hurricane Katrina. From August 17 to 23, 2005 and beyond, Israel experienced one of the most excruciating moments in their nation's history. From August 29 forward, the U.S. experienced the largest and most devastating disaster in its history. (End of excerpt from Eye to Eye, William Koenig)

ARIEL SHARON

Just a few months later on December 18, 2005, Prime Minister Ariel Sharon was hospitalized after suffering a minor stroke. During his hospital stay, doctors discovered a heart defect requiring surgery. He was put on bed rest until a scheduled surgery to try and correct the heart defect on January 5, 2006. A day before the scheduled surgery, Sharon suffered another stroke that caused a brain bleed. After two surgeries, lasting 7 and 14 hours, doctors stopped the bleeding in Sharon's brain; but they were unable to prevent him from going into a coma.

Ariel Sharon would remain in that coma until January 11, 2014, when he died. For over eight years, he remained in a vegetative state. (Wikipedia, the free encyclopedia, https://en.wikipedia.org/wiki/Ariel_Sharon) Jim Hollander (26 December 2005).

We see that the "Gaza Land for Peace" deal was a complete failure and devastation arose on many fronts. From 2005 onward, Israel was attacked from the Gaza Strip as Hamas used Gaza as a fortress to attack Israel.

WE WERE ATTACKED

On one of my trips to Israel, we experienced first-hand what the Israeli's must live with all the time. Several days of attacks occurred during our stay, with rockets being launched from Gaza into Israel. While staying in a hotel in Jerusalem one night, we were alerted that there were incoming rockets and put on lock down.

A few days later at the end of our trip, we were near Tel Aviv, on our way to the airport and we stopped at a restaurant for a meal. As we waited for a table, our group of about 20 people suddenly heard sirens as Jewish people started running out of the restaurant and yelling for us to flee to the bomb shelter. As a group, we followed the Jewish workers as fast as we could to the bomb shelter. It was then that I noticed one of the people in our group who was unable to move quickly was being escorted by one of our board members from our ministry. Then I looked up into the sky and saw the incoming missile streaking across the sky and making a downward turn towards us, as if it knew exactly where we were.

In that moment, I felt fear and helplessness as I have never felt before in my life. I said, "Lord, I don't want to leave my wife as a widow, and I still have so much that I want to do for you." As I looked up into the sky, watching the incoming missile closing in on us, I knew that our dear sister and board member didn't have enough time to make it to the bomb shelter. In my panic and not knowing what to do, I then witnessed a miracle. Another missile moved in at a faster speed than the incoming Hamas missile from Gaza. As they collided, there was a midair explosion right above us. After everyone in our group safely arrived in the bomb shelter, we felt the ground under our feet shake from the shrapnel as the remains from the rockets hit the ground just a few miles from our location. It was the "Iron Dome" Israeli defense system that saved our lives. This technology was given to the Israeli government by the United States. I thought to myself, "here I am, almost 7,000 miles away from my home in the United States, and my own country just saved my life and everyone in our group." I was never prouder to be an American then on that day.

We remained in the bomb shelter for about 20 minutes until we were given the clearance to come out. The workers then served us dinner that night as planned. It was then that I realized what life in Israel is really like. Our Israeli tour guide asked us an interesting question. She asked, "How long would your country allow Canada or Mexico to do what Gaza is doing to Israel?" She then answered her own question and said, "Not very long, but the United Nations expects Israel to show restraint from going to war with our enemies who continue to attack us unprovoked."

After dinner, our group headed to the Tel Aviv airport by bus. As we were a few miles from the airport, we were alerted to another incoming missile targeting the airport. We literally looked out our bus windows and saw another incoming rocket being taken out by the Iron Dome Defense System. I must say that I was never more anxious to board a plane than that day. Once safely in the air, I was so relieved to be heading back to the United States. But then I thought of my dear Jewish friends and our precious tour guide and her family who must stay behind and deal with such attacks. How incredibly sad! All I can say is, "come quickly Lord Jesus!"

CONNECTING THE DOTS

If only man could make the connection between sin and calamity instead of believing in mother nature, climate control or that God sits up in Heaven (if they believe in a God at all) unaware of sinful lifestyles, looking the other way. On the contrary, God is highly active in the world, and He has laid down a spiritual law that says, *"God is not mocked, whatsoever a man (or nation) sows, this they shall also reap"* (Galatians 6:7).

The truth in Jeremiah's day was that the Babylonians were coming to kill, steal and destroy them and everything they owned. They were being sent by God to punish His people for the sowing of their sins, which they continuously committed without any fear of God and no thought or plan to repent of their sins. They had no care that what they were doing was an abomination before God, and that He would hold them accountable. The Word of God says:

> *"Thus says the LORD, Behold, a people comes from the north country, and a great nation shall be raised from the sides of the Earth. They shall lay hold on bow and spear, they are cruel, and have no mercy; their voice roars like the sea; and they ride upon horses, set in array as men for war against you, O daughter of Zion"* (Jeremiah 6: 21-23).

The nation of Israel refused to admit their guilt and turn from their sins, but instead believed they were innocent of any wrongdoing in their self-righteousness mind. When a person has no guilt of their continual sin, and no plans to stop sinning then God has no alternative but to pour out His justified wrath and destruction. How sad that sinners rarely ever connect the dots between their sin and the judgement they receive from God. They instead believe that calamities they go through are the result of just some random acts. They never put two-and-two together, realizing and admitting that it was "Father God" not Mother Nature who sent judgment for their continual sins for which they gave no repentance. The destruction caused by sin is so avoidable if we would only believe that God is watching and holding us all accountable to the way we live. God has said in His Word: *"If My People, who are called by My name, shall humble themselves, and pray, and seek My Face, and turn from their wicked ways; then will I hear from Heaven, and will forgive their sin, and will heal their land"* (II Chronicles 7:14).

If only the leaders and people of America would believe in just this one verse, things could be so different. God wants to bless His people and cause them to prosper, but He cannot bless sin and blatant disregard for His Commandments.

CHAPTER 6

FALSE PROPHETS IN THE LAND

God told Jeremiah to make *"bonds and yokes"* and send them to the other kings of the nations that surrounded Israel at that time. He was to send them with a letter that the yokes were to be worn around their necks. This was to symbolize the yoke of slavery that they were all going to be bound by.

Perhaps, these nations were discussing a defense against the Babylonians with Zedekiah, King of Judah. These yokes were sent to the Kings of the nations of Edom, Moab, Ammonites, Tyrus, Zidon, who had come to Jerusalem to meet with Zedekiah. The message that Jeremiah sent with the yokes read:

> *"Thus saith the LORD of Hosts, the God of Israel; Thus, shall you say to your masters. I have made the Earth, the man and the beast that are upon the ground, by My great power and by My outstretched arm, and have given it unto whom it seemed meet unto Me. And now have I given all these lands into the hand of Nebuchadnezzar, My servant; and the beasts of the fields have I given him also to serve him. And all the nations shall serve him, and his son, and his son's son, until the very time of his land come: and then many nations and great kings shall serve themselves of him. And it shall come to pass, that the nation and kingdom which will not serve the same Nebuchadnezzar, the king of Babylon, and that will not put their neck under the yoke of the king of Babylon, that nation will I punish, says the Lord, with the sword, and with famine, and with the pestilence, until I have consumed them by his hand"* (Jeremiah 27:4-8).

Can you imagine what the reaction was of these kings when they received their yokes with the message above. Jeremiah was saying that God called Nebuchadnezzar His servant. Now why would God call an evil and wicked man, who was not a Jew, His servant? Because he was referring to him as an instrument or tool of His Judgment. He was not speaking of Nebuchadnezzar as a servant in terms of him having a relationship with God.

The key truth here is that God sometimes uses that which is evil to be a judgment arm of His wrath for His people who have rejected Him or have gone their own separate way. God warns His people of the judgment that will come to them if they do not repent. However, when they don't turn from their rebellion, God said that He would put them under the rule of Nebuchadnezzar and the Babylonians.

THE LAW OF RETRIBUTION

God, who is Holy and perfectly righteous, has obligated Himself to judge unrepented sin just as He has obligated Himself to bless repentance and obedience. The Bible says, "*Be not deceived; God in not mocked: for whatsoever a man sows, that shall he also reap. For he who sows to his flesh shall reap of the flesh corruption; but he who sows to the Spirit shall of the Spirit reap life everlasting*" (Galatians 6:7-8).

When God's people continue in sin with no repentance, God will chastise them. This purpose of chastisement is always to bring His people back to Him and to have them understand that He is Holy and sin will not go unpunished. What kind of a parent would you be if your son or daughter kept stealing money from your wallet and you did not discipline them? If you, who are evil, know how to chastise your child; how much more should a thrice Holy God chasten His children? The Bible says:

> "*And you have forgotten the exhortation which speaks unto you as unto children, My son, despise not you the chastening of the Lord, nor faint when you are rebuked of Him. For whom the Lord loves He chastens and scourges every son whom He receives. If you endure chastening, God deals with you as with sons; for what son is he whom the father chastens not?*
>
> *But if you be without chastisement, whereof all are partakers, then are you bastards and not sons. Furthermore, we have had fathers of our flesh which corrected us, and we gave them reverence: shall we not much rather be in subjection unto the Father of Spirits and live? For they verily for a few days chastened us after their own pleasure; but He for our profit, that we might be partakers of His Holiness. Now no chastening for the present seems to be joyous, but grievous: nevertheless, after it*

yields the peaceable fruit of Righteousness unto them which are exercised thereby" (Hebrews 12:5-11).

If we can all learn these scriptures and believe them and live by them, we would save ourselves a boatload of pain and suffering. If only the kings of Israel and the kings of the surrounding nations would have believed the message that Jeremiah sent to them, so many lives could have been saved. How tragic it is that the human heart is so rebellious to the ways of God.

Today, our nation and the nations of the world are in the exact same place as Israel and the other nations that Jermiah sent his letter to over 2,500 years ago. Because most of the world has rejected the Lord Jesus Christ, God will send a strong delusion, the Antichrist, who will claim to be the Jewish Messiah and begin to rule the world. The Bible says, *"And for this cause God shall send them strong delusion, that they should believe a lie. That they all might be damned who believe not the Truth but had pleasure in unrighteousness"* (II Thessalonians 2:11-12).

Because Israel and most of the world do not want the truth nor want to believe that Jesus is God's Messiah who was sent to die for their sins, God (not Satan) will *"send them strong delusion."* This strong delusion is speaking of the "man of sin" who is called the *"Son of Perdition."* This is speaking of the Antichrist, who comes as the workman of Satan and *"with all power and signs and lying wonders"* (II Thessalonians 2:9).

The Bible also reveals that at the mid-point of the seven-year Tribulation, Michael the Archangel wins a war with Satan in the heaven, and the devil is thrown out of the heavens and down to the earth. This marks the beginning of the Great Tribulation, which will last exactly three and a half years (42 months or 1260 days). As a result, Satan will greatly persecute the woman (Israel) during the last half of the Tribulation period (Revelation 12:1-13). All of this teaches us that the Lord is the One who oversees the earth. He is the one who oversees nations and limits even the Devil himself with what he is allowed to do. This is the message sent to the kings of the nations in Jeremiah's day, which symbolizes not only judgment in their day, but also in the last days; the days we are living in right now.

GOD'S SOVEREIGNTY

Many Christians can't accept the fact that it was God who put Joe Biden in as the President of the United States. They believe that the election was stolen. Even if that was true, the Bible teaches that God allowed it. Why? I believe because just like Israel of old, we are getting exactly what we deserve. You say, yes, but there are still a lot of good people in our nation who love the Lord and love America. I would agree with you; however, the percentage of people who really follow God and His Word has shrunk to just a small percentage of the population in America today. The reason the world and most of the modern church cannot accept the truth that God is sovereign is because they have not been taught about the true God of the Bible. They instead have falsely been taught that God would never send wrath and judgment to His people.

I had a pastor of a church say to me after 911 that he could never serve a God who caused 911. He could not accept that the Muslim terrorists who highjacked planes and caused that evil destruction on our land and killing over 2,000 people was either cause or allowed by God. But then, what do you do with the scripture that says God called evil king Nebuchadnezzar, His servant, to judge Israel? You see, if your theology does not line up with the Bible, then you have the wrong theology.

Let's be clear. God either causes things to happen or He allows things to happen. So, we can all agree (I think) that God allowed 911 to happen. The question is why? This nation must come to grips that we as a nation have turned away from the God of the Bible and disobeyed His Word. We have committed abominable sins as a nation and that is why our nation is vulnerable to the lurking evil that is all around us. Do we realize that at any moment, God can lower the hedge of protection and make this nation vulnerable to the attacks of our enemies. He did it with Israel, so why wouldn't He do that with the United States of America?

One must keep in mind that God is Holy. He is righteous and will hold you accountable for your sin. In other words, as the Bible says, *"your sin will find you out."* Man does not want to accept this. He doesn't believe that he is a sinner and worthy of death. We must understand that the only thing standing between Heaven and the judgment of Hell is the Cross of our Lord Jesus Christ. When one puts their faith in Christ and what He did for them on the Cross, only then does the Bible start to make perfect sense. Remember that the Bible was physically written by man, but it was the Holy Spirit who inspired every Word written.

We must understand that the Bible teaches that God does not tempt man into sin, that is the work of the devil. However, God does test man. He will test the faith of His people. He does so by allowing evil to attack us. Sometimes, it is because of our sin and our refusal to repent after multiple warnings. Other times (as in the case of Job), God allows a test to make us more sanctified, humble, and committed to the Lord's direction for our lives. Either way, the Bible teaches us that God will use evil man and even the devil himself to accomplish His work.

You may not like the above truths and it may not be the God who you have been taught about in your church or from your favorite preacher you watch over television. However, like it or not, this is the God of the Bible. Let me assure you that everything God does is right, perfect, and just. If what you are reading goes against what you have been taught and you are struggling with this truth, then maybe it is time to stop watching preachers like Joel Osteen and start studying your Bible for yourself.

The Great Deception is all over the TV, the internet, on social media and in many of the modern churches today. So, it's time my friend, that the true Church shun the "prosperity pimps" who are more interested in your money, than they are concerned about your soul and where you are going to spend eternity. It's time to start following the God of the Bible!

Yes, I do call them "pimps" because that is what they are. They appear to you as nice easy-going men or women, and they tell you that God wants to bless you (which He does); however, they never really deal with sin and very seldom if ever talk about repentance. They give messages that tickle your ears and make you feel comfortable, but the preachers of the Bible like Jeremiah made the people feel uncomfortable. Why? Because the people loved this world, more than the one to come.

Most of the modern preachers today are what the prophet Isaiah called *"blind watchmen"* and *"dumb dogs"* who will not bark. Our dog, Johnny, has a high-pitched bark and uses it every time he sees someone walk past our house. Our house is on the corner of our street, and it has a lot of windows. A lot of people walk by house as they take their own dogs for walks. We constantly try to get Johnny to stop barking, as it is his daily routine for him to run from window to window and bark at all the activity going on outside of our home. But you know what Johnny is? He is a good watchdog; he is just doing the job that God created him to do; which is to protect his loved ones.

Isaiah's words should be shared with every modern preacher who refuses to preach about sin, the Cross, and repentance and who will not give weekly altar calls for people to come forward to get their hearts and lives right with God. Read the scathing words of the great Messianic prophet Isaiah:

> *"His watchmen are blind: they are all ignorant, they are dumb dogs, they cannot bark; sleeping, lying down, loving to slumber. Yes, they are greedy dogs which can never have enough, and they are shepherds who cannot understand: they all look to their own way, every one for his gain, from his quarter"*
> (Isaiah 56:10-11).

Do you want to know why most Christians and most Americans are spiritually blind and under the Great Deception today? Because the watchmen, the preachers they follow are sleeping and they are dumb (mute) dogs who won't bark to warn the people that judgment is coming. The reason they will not do their job as Watchmen is because they want your *"quarter"* (i.e., your money). That is what the Word of God says (Isaiah 57:11).

Just like in Jeremiah's day, the other nations would not heed the warnings of God, sent by the prophet Jeremiah. So, they were judged, and many people died. I believe the same thing is about to happened again to not only the United States, but also to the nations of the world. God's judgment is coming, and it is called the Great Tribulation, and the Great Tribulation is going to happen mainly because of the Great Deception.

THE LYING PROPHETS

In Jeremiah's day, the following leaders falsely led the nations in the opposite direction from God and His Word.:

- The Prophets (those who were to foretell future events)
- The Diviners (i.e., soothsayers)
- The Dreamers (those believing their dreams were of God, but were not)
- The Enchanters (one who practices witchcraft)
- The Sorcerers (occult, magic)

God said that these false prophets were saying the opposite of what God said through His true prophet Jeremiah. They were saying *"You shall not serve the King of Babylon"* (Jeremiah 27:9). God said they *"prophesy a lie unto you"* (Jeremiah. 27:10).

God gave those nations a promise that if they submitted to the judgment of God, they would remain in their land; but with their land being ruled under the control of the Babylonians. If they did not yield to the Babylonian's rule, they would be judged and suffer great destruction (Jeremiah 27:11). So, even in Judgment God gave Israel and the other nations an opportunity to take the lesser punishment. But they would not listen to Jeremiah's message.

COMMANDS TO ZEDEKIAH, KING OF JUDAH

God also spoke to the King of Judah the same message that He spoke to all the other nations saying, ***"Bring your necks under the yoke of the King*** *of Babylon, and serve him and his people, and live"* (Jeremiah 27:12). God would ask the question to the kings, *"Why will you die, you and your people by the sword, by the famine, and by the pestilence, as the LORD has spoken against the nation that will not serve the King of Babylon?"* (Jeremiah 27:13).

The love that God has for people is amazing to me. He even offers mercy in His Judgment if we would just follow His Word. But the kings still would not follow the Word of God. Oh, how wicked and stubborn is the sinful heart of man. The three great judgments that God would send to Israel and to the other nations who rebelled against Him were: (1) The Sword (violence and death), (2) The Famine (hunger) and (3) The Pestilence (disease, plagues).

In the year 2020, I believe God allowed or may even have sent the COVID-19 pestilence to the world as a warning. He is trying to warn the world of even greater destruction that is coming if we do not repent and turn to the God of the Bible.

Shortly after this virus began to spread, our country went into shutdown. Again, I believe this virus was and still is a warning sign from God that He is not pleased with our nation and the world, and we must turn back to Him before it is too late. Only prayer and repentance can remove these judgments that are coming. God said:

> *"If I shut up heaven that there be no rain, or if I command the locusts to devour the land, or if I sent pestilence among My people; If My People, who are called by My Name, shall humble themselves, and pray, and seek My Face, and turn from their wicked ways; then will I hear from Heaven, and will forgive their sin, and will heal their land"* (II Chronicles 7:13-14).

Now, notice 3 very important truths from the above scripture: God says it is Him who sends the draught, locusts, and the pestilence. He sends the judgments to judge His people for their sins of which they will not repent.

Only His people who are called by His Name can stop the judgment. How? By humbling themselves, and praying, and seeking His Face, and turning from their sin. But this is not what the false prophets were telling the people in Jeremiah's day. The false prophets were telling lies in the Name of Jehovah. They were mimicking Jeremiah by using the same phrase that Jeremiah used: *"Thus saith the Lord,"* but they were not speaking the same message, they were in fact speaking lies and were committing blasphemy by attempting to make God a part of their lying schemes. Consequently, they would perish in the judgment for this sin.

A FALLING AWAY FROM THE FAITH

A significant end-times sign given in scripture is the falling away of the church from the true faith. The Holy Spirit explicitly revealed this to the Apostle Paul as he wrote: *"Now the Spirit speaks expressly, that in the latter times some shall depart from the Faith, giving heed to seducing spirits, and doctrines of devils"* (I Tim. 4:1). The words *"shall depart"* mean "to remove, revolt or desert." You cannot remove or desert from something unless you were already there first. Therefore, what the scripture is telling us is that in the end times, just before Jesus comes back, there will be Christians and Churches that are going to desert the true faith of Christendom in which they once believed.

The true preacher of the Gospel preaches and teaches about the spiritual riches we receive through faith in Christ's sacrifice on Calvary, whereas the new modern-day preachers focuses on materialistic riches in this present world. This new preaching wants to move the church from emphasizing Christ and denying self to preaching about self and the promotion of self. So many Christians across this nation have bought into this new self-absorbed teaching and have drunk the cool aid so to speak. "New Age" teaching has slipped into the modern church, and it fails to preach a death to self and living for God's Kingdom to come. It rather preaches self-promoting ideas and promises that God will fulfill their personal dreams to achieve their destiny in this world.

The modern seeker sensitive preachers treat God as almost their eternal bell hop, waiting to serve man. However, the true biblical preachers talk about going to the Cross and dying to self (Galatians 2:20). The old-time preacher didn't worry about offending the sinner, while the modern-day preacher is more concerned with making the sinner feel comfortable and confident in their riches in this world.

Old-time preachers say that this world is not our home, we are just passing through. Modern preaching emphasizes this world and the blessing of it. Many of the churches today do everything they can to be seeker sensitive by providing entertainment, shorter services, big fancy lights and video productions, coffee, and bagel shops in the church in order to offer an atmosphere where people feel comfortable. They want people to come to church and hang out at their facilities. The old-time church called sinners to the altar to surrender their lives to the Lordship of Jesus Christ and repent from immorality and every form of wickedness. The modern preacher says, "eat and be merry" and the old way said, "repent or be judged." The question is, what message are you listening to and believing? What kind of church are you attending?

I started in ministry in 1987, and I can honestly say that I've never seen the church in a more spiritually weakened state then it is right now. Like Samson of old, most of the modern church has lost its spiritual power, and its vison, and the most troubling aspect of this is most don't even have the discernment to know it. The Bible says after Samson's hair was cut, he was awoken out of his sleep one night with the words: *"The Philistines be upon you, Samson."* The Bible says that Samson went out as he did other times to battle, but *"he wist (knew) not that the LORD was departed from him"* (Judges 16:20). (There is nothing worse that can be said of a person than that the Spirit of the Lord has departed- ESB page 447 Old Testament).

The truth is most of the modern church functions in activities and programs without the power and might of the Holy Spirit. They fail to recognize that the Holy Spirit is grieved and quenched. They don't even understand what grieves and quenches the Spirit of God. One of the greatest sins in the church is lukewarmness. Jesus said it was the lukewarm that He will spit out of His mouth (Revelation 3:16). But to the outside world, the church looks like it is in the best financial shape ever. Similarly, this is what is happening in our public schools. The physical facilities of public schools are amazing to look at, the athletic sports fields in many schools today are equal to most NCAA Division III colleges or better. As I look at our local high school campuses with their thousands of square feet of Astro Turf for football, baseball, soccer, softball, etc. I wonder where all the money came from to build these incredible fields.

But, as beautiful as these facilities are, the public schools of America have never been more dangerous and the students more hopeless. School violence is increasing at alarming rates as our youth are becoming more violent, obscene, depressed, suicidal, etc., then at any time in our nation's history. Just like many of our churches, which have put a lot of money into their facilities while at the same time the people have become more worldly and lost. It is just like Jesus said: *"Now do you Pharisees make clean the outside of the cup and the platter; but your inward part is full of ravening and wickedness. You fools, did not He Who made that which is without make that which is within also?"* (Luke 11:39-40)

Jesus said of the last church age, which is symbolized by the Laodicea Church, *"So then because you are lukewarm and neither cold nor hot, I will spue you out of My mouth because you say, I am rich, and increased with goods, and have need of nothing, and know not that you are wretched, and miserable, and poor, and blind, and naked"* (Revelations 3:17). This Laodicea church was not just a reference to a church on the earth after Christ ascended up to heaven, 2,000 years ago, but it speaks of the last church that exists right before Christ comes again, which is the time in which we are living right now.

The Greek word Laodicea is "Laodikeia," and has a two-part meaning. The first part is "Lao," and means, people, nation, specifically people of God's choice. It figuratively speaks of Christians. The second part of the word is "dike," and it means, judgment, punish, vengeance. When you put it together, it means, "the justice of the people." The generation that we are living in right now is the generation of His wrath. The Bible says, *"For the time is come that Judgment begins at the House of God: and if it begins in us, what shall the end be of them who obey not the Gospel of God"* (I Peter 4:17). God is getting ready to judge this nation, but He will first Judge His church. Why? Because as the church goes, so goes the nation. The truth is the church is responsible for the spiritual decline of our nation.

The financial prosperity of the modern church has set pride in motion, contributing to losing its hunger and thirst for God and lost souls. Because of our financial prosperity, modern churches have been made into comfortable operations that lack passion for the Holy Spirit. The Bible teaches that right before the Second Coming of Christ there will first be a *"falling away"* (II Thessalians 2:3). The Greek word for *"falling away"* is *"Apostasia"* and means a departure from the faith.

When I first entered the ministry and attended pastoral fellowship meetings, I must admit I was personally intimidated. Most preachers that came to the meetings were dressed in a suit, carrying their Bibles with them, and they often quoted scriptures from the Old and New Testament with precision, without even opening their Bibles. They would articulate their viewpoints using the Word of God in powerful ways. The true Gospel preacher was the salt and light of the community. One could clearly see that he or she spent much time studying the Word of God.

Today, a pastor would look out of place if they wore a suit to a pastoral meeting. The new preachers come to the meetings in ripped jeans and t-shirts and their dress is only an indicator of the way they handle the Word of God, sloppy and without reverence. They are most interested in promoting events and programs, or how to grow a church numerically. Today's preachers focus on practical steps to make a church more attractive to the outside world. If prayer and seeking God is included at all, it is usually centered around social issues rather than the actual Word of God.

For example, as the COVID-19 virus hit our nation and world, I attended pastoral meetings that were all about how to cope with the pestilence rather than why God was allowing the pestilence. We seldom heard what the Church should do to see God heal our land. When the violence began in the streets our nation, the preachers spent a lot of time on the topic of racism instead of the judgment of God that is soon to come (i.e., The Great Tribulation). I didn't hear any preacher speak about the Rapture of the Church, which is the next prophetic event on God's calendar, nor was there any mention of repentance or turning to God (II Chronicles 7:13-14).

What has happened to the modern preacher is they are afraid to preach on end times. Today, many preachers don't even have a position on the Rapture of the Church, the coming Apocalypse, or the Second Coming of the Lord Jesus Christ. Most do not understand God's plan for mankind in the end times or for the nation of Israel. Most don't even preach from the book of Revelation, the book of Daniel, or Isaiah, Jeremiah, etc. And even more troubling is some of them tell their congregations not to study the book of Revelation because they say it is too hard to interpret. So, in turn most Christians in America are ignoring the end-time prophecies of the Bible all together and this is why so many Christians are apostate as they are caught up in this world and are not watching and praying for the soon return of Jesus. How very sad this all is!

CHAPTER 7

THE APOSTATE CHURCH

The Bible teaches us that there will be a great falling away from the truth in the time right before Jesus comes to Rapture His church away. My friend, we are living in that day. The big question is, how did we get here? How did the church become more in love with the pleasures of the world than lovers of God? How did the church, like Samson, get so seduced by the Delliah's of this world, that we forfeited the power of the Holy Spirit?

All we have do is look back at the nation of Israel and see how they were lured away from the truth and started to worship other gods. This will show us exactly what the devil has done to the modern Church and our Nation. As it has been said, there really is nothing new under the sun, it is just history repeating itself.

The Bible says that the Lord spoke to the prophet Jeremiah and said, *"And I have seen folly in the prophets of Samaria; they prophesied in Baal and caused My people Israel to err"* (Jeremiah 23:13). The word "Baal" in Hebrew means, "Owner or Lord." Israel really believed that they were following Jehovah because the prophets told them that all was good. However, the reality was that they were following another god, the god of Baal.

Today in America, many Christians think they are worshipping the Lord; but they are in actuality following another Jesus, another spirit, and they are believing in another gospel (II Corinthians 11:3-4). One must be reminded that just because a particular preacher over television or at the pulpit is using the name of Jesus, or the name of the Holy Spirit, does not mean it is the Jesus of the Bible or the true Holy Spirit. God told Jeremiah to tell the people, *"Thus saith the LORD of Hosts, Hearken not unto the words of the Prophets who prophesy unto you: they make you vain: they speak a vision of their own heart, and not out of the mouth of the Lord"* (Jeremiah 23:16).

Many people in America today are following the wrong voices who have given them the wrong message. Most are following voices that appeals to the flesh. For example, the message that Donald Trump ran on in his last campaign, "Make America Great Again" (MAGA) is not a correct message. God's message is not, "Make America Great Again," it is, "Make America Good Again." Unless we repent and come back to the God of the Bible, we are going to face a similar judgment as Israel did in the time of Jeremiah. By the looks of things, that judgment has already begun; however, nothing compares to what is coming.

Jeremiah pleaded with Israel to turn back to God before it was too late. God said through the true prophet, *"If that nation, against whom I have pronounced, turn from evil, I will repent of the evil that I thought to do unto them"* (Jeremiah 18:8). This is God giving Israel one last chance. However, Israel would not repent and obey this last-minute warning and urgent plea, therefore their nation was severely judged, and history recorded it.

Today the churches in America have gone in many different directions and most of them have not been good. We have seen the churches turn to human psychology, using programs of man, like the 12 steps, 6 steps, 4 steps etc., to try to set people free. We have built churches based on what man wants (i.e., the seeker) rather than what God wants. We have allowed extreme manifestations in the Charismatic and Pentecostal churches that are extrabiblical and even mystical to come in the church, and we have called it the anointing of the Holy Spirit. We have seen church leaders act proud, haughty, high minded and even commit blaspheme from the pulpits of America. All the while, most of the church doesn't have enough discernment to spot it and call it out for what it is, deception. It is all so sad and very dangerous.

I would like to list ten different theological positions or movements in the church that I have personally witnessed over the past 35 years of being in full time ministry. I believe these are the bedrock as to why the American churches today are so lukewarm, backslidden, and apostate. The Bible told us it would be just like this before Jesus returns. There are more than ten, but this will give you an idea of the most popular movements that have caused so much confusion and deception among Christians in our nation.

Now, I want you to know it is not my intent to judge the people in these movements in terms of their salvation. I am only naming these movements and some of their leaders to protect and warn the reader that these are not presenting the true Gospel message. I should also point out that there are millions of people in these movements who love God, but I believe they have been deceived and continue to be deceived. I know because upon a day I was there among them and as a young preacher, I couldn't see at that time how far off these churches and leaders had gone.

I have friends that I love very much who are caught up in these movements and my prayer is that they will see the true Gospel message and repent of these false ways. The true Way is Jesus Christ and Him Crucified, and any other way quenches and grieves the Holy Spirit. Now, buckle your seatbelt as we begin to share with you these deceptive movements.

THE NICOLAITAN CHURCH

Jesus said to the Church of Pergamos: *"So have you also them who hold the doctrine of the Nicolaitanes, which thing I hate"* (Revelation 2:15). If there is something in the Bible that Jesus says He hates, I think it might be a good idea for you and me to figure out what it is. The meaning of the word "Nicolaitans" means "laity-conquerors" or in other words "victory over the people." This refers to an unscriptural Church Government whereby the people of the church look to the leadership of the Church as their mediator and spiritual covering before God. These are those in church leadership who exploit the people and use them. The leadership serves over them in a controlling fashion.

Today we see clergy using titles such as "Apostle" or "Pope" to command greater respect and present a spiritual covering that was never intended by God. The Nicolaitan Church forms a church government that elevates man and places an unscriptural emphasis on the leaders, removing if you will Jesus as the Head of His Church. It replaces Jesus as being in His mediatorial role, and the Holy Spirit is replaced by a man dressed in religious garments that tries to impress the common man. However, the Bible says, *"For there is one God, and one Mediator between God and man, the man Christ Jesus"* (I Timothy 2:5).

The Truth is that when we get to heaven the Pope will not have one iota of authority there, no pastor, church committee, nor bishop who will be your mediator to God. No, only Jesus, He is the One mediator between sinful man and the Father. But man loves to take the place of Jesus in religious institutions to control the people. There are many unscriptural church governments where man places himself in positions where the people must answer to them.

The spirit of the "Nicolaitans" is alive and well in the church today. I was in a church leadership meeting some years ago where they held a seminar for pastors and church leaders on the topic "transferring the wealth of the world" to the church. It was led by a man who was working for an organization called "New Apostolic Reformation" started and led by C Peter Wagner (who is now deceased).

Through a minister friend of mine, I was introduced to the seminar leader who I heard was the third ranking official in this organization's leadership chain at that time. In other words, he was a "big wig" within that organization. After our initial greeting, he very quickly asked me, "Who's your Apostle?" I was surprised and taken back by the question, not really knowing how to answer the man. No one had ever asked me that question before. I thought why was he asking me such a question? In essence, he wanted to know "who was my covering in my ministry?" This is the Nicolaitan spirit about which Jesus said, "I hate." The modern church bought the lie of unscriptural teachings, that every church needs an "Apostle" or a "Spiritual Covering." However, what does the Word of God say? *"Woe to the rebellious children, says the Lord, who take counsel, but not of Me; and who cover with a covering, but not of Spirit, that they may add sin to sin"* (Isaiah 30:1).

The Word of God teaches that only the Spirit of God can spiritually cover someone. However, a religious man thinks that he can receive covering from the church or denomination, for that is what the modern church has taught him. Ask yourself some simple questions: How can sinful man cover sinful man? Who was Moses, Joshua, or David's spiritual covering? It was God alone!

Many in the modern church follow unscriptural church governments who desire to control the laity. They do so simply because the people lack discernment due to not studying their Bibles. They are mesmerized by these charismatic leaders who, *"professing themselves to be wise, they became fools"* (Romans 1:22). The Nicolaitan Church goes back to Judaism and the Sanhedrin in Jesus' day who were responsible for the death of Jesus. Even though we know that no man took Jesus' life, but He freely gave it (John 10:18); it was the Jewish Sanhedrin who turned Jesus over to the Romans to be executed. Why? Because they could not control Jesus; He would not submit to their unscriptural hypocritical Temple Governmental control.

The Christian Church began to see this same spirit come in around 300 A.D. with a man by the name of Constantine, the Roman Emperor. During his rule from 306 to 337 A.D., he launched what is known by historians as the State Church of the Roman Empire. During the dark ages (approximately 500 to 1500 AD), we see the Roman Catholic Church emerge with all its "Laws" and "Rituals" that set up a religious government which called the people into submission to the church. They instituted creeds, washings, forms, Christian "works" and demanded allegiance to the Church (i.e., the Romans Catholic Church), even going so far as to tell the people that if they left the Catholic Church, they would lose their salvation.

Basically, the Catholic church is a Roman institution that arose from the ruins of the Roman Empire, and it has been referred to as "The ghost of the Roman Empire come to life in the garb of Christianity." It brought itself into power through the glory of Rome and the name of Christ by deception and force; and by force and bloodshed it maintains that power. (Catholicism and Christianity by Jimmy Swaggart introduction.)

Roman Catholicism should be classified as a false church since its doctrine of salvation is not consistent with the Bible. The Bible teaches, *"By grace are you saved through faith; and that not of yourselves: it is the gift of God: not of works, lest any man should boast"* (Ephesians 2:8-9). In other words, "justification comes by faith alone," that which Jesus did on the Cross alone saves the sinner. The Catholic church teaches a works-based salvation (i.e., infant baptism, joining the catholic church, penance, etc.). Any church that teaches you must do a "religious work" to be saved should be classified as a false way that God hates. Religion is man-made and teaches the people to "do, do, do" to be accepted by God. True Christian faith teaches "done, done, done" by what Christ did on the Cross. Christ did it all at Calvary and the only thing sinful man has left to do is to repent of depending on self to save and trust in the finished work of the Cross alone (John 19:30).

A religious church adds works to faith. After the day of Pentecost, the early church had to deal with this as Gentiles (non-Jews) were being brought into salvation and received the gift of the Holy Spirit. There arose a dispute among Jewish disciples about whether these new gentile converts needed to be circumcised as Jews, as was taught in that day.

In Acts chapter 15, we see a meeting taking place in Jerusalem among the leaders to discuss this disagreement in the early church. Some spiritual giants were involved in this meeting such as Paul, Peter, James (Jesus' half-brother), Barnabas, etc. The Bible tells us that *"certain men which came down from Judaea taught the Brethren (Christians), and said, Except you be circumcised after the manner of Moses, you cannot be saved"* (Acts 15:1). If this teaching remained in the early Church, the early Church would have gone straight into apostasy.

This was a huge meeting, with serious ramifications taking place in Jerusalem; and if the early church leaders were to get this wrong, the early movement would have been greatly hindered and tainted. God would have had to raise up another church because the teaching of how one is saved is paramount to the work of God and the most important doctrine in all the Church. There can be no wiggle room when it comes to God's plan of Salvation as should be obvious. Paul the Apostle said, *"But though we, or an angel from heaven, preach any other gospel unto you than that which we have preached unto you, let him be accursed"* (Galatians 1:8). The word "accursed" means eternally condemned. When it comes to the teaching of how one is saved there can be absolutely no compromise. It must be totally based on scripture, or it must be rejected. Therefore, whoever teaches an alternative way of salvation than that which the Bible teaches must be utterly rejected.

The Bible says:

> *"And when there had been much disputing, Peter rose up, and said unto them, men and Brethren, you know how that a good while ago God made choice among us, that the Gentiles by my mouth should hear the Word of the Gospel, and believe. And God, which knows the hearts, bear them witness, giving them the Holy Spirit, even as He did unto us. And put no difference between us and them, purifying their hearts by faith"* (Acts 15:7-9).

Peter was telling the leaders of his day that the gentiles who were in the house of Cornelius received salvation and the gift of the Holy Spirit by simply believing on what Jesus did on the Cross for them (Acts 10:44-46). They did not do anything religious, and they certainly were not circumcised by Peter before they received the gift of the Holy Spirit. They simply believed, and God gave them the gift of the Holy Spirit, this was Peter's argument. Peter confronted the religious Jews (i.e., pharisees) by saying *"why do you tempt God to put a yoke upon the neck of the disciples, which neither our Fathers nor we were able to bear"* (Acts 15:10). He then makes a powerful statement that separates all religions from true biblical Christianity: *"But we believe that through the Grace of the Lord Jesus Christ we shall be saved, even as they"* (Acts 15:11).

This is the number one reason we must denounce the Roman Catholic Church as well as any other religious organization or church who adds works to salvation. Unfortunately, there are a lot more religious churches today than there are true churches of the faith.

It is shocking to see the many practices in the Catholic church that are not referenced in the Bible at all but were instead added by man under this religious system. It is safe to say that Roman Catholicism has deceived more people into following a false way of salvation than any other religion on the face of the earth. A preacher once said that Roman Catholicism is the greatest counterfeit Satan has ever come up with. I must agree!

I know some will take offense to what I have written and will disagree with me; however, I challenge them to find Biblical references to substantiate many of the Catholic teachings such as:

- Infallibility of the Catholic Church. This is not Biblical. Read, ROMANS 3:10-20.

- Sinless perfection of the Pope and the Virgin Mary. This is not Biblical. Read ROMANS 3:23. Mary called God her Savior. Read, LUKE 1:47.

- Penance being necessary for salvation. This is not Biblical. Read, GALATIANS 2:16.

- Mary delivers souls from death. No Bible for this.

- Prayers made to the Saints- The Bible teaches against this. DEUTERONOMY 18:11.

- Worshipping man. Read, REVELATION 19:10.

- Communion elements becoming the actual body and blood of Christ (transubstantiation) Read, HEBREWS 7:26-27.

- Purgatory, souls in waiting before they go to heaven. This is Not scriptural. Read, EPHESIANS 4:8-11.

- Indulgences, the giving of money to get souls out of purgatory. No Bible for this.

- Rosary, praying a repetitive prayer that includes praying to Mary, The mother of Jesus. This is against what Jesus said. Read MATTHEW 6:7

The truth is that not only are the above teachings not found in the scripture, but on the contrary, they go against what the Bible teaches. Any religion that includes beliefs and practices that goes against what the Word of God teaches must be classified as a false church. Sadly, this is Roman Catholicism.

There are nearly one billion people in the world who claim the Roman Catholic church as their spiritual covering or church. At the Great White Throne Judgment, it is going to be a very sad day to see how many people trusted in the Roman Catholic teaching and as a result will lose their soul.

On that day, many will learn that God considers Roman Catholicism as a part of the "Great Whore" like all the other false religions of the world

(Revelation 17:1, 20:11-15). I should point out that there are those who are saved but yet still attend Catholic churches, but after coming to Christ they should leave that teaching and that church all together.

Any church Catholic or Protestant that sets itself up as the spiritual covering for the people is classified as a Nicolaitan church which is what God said, *"I hate."* Now church authority is to be respected and honored when it is biblical, but never should a church or a church leader take on the role of your spiritual covering. God, the Holy Spirit is our covering, as God is the only One who is sinless and can lead us into all truth. There are those today who go in the other extreme and say they don't need the church and they don't need to submit to a pastor or church leadership. This is also an erroneous idea and will only lead that person, whomever they are, into further problems from their rebellious attitude.

God has set up the Church to be a spiritual guide in each believer's life. God's Word commands us to not forsake the church as it says: *"Not forsaking the assembling of ourselves together, as the manner of some is; but exhorting one another: as so much the more, as you see the day approaching"* (Hebrew 10:25). God in fact has chosen the Apostle, Prophet, Evangelist, Pastor, and Teacher to lead His church and to teach and equip the saints in the church for the work of the ministry (Hebrews 10:25, Ephesians 4:11-12). All of this is biblical and good.

THE HEBRAIC CHURCH

There is another Church movement that is trying to take the New Testament Church back under Mosaic Law. Basically, it is gentiles who try to be Jewish. They want to bring back things like adhering to the Torah by seeking a better understanding of the culture, history, and religious-political backdrop of that era that led to the core differences with both the Jewish, and later, the Christian communities.

This movement teaches a need for the church to keep a 7th day sabbath (i.e., Saturday), celebrate the annual Jewish feasts, wearing of the Jewish prayer shawl's, blowing of the Shofar's, and to follow Jewish rituals and traditions. Starting in the 1990's, this movement became more prominent and continues today.

The Hebraic movement is just another attempt by the church to put man under Law, which only leads to sinful bondage instead of the freedom we find in Christ. The New Testament teaches freedom from being under the Law as Christ fulfilled the Law and now, we are under Grace. This freedom in Christ provides us with a personal relationship with God through the blood of Christ and not through anything that man does to try to justify or sanctify himself.

Followers of the "Hebrew Roots" movement believe that sin breaks the Torah (1 John 3:4). This includes the purity laws, such as adhering to dietary restrictions as explained in the Torah. They consider it sinful when a strict adherence to the sabbath is not kept, when one eats forbidden animals, or if social and religious laws are not observed.

They believe that a person is not really a Christian if they do not keep the Sabbath or observe the dietary restrictions. Obviously, this goes against New Testament teachings as Paul wrote to the Colossians, *"Wherefore if you be dead with Christ from the rudiments of the world, why, as though living in the world, are you subject to ordinances (Touch not, taste not; handle not; Which all are to perish with the using;) after the commandments and doctrines of men?"* (Colossians 2:20-22). This verse teaches that salvation is found only in the death of Christ on the Cross and trusting in Him alone. There is no salvation or victory from sin in the following of any rules or regulations since scripture clearly teaches that we have been set free from these laws and traditions.

The Hebraic movement ignores Acts chapter 15, Colossians chapter 2, and other scriptures that teach against adding to the grace of Jesus Christ. This movement wants to bring Jews and Gentiles back under Old Testament Law because they misunderstand that salvation is in the Cross of Christ alone and no longer includes having to follow the Old Testament Law. The "spirit of religion" controls people and puts them under a man-made system of rules. True Christianity sets you free from all of that. In fact, the freedoms that Gentiles enjoy is supposed to make the Jews jealous of what the Gentiles now possess, as we are no longer under the yoke of having to abide by Jewish laws and rituals. For Romans 11:11 says: *"I say then, have they stumbled (the Jews) that they should fall? God forbid: but rather through their fall Salvation is come unto the Gentiles, for to provoke them to jealousy."*

The child of God does not need to go back and find their Jewish roots. That is a lie from the devil. We are living under a better covenant now. This does not mean studying the Old Testament scriptures is not important. Every Christian should study the entire Bible. However, it is to be done with the intent to learn how the Old Testament reveals, through the Jewish feasts and all the Laws of the coming Messiah Jesus. The Old Testament is amazing how God was with the Jewish people and delivered them from their enemies supernaturally, even as Jesus does for all of us today who believe in His Name. To study and learn these scriptural truths found in the

Torah (first five books of the Bible) and elsewhere in the Old Testament, are tremendous revelations. However, we are not to put ourselves back under Old Testament Law, to do so is a great insult to the work of the Cross.

The Word of God says:

> *"I marvel that you are so soon removed from Him Who called you into the Grace of Christ unto another gospel: which is not another; but there be some who trouble you, and would pervert the Gospel of Christ. But though we, or an Angel from Heaven, preach any other gospel unto you than that which we have preached unto you, let him be accursed"* (Galatians 1:6-8).

The word *"pervert"* means to twist. Most false teachers in the church do not remove truth, They just change it. Only through the study of the scriptures can the believer have the proper discernment to spot these subtle perversions.

THE REFORM CHURCH

There is another movement in our nation today that is called "Reform Theology" or others have labeled as the "Grace Movement." It comes out of the Presbyterian Church and is more commonly known as "Calvinism" and named after its founder, John Calvin. These followers are marked by a strong emphasis on the sovereignty of God, the depravity of humankind, and the doctrine of predestination." (Merriam Webster https://www.merriam-webster.com/dictionary/Calvinism)

Whenever there is a single man associated with a teaching or doctrine, you should get a check in your spirit, as I have with John Calvin. He was a French theologian and reformer in Geneva during the Protestant Reformation and lived from 1509 to 1564. Aspects of his teachings include the doctrines of predestination and the absolute sovereignty of God in salvation.

Calvin was originally trained as a humanist lawyer. He broke away from the Roman Catholic Church around 1530. After religious tensions erupted in widespread deadly violence against Protestant Christians in France, Calvin fled to Basel, Switzerland. In 1536, he published the first edition of the Institutes. In that same year, Calvin was recruited by Frenchman William Farel to join the Reformation in Geneva, where he regularly preached sermons throughout the week; but the governing council of the city resisted the implementation of their ideas, and both men were expelled. At the invitation of Martin Bucer, Calvin proceeded to Strasbourg, where he became the minister of a church of French refugees. He continued to support the reform movement in Geneva, and in 1541 he was invited back to lead the church of the city. (Wikipedia, the Free Encyclopedia https://en.wikipedia. org/wiki/John Calvin).

Out of the teaching of John Calvin came what is now known as the "TULIP" doctrine. These 5 basic teachings make up what is called Reform Theology or Calvinism. Here are the 5 main points of Calvinism:

- Total Depravity: There is nothing inherently good in man; Salvation is all of God and none of man's responsibility.

- Unconditional Election: God chooses who receives eternal life and who goes to eternal damnation.

- Limited Atonement: Jesus did not die for the whole world, but only for the elect of God.

- Irresistible Grace: If God gives you His Grace, you will not reject it.

- Preservation of the Saints: "Once saved, always saved." You didn't choose it, so you can't lose it. This means unconditional eternal security.

If you take the five points of Calvinism and do a biblical study, you will find that every point, although containing some truth, is flawed and thereby unscriptural.

As far as total depravity goes; yes, man is sinful, lost, and depraved. But that does not mean that man's free will, which has been put into man by God, can't be convicted of sin and want God to change his or her life. Jesus said of the sinful tax collector, *"And the Publican, standing afar off, would not lift up so much as his eyes unto heaven, but smote upon his breast, saying God be merciful to me a sinner. I tell you, this man went down to his house justified"* (Luke 18:13-14).

Number two I do not believe that the Bible teaches predetermination that God predetermines who goes to heaven and who goes to hell. I do believe that the Bible teaches predestination, which means that those who receive Christ are predestined to spend eternity with Christ forever. Obviously, God Who is all knowing, does know who will choose Him and who will reject Him, however He does not program (i.e. create) or manipulate those who will accept and those who will reject Him, this would be a violation of man's free will.

The Bible says:

> *"For whom He did foreknow, He also did predestinate to be conformed to the image of His Son, that He might be the First born among many Brethren. Moreover, whom He did predestinate them He also called: and whom He called, them He also justified, them He also glorified"* (Romans 8:29-30).

The key word is *"for whom He did foreknow"* which means in the foreknowledge of God He then predestined. If God predetermines everything, then why would we need to preach the Gospel? In a pre-determination world, every soul who goes to hell could blame God for creating him that way. Isn't that the argument of the homosexual today, they say, "God made me that way." The Bible says that God loves the whole world, and He is not willing that any perish, but all come to repentance and be saved (John 3:16, II Peter 3:9).

The Bible says that man is the one who determines if he goes to heaven or spends eternity in hell. Romans 10:13 reads, *"For whosoever shall call upon the Name of the Lord shall be saved."* The scripture does not say, "for when the elect shall call" but it says, "whosoever." This means anyone and anywhere.

God said in Hosea 4:6: *"My people are destroyed for lack of knowledge: because you have rejected knowledge, I will also reject you."*

The teachings of "Limited Atonement" insinuates that John 3:16, doesn't really mean what it says: John 3:16 says, *"For God so loved the world, that He gave His Only Begotten Son, that whosoever believes in Him should not perish, but have everlasting life."* But they take it to mean, "For God so loved just His elect, that He gave His Only Begotten Son, for just His elect, as in His election, are not going to perish but have everlasting life." So, if we believe in predetermination then we must change the Bible such as II Peter 3:9 would be changed to say, "He does not want all to repent, but only the ones He predetermines, and because he predetermined it, they will repent.

I really don't know how anyone could believe this kind of teaching. I understand that there are some very intelligent people within Calvinism, but maybe the underlining problem is they are too smart for their own good. Those who teach Calvinism really lack the proper discernment of the love and mercy of God that is clearly taught throughout the scriptures.

The fourth principle of Calvinistic teaching is "Irresistible Grace," which is another belief that takes away the free will of the individual. It teaches that if God extends His Grace to a person they would never resist or reject it. Why? Because it is too good for anyone to reject, so they teach. Of course, this removes Satan's ability to "steal, kill, and destroy" a person's faith (John 10:10).

In the life of Judas, we see a man chosen by God through grace to be one of the 12 disciples. He saw all of Christ's great miracles and was even used himself in the power of God. However, he walked away from Jesus and betrayed Him because his heart was wicked, and he loved money more than he loved God. He is in hell today; so, in the case of Judas, he rejected the grace of God in the end. There are other examples in the Bible of men and women who started out right but then walked away from God. In fact we see this in the very beginning with Adam and Eve, we also see in the nation of Israel, and we see it today in the modern church, where man begin to follow Christ, but then they are tempted by the world's pleasures, and they fall away and stop following Christ.

Finally, the teaching of preservation of the saints (once saved, always saved) is simply not scriptural, but and in fact it is a very serious teaching error. It ignores many scriptures that speak of the opposite. Consider what Jesus said to the Church at Sardis: *"He who overcomes, the same shall be clothed in white raiment; and I will not blot out his name out of the Book of Life, but I will confess his name before My Father, and before His angels"* (Revelation 3:5). If it weren't possible for your name to be blotted out of His book and for you to lose your Salvation, then why would Jesus even say so?

Even though there are many scriptures that refute the teaching of unconditional eternal security throughout the Bible, this teaching continues and is believed by many. The truth is that the Bible doesn't teach unconditional eternal security, but it does teach conditional eternal security. If one keeps his faith in Christ and what Christ did at the Cross to save them, their name will not be blotted out. For Jesus said, *"And I give unto them Eternal Life; and they shall never perish, neither shall any man pluck them out of My hand"* (John 10:28). In other words, our Salvation is secure if we keep our faith in Christ.

Remember what Jesus said to Peter. He said: *"Simon, Simon, behold, Satan has desired to have you, that he may sift you as wheat: But I have prayed for you, that your faith fail not"* (Luke 22:31-32). Notice here we see that the fight is all about our faith. The Bible tells us to *"fight the good fight of faith"* (I Timothy 6:12). The Blessings of God promised in the Bible are always conditional and not automatic. The condition is based on us keeping our faith in Christ and the blood that He shed for the remission of our sins.

Our confidence is in the fact the Bible teaches God will not change His mind about your salvation and no man or devil can take you out of God's hand. This means that no outside force can take you out of God's hand. However, God doesn't remove man's free will (except in extreme cases); so, if a person desires to walk away from God, and go back into a life of sin and deny the existence of God, then they can take themselves out of the hand of God and forfeit their salvation. Regrettably, many people have done this very thing down through the ages.

What makes Reform Theology so dangerous is that it removes all human responsibility and free will. If you study it closer, you will notice that it does not teach the mighty baptism of the Holy Spirit as experienced by the early Church in the Book of Acts. They believe that this experience has not continued to all generations and to as many as the Lord calls as the Bible has clearly taught (Acts 2:39). The reformers teach that the gifts are not for today and in essence they have denied the power of the Holy Spirit.

When the gifts of the Holy Spirit are denied as being for today, it removes the supernatural demonstration of God. All you are left with is mainly your own intellect. One of the gifts of the Spirit is discernment; so, when you deny the gift of the Holy Spirit, that gift is not present in one's life or it is very limited. Obviously, it is God's Word that guides our life; but it is also the Holy Spirit Who is our teacher and the One who possesses all wisdom and discernment (John 16:13, Romans 8:14, 26-27). We must not limit or deny Him in any way or else we are left to our own reasoning and will power which are woefully inadequate.

One of the present-day leaders of Reform Theology is John MacArthur. Although he is a very gifted speaker and oftentimes conveys solid biblical truths, however when it comes to the baptism of the Holy Spirit and the gifts of the Spirit, he is a Cessationist, which means he believes the gifts of the Spirits have ceased or ended.

John MacArthur said:

> "My Pentecostal and Charismatic brothers and sisters in Christ say that none of these gifts have yet ceased. So, their answer to the question of when they will cease is, "In the future." Charismatic people who say that all the gifts are still in effect today often give the following argument. They say, "There isn't one verse in the entire Bible that says tongues have ceased. So, that settles it for us. They haven't ceased!" Well, they're right about the fact that there isn't a single verse in the Bible that specifically states that tongues have ceased. But do you know what? There isn't a single verse in the Bible that specifically states that God is three in one, either. But He is, isn't He?"

MacArthur goes on to say,

"To argue that something isn't true because the Bible doesn't specifically say it, is weak. And to argue that one needs a specific biblical statement to prove a point is also weak. Why? Because there are many truths in the Bible that are indicated to us by the totality of Scripture rather than any one given statement. For example, there isn't a verse that specifically says, "Jesus is 100% God and 100% man at the same time in an indivisible oneness." But that is the essence of the God-Man character of Christ, isn't it? You say, "How do you know?" Well, we have to piece together all the biblical facts of Christ's character in order to see the whole portrait. So, to argue that tongues haven't ceased because there isn't a verse specifically stating that fact, is not a good argument to use." (John MacArthur, Grace to You)

If you listen to Dr. MacArthur's logic in his above statements, you will think that he would conclude that the gifts of the Spirit (i.e., speaking in other tongues) is still in effect today. First, he uses the words, "Well, we have to piece together all the biblical facts of Christ's character in order to see the whole portrait."

So let's do that. Jesus said:

"And these signs shall follow them who believe; In My Name shall they cast out devils; they shall speak with new tongues; They shall take up serpents; and if they drink any deadly thing it shall not hurt them; they shall lay hands on the sick, and they shall recover" (Mark 16:15-18).

We have the whole book of Acts that shows how the Holy Spirit baptizing believers with the Holy Spirit with the evidence of speaking with other tongues. In Acts 2:39 the Bible says that the Promise of the Father (i.e., the Baptism with the Holy Spirit with the evidence of speaking with other tongues) is for all generations.

We have the teaching on the gifts of the Holy Spirit in Paul's letter to the Corinthian church (I Corinthians chapters 12-14). If the gifts were going to cease at the time around 100 A.D. as some teach, then why did God put these three chapters in the Bible to explain to us how the gifts should operate in the church? Why would we need to be instructed in this if the gifts have ceased.

So, based on John MacArthur's own logic he should conclude that the gifts of the Holy Spirit are still in existence today. But John MacArthur would rather choose to throw all that out and just be a non-believer of the supernatural gifts for today. Why? Because his intellect gets in the way of the supernatural power of God. What he personally hasn't experienced, he chooses not to believe. Also, he looks at the abuses of the gifts of the Spirit and throws out what the Bible clearly teaches.

Some years ago, Pastor MacArthur concluded his study on the gift of speaking in other tongues with this statement:

> "Well, after spending seven years studying this question and reading all sides of the issue that are in print, and after spending many hours discussing it with Charismatics and trying to evaluate it from their perspective, I am convinced, beyond all reasonable doubt, that tongues ceased in the Apostolic Age nineteen hundred years ago."

Because John MacArthur came to this conclusion that the gifts have ceased and because he is a well-known author and Bible teacher heard over national radio, many in the modern church have followed him in this same belief. By the way notice in his above statement, he said he discussed it with Charismatics, but he never said He went to the Lord to ask God about it. God said: *"Call unto Me, and I will answer you, and show you great and mighty things, which you know not"* (Jeremiah 33:3). I believe if Pastor Macarthur would do this, the Lord would show him that he is wrong in his beliefs concerning the gifts of the Spirit.

The belief of Calvinism has had a massive impact on how the modern church operates with limited to no power flowing through it. In this case, the devil has used man's intellect to remove the Power of God working in many churches. Please understand Satan is never threatened by man's wisdom, but he does shake in his boots when there is a demonstration of the Power of the Spirit. So, he works very hard to defuse the Church from the Power of the Holy Spirit and in this case, it looks like he has done a pretty good job.

Without the Power of the Holy Spirit the church loses its vision, sin begins to bind us, and life becomes just a grind. However, when the Holy Spirit baptizes a believer (i.e., fills) and that believer continues to be refilled with the Holy Spirit, life is going to be a life with God's vision, deliverance, and joy in the Holy Ghost. Reform Theology removes the Power of the Holy Spirit through unbelief. This hurts the church in unmeasurable ways as should be obvious. A powerless church is a defeated church as it is dry, lifeless and lacks vision. God never intended for His church to rely on the intellect of man, but to instead lean on the Power of God and all His gifts.

Paul said,

> *"And my speech and my preaching was not with enticing words of man's wisdom, but in the demonstration of the Spirit and of*

power: that your faith should not stand in the wisdom of men, but in the Power of God" (I Corinthian 2:4-5).

THE SEEKER-SENSITIVE CHURCH

The seeker sensitive church is a movement today that attempts to make church more attractive to an unchurched person, which is probably the bedrock to the backslidden church that we see in America and Canada today. The idea of the Seeker-Sensitive Movement is to create a church model that is desirable, more attractive, more culturally relevant, and more person-centered than the traditional Church model.

Followers and churches of this movement are in the thousands and some of the most well-knowns leaders of this movement are men like Rick Warren who authored the bestselling books, "The Purpose Driven Life" and "The Purpose Driven Church" which outlines how Pastor Rick Warren, and his team went house to house in his community asking the people what they were looking for in a local church. After his intense survey of the people, he built a church that the people wanted, right down to how long they wanted a Sunday morning service to last.

Today, leaders like Stephen Furtick of Elevation Church are followers of the Rick Warren model and they are having great success in building very large churches. However, the guru of this movement was a man by the name of Bill Hybels who built a thrilling seeker-sensitive church in the suburbs of Chicago, Illinois, called Willow Creek. He formerly worked with Youth for Christ (YFC) where he learned an evangelistic strategy where you create meetings for unsaved youth from the public school that are fun and exciting. Bill Hybels basically took the concept of YFC and first developed a strategy for the youth in his church. When he later became a pastor, he took this same concept to a whole other level as he implemented it for adults in a church setting. Hybels went as far as designing his church to look more like a theater than a church. He removed everything that looked churchy such as crosses, stained-glass windows, religious images, and emblems that he thought might offend those visiting for the first time. He wanted his church to be a nice, friendly, spacious amphitheater that was designed to look more like a movie theater with a Broadway stage than a traditional church.

His idea was to build a church that had multiple programs for the seeker (i.e., unbeliever) but at the same time appealing to the believer. He utilized things like drama, storytelling, secular music, shorter services, and a variety of programs and services for the family. His church had the appearance of almost like mini mall, car repair shop, and movie theater all rolled up into one. Everything was developed through the mindset of being relevant to the culture in which they were trying to reach.

Pastor Bill Hybels created a church in essence that was geared towards the seeker and not the One who was being sought, Jesus Christ. He made a church that was user-friendly, comfortable, and accommodating rather than convicting, confronting and challenging. Basically, Bill Hybels developed a church with a completely different paradigm than anything the church had ever seen before.

The result was that his church grew from a small group of people into a thriving megachurch; Willow Creek Church soon became known as "Willow World" located on a 90-acre parcel of land in South Barrington that eventually grew to 155 acres. They built a worship center that held 7,000 seats and developed it into a mall-like facility.

I was told that they even had an auto repair shop at the church so that single moms who had car problems could pull up on a Sunday morning and turn their keys in at the front door of the church and go and sit through the service while their car was being serviced. They thought of everything to make their church seeker friendly, so that people wanted to go to Willow Creek Church. However, there was only one problem. It was not biblical!

The Church in the New Testament and in the Old Testament was never meant to be built to please man, but it was to be built to please God. If God was pleased by His Church, then the Holy Spirit would be present to save souls, heal the sick, break the bondages of sin and lives would be restored by the Power of Almighty God.

Bill Hybels made the grave mistake of building a church from a worldly and fleshly mindset, which was void of the Holy Spirit's wisdom and power. He built Willow Creek on a seeker-sensitive premise instead of being Spirit led and Spirit designed. He wanted to please man more than wanting to please God, although he would not say that, however his actions spoke louder than his words. From the natural eye, his idea looked good; but, through spiritual eyes, I believed it grieved the heart of God.

In 1994, I visited Willow Creek back in the heyday of this movement. I must admit, the facility was impressive and some of what was observed, particularly for the youth ministry, didn't seem all that wrong or bad. We must realize that the devil doesn't create something that looks all evil. He is more cleaver than that. He mixes truth with lies, and he mixes holiness with a mixture of unholiness. But the Bible teaches: *"A Little leaven, leavens the whole lump"* (Galatians 5:9).

When I attended the Sunday morning service, the church service was attempting to use "relevant biblical teaching, music, and drama." But it was missing the Cross, the power of the Holy Spirit, and it was lacking real conviction, and there was no altar call at the end of the service for people to get right with God. It was for the most part, a good show with some biblical truth mixed in. I will admit that Bill Hybels was a very good communicator, very likeable, and he did teach on Christ and used scriptures, but he just didn't go far enough with what matters to God (in my opinion).

Willow Creek Church grew very fast and caught the attention of many church leaders across the nation and soon Bill Hybels developed what was called the Willow Creek Leadership Conference to teach the principle of "Willow World" to the nation's pastors. Now the deception was spreading and spreading fast.

The Conference taught American pastors and leaders how to start their own "Willow Creek Church" (i.e., Seeker-Sensitive churches). The conferences included high registration fees and a line-up of speakers who were nationally known leaders; some of which were not even Christians, but people Bill Hybels believed were innovative leaders and thinkers with skills and concepts that would benefit the church. There was a yoking together, a marriage if you will with the Church and secular CEOs of companies and corporations.

Churches across America were now trying to copy the Willow Creek Church model. The Great Deception was on as hundreds of pastors went in the direction of building seeker sensitive churches like Willow Creek. The hearts of the pastors were right in that they wanted to reach the "seeker" (i.e. the lost), but they were just going about in the wrong way.

CARRRYING THE ARK IN THE WRONG WAY

We see this in the life of King David when he wanted to bring the Ark of the Covenant to Jerusalem. The Ark represented the presence of God, and it was the right thing to do to bring it to Jerusalem. So, David had the right idea, but he went about it in the wrong way.

The Bible says David consulted with his leaders instead of consulting with God and His Word. This approach of course never ends well. The result was they decided to move the Ark on a "new cart" and two men "Uzza" and "Ahio" drove the cart as it was pulled by oxen. When they came to what the Bible called the *"threshing floor of Chidon"* the cart slipped as the oxen stumbled. When the Ark began to slide Uzza reached out his hand to steady it, and when he touched the Ark, God smote him and took his life. (I Chronicles 13:1-10).

This confused David as to why God took Uzza's life, and the Bible says that David was afraid of God. But when David went back to scripture, he learned that he was attempting to move the Ark of God in the wrong way. He then repented and moved the Ark of the Covenant in the biblical way. He learned that only the priests (and not common man) were to carry the Ark by the poles that were designed by God.

Today I believe many pastors in churches have the right heart to reach people for God, but they are using the wrong methods. The truth is God's Word doesn't instruct us to build a church for man, it instead instructs us to build a church for God, a church that glorifies Him.

David saw a man die because of attempting to go in an unscriptural way and unfortunately churches today in the modern church are doing the same thing as tens of thousands of people are dying spiritually. My prayer is for Willow Creek Church and all the seeker-sensitive churches in America, would do what David did; repent, and go back to the scriptures and learn how to build God's Church, God's Way. If America's pastors would decide to begin to handle the things of God with reverence and biblical accuracy, then I believe we would see a mighty move of God again in our nation.

On April 10, 2018, following allegations of sexual abuses, Bill Hybels announced his immediate retirement as senior pastor for the church. (1) "Willow Creek Announcement". www.willowcreek.org. Archived from the original on April 11, 2018. Retrieved April 11, 2018. The church went through extensive legal issues that not only included sexual allegations, but also led to more resignations, financial shortages due to the high legal fees, staff layoffs and a reduction in church attendance because of the allegations. It was all very sad to hear and see the "Willow World" come crashing down.

When something is of the flesh and not of the Spirit, you will find that even though it's beginning can look very good in terms of growth (numerically and financially); if it is not of God, or it begins to move away from the biblical way, it won't have a good ending. God is gracious and offers us time to repent, but if repentance does not happen and there is no turning back to God, the Lord will eventually judge it.

Thank God we serve a forgiving and gracious God who, if repentance occurs and God's ways are followed, He offers redemption. I pray this is the case for Bill Hybels. I have no doubt that he was sincere in what he wanted to build at Willow Creek, as were his leaders and staff. But I believe that the concept of a seeker-sensitive church is scripturally flawed, and the root flaw is that the central focus is the Seeker and not Jesus Christ and the Cross. We must build our churches to please an audience of One. If God is pleased, then we will see His Holy Spirit moving and operating.

I once challenged a pastor friend of mine who was beginning to study the seeker-sensitive church through the book "The Purpose Driven Church." I ask this Pentecostal pastor why he would be studying a church growth method from a pastor who did not believe in the Gifts of the Holy Spirit (i.e., Rick Warren). His answer was because Rick Warren had built a large church that has over 15,000 people attending it. I responded to this man's reason by saying to him: "Since when is big considered healthy, a 400-pound man might be big but he is not healthy."

This is what has led to the deception of many pastors, they are more concentrating on how to build bigger churches, rather than building spiritually healthy churches. The Roman Catholic church is big, but it is certainly not spiritually healthy.

THE WORD OF FAITH CHURCH

The 5th church model that has greatly affected American churches is the Word of Faith movement. Names like Kenneth Hagin, Kenneth Copeland, Jesse Duplantis, Benny Hinn, Joyce Meyers, Joel Osteen, TD Jakes, Rodney Howard-Browne, are some of the most popular Word of Faith preachers over the past 50 years.

The Word of Faith teachers promote that your confession and your faith is how you receive everything from God, namely divine healing, financial prosperity, and success in this life. What these ministers promote has caused their ministries to obtain great wealth. They promote a belief that if you "confess it," you can "possess it." They teach their people to stand firm on God's Word, because then God is obligated to respond with what you confess and believe in.

The main problem with this teaching as I see it is three-fold:

- It removes the Sovereignty of God and places it in the hand of man. Man in essence becomes a "demigod." I can have what I say, or what I believe. This teaching even at one point went so far as to teach that we are "little gods" where we can call things into existence by our words and our confession.

- It places its main objective on earthly rewards.

- The object of faith is faith in this movement, is not faith in Christ and Him Crucified but faith in your faith (i.e., your confession) It mostly is a greed gospel more than a need gospel (as I see it).

Let's first establish that there is biblical truth in this movement, however, it is mixed with errors. The truth is that God does honor faith in His Word and will save and will heal and will bless those who stand on His Word.

The error happens when the object of faith moves away from Jesus Christ and the Cross, and the motive becomes self-gratification or self-promotion instead of for God's Glory.

Let me give you some Word of Faith statements made by their teachers that might appear good to the biblically illiterate ear, but not to the discerning student of the Word of God.

Kenneth Hagin said, "They must have seen them acting as they were drunk." This was Brother Hagin's logic to the verse in Acts 2:13 when the people mocked the early church on the day of Pentecost who were all filled with the Holy Spirit and spoke in other tongues. The mockers said: "These men are full of new wine" (Acts 2:13).

This assumption by Kenneth Hagin was made to try and substantiate the very weird and extra-biblical manifestation of Christians acting like they were drunk with the Spirit. He himself towards the end of his ministry displayed erratic and out-of-control behavior while preaching, which was supposed to display a man "drunk in the spirit."

Kenneth Hagin is known as "Daddy Faith," as he was one of the founders of the Word of Faith Ministry. He started a Bible school in Tulsa, Oklahoma called Rhema Bible School. Towards the end of his ministry, he got caught up in the "laughing revival" where people started to laugh uncontrollably in services while the minister preached.

In Tampa, Florida, Rodney Howard-Brown pastors a large church. He is a preacher who came from South Africa and began the "laughing revival." He received the nickname the "Holy Ghost Bartender." In his meetings people displayed bodily actions as though they were literally "drunk in the spirit."

There is nothing in the Bible that gives evidence of these strange manifestations that has been seen in these meetings. To the contrary, the Bible teaches that when the Holy Spirit comes into a life, that person is filled with the fruit of the spirit of self-control (Galatians 5:23).

I have been in church meetings where the people would act weird and begin to laugh uncontrollably and carry on like they were literally drunk. They would even go so far as to make animal sounds or carry out animal like gestures. Very bizarre behavior, but all supported by the leadership of these charismatic churches telling the people that these are manifestations of the Holy Spirit.

As with any teaching in a church or any supposed manifestation, the Word of God must be our guide. I can tell you that in the ministry of Jesus, there are no scriptures (no, not one) where people laughed uncontrollably, acted drunk when Jesus touched them, or made animal sounds, calling it the power of the Holy Spirit. Jesus Himself, who had the Spirit without measure, never demonstrated anything even close to what these Word of Faith preachers and teachers call a manifestation of God. In fact, the Bible to the contrary the Bible says: "Wine is a mocker, strong drink is raging: and whosoever is deceived thereby is not wise" (Proverbs 20:1).

Why would God's Holy Spirit make someone act as though they were drunk when the Bible calls wine a mocker? The Bible also says, *"And be not drunk with wine, wherein is excess; but be filled with the Spirit"* (Ephesians 5:18). Here, the Holy Spirit's direction is the opposite of being drunk with wine.

Where is the scriptural evidence of "laughing in the spirit" and carrying on like one is drunk? It first came from one scripture, which is Acts 2:13. It says, *"Others mocking said, these men are full of new wine."* This verse refers to the 120 people who were filled with the Spirit on the day of Pentecost. They came out of the Temple speaking in other tongues. It was mockers who said that the 120 people were drunk. However, Peter stood before them and said, *"For these are not drunken, as you suppose, seeing it is but the third hour of the day"* (Acts 2:15).

This is the passage they erroneously use to back up the unscriptural teaching of where the "laughing revival" came from. What makes this so ridiculous is that there is no other scripture in the New Testament that even remotely describes people being filled with the Spirit and acting in an uncontrollable way. In fact, the Bible teaches the opposite for a child of God. It says, *"For God has not given us the spirit of fear; but of power, and of love, and of sound mind"* (II Timothy 1:7). The word for "sound mind" in this scripture means "a spirit of self-control." In scripture, the Holy Spirit never has believers act out of control, either acting like they are drunk, or laughing uncontrollably while the minister preaches the Word. To the contrary, scripture teaches order and not confusion in God's House.

However, God put King Nebuchadnezzar in a state of insanity for seven years due to his pride (Daniel 4:33). Therefore, I don't think that the Church wants to exhibit a spirit of being out of control and looking like they are temporarily drunk as God may just fix it that they stay in that state. One ought to be careful about what they call a manifestation of the Holy Spirit. The Bible declares, "*Be not deceived; God is not mocked: for whatsoever a man sows, that shall he also reap. But he who sows to his flesh shall of the flesh reap corruption. For he who sows to the Spirit shall of the Spirit reap life everlasting*" (Galatians 6:7-8).

It amazes me how gullible some Christians can be. But remember that whenever someone leaves the teaching of the Cross, they are not far from the golden calf. I am not saying that Kenneth Hagin didn't teach truth, but I believe he went too far in his teaching as many others in this movement have and in so doing have made a mockery of Christianity to so many.

Bible teachers who allow this kind of out-of-control behavior in the Church, in the name of "freedom," are causing confusion for the unlearned and unsaved not to mention opening up their congregation to familiar and strange spirits. God made it clear that in an open church service, people are not to speak out in tongues unless there is an interpreter. Why? The Bible says that the unlearned or unbeliever will say that the people are all mad or crazy (I Corinthians 14:23). If God teaches us to avoid confusion that occurs when everyone is speaking in other tongues in a service with no interpreter, how much more will the unlearned and unbelievers say about people who act drunk, make strange animal sounds, and or laugh out of control during a service?

I believe that preachers like Rodney Howard-Browne, who allow this "strange spirit" to come into the church, need to repent and renounce this unholy, weird, strange, and confusing spirit. These teachings have caused untold damages to people's faith and have cause many to walk away from the Lord. These teachers have given a bad name to the overall movement of the Pentecostal and Charismatic church.

Joyce Meyer

Over the past 20 years, Joyce Myer has been one of the leaders in the Word of Faith movement. She has captivated large audiences with her humor and direct approach. She is obviously a gifted communicator who made a lot of money selling her books and speaking at large conferences and has become very successful in the eyes of the church. However, what is she teaching? Joyce Meyer clearly focuses on making a better "YOU." Here are just a few titles of some of her many self-help books:

- Power Thoughts
- Healing the Soul of the Women
- The Confident Woman
- Living Beyond Your Feelings
- Change Your Words Change Your Life
- The Mind Connection, Look Great Feel Great

Most of her books' themes are centered on self because self-centered books, or self-centered churches bring in large American crowds, especially when the speaker has a charismatic personality. But the problem with this is that the Bible is not a self-centered book; it is a Jesus-centered book. The Bible calls sinners to repent and crucify self; it says to come out of the world's system of lust and instead live for the world to come. The Bible preaches and teaches Christ and Him Crucified (I Corinthians 2:2, Galatians 5:14).

Joyce Meyer wrote in one of her books:

> "The Devil thought he had it, the devil thought he had won. Oh, they were having the biggest party that has ever been had. They had my Jesus on the floor, and they were standing on his back jumping up and down laughing and he had become sin. Don't you think that God was pacing wanting to put a stop to what was going on. All the hosts of hell were up on him, up on him, up on him.
>
> The angels are in agony, all the creation is groaning. All the hosts of hell were up on him, up on him, they got on him. They got him down in the floor and got on him and they were laughing and mocking, "ha-ha you trusted God and look where you ended up. You thought he would save you and get you off that cross – he didn't ha-ha." (a sermon she preached "From the Cross to the Grave" July 17, 2014- Jesus went to hell)

Her statement references her teaching where she says that after Jesus died on the Cross, He went to hell and was tortured by the devil for three days. She once taught (and I should point out does not teach this anymore) that after Jesus died on the Cross, He went to hell to be punished for sin. She then taught that after three days and three nights of demons jumping all over Him and laughing at Him, God finally had enough and seeing that the price was finally paid, God ended the suffering and Jesus then physically rose from the dead as the first born-again man.

All this of course is erroneous and utterly blasphemous, having no biblical reference. In fact, the Bible teaches the very opposite of what Joyce

Meyer once proclaimed to her gullible audiences. Jesus, when He died on the Cross, said *"It Is Finished"* (John 19:30). In the Greek, this phrase means "paid in full." The Work of the Cross, where Jesus shed His Blood for the sins of the world and died, was enough in the eyes of God the Father for the penalty to be paid for sin.

Jesus did go down into hell for three days, but not to be mocked and stomped on by the devil as Mrs. Meyer ridiculously proclaimed. When He went into hell, the Bible says he preached unto the spirits in prison. It is believed that Jesus preached to the fallen angels who are locked away in the underground prison of hell (I Peter 3:19-20).

Jesus also went into a place called "Abraham's bosom," (i.e. paradise) where the Old Testament saints who died, were waiting for their coming Redeemer. They were waiting for the work of the Cross to be finished so that their spirits and souls could go to heaven. So, Jesus did go down into this place called "Paradise" and He led captives out of hell into the portals of Glory (Luke 16:22-26, Ephesians 4:8-9).

One must be incredibly careful to not believe false teachings related to the work of the Cross because you are dabbling in the very essence of your salvation. It is very advisable that you run away from any teacher that tampers with the work of the Cross. It is a finished work, and nothing is to be added or taken away from the biblical account of the death, burial, and resurrection of Jesus Christ.

Kenneth Copeland

Pastor and teacher Kenneth Copeland became the leader of the Word of Faith movement after his mentor, Kenneth Hagin, died. He is probably one of the richest leaders in the Word of Faith movement today.

On June 23, 2014, Kenneth Copeland met with Pope Francis along with James and Betty Robison and other evangelical leaders. Kenneth Copeland had this to say about his meeting with Pope Francis:

> *"I am so blessed! What Jesus asked the Father for in John 17:21, "that we may all be one in Him," is finally coming to pass. Pope Francis is a man filled with the love of Jesus. All eight of us in our meeting together with him were moved by the strong presence of the Holy Spirit, and our love for one another was strengthened beyond measure. Like I said, I am so BLESSED! What a time to be a believer!"* (Kenneth Copeland Ministries, June 26, 2014, https://blog.kcm.org/kenneth-copeland-reports-in-about-his-meeting-with-pope-francis/)

First, the prayer of Jesus recorded in John 17 was not a prayer for unification of all religions to be one. That is a gross error and, to be frank, it is so dangerous for anyone to even make that statement regarding Roman Catholicism. Jesus' prayer to the Father was unity among true followers of Jesus, which includes only those who are born again, and believe that one is justified by faith in Christ alone. Salvation has nothing to do with any works, which is what the Roman Catholic Church teaches and believes. In fact, Pope Francis has made statements that are clearly not biblical, such as:

> "Many think differently, feel differently, seeking God or meeting God in diverse ways. In this crowd, in this range of religions, there is only one certainty that we have for all: we are all children of God." (Vatican City, Jan. 7, 2016, CNA Catholic New Agency, https://www.catholicnewsagency.com/news/in-first-video-message-pope-francis-stresses-unity-we-are-all-children-of-god-39381)

This statement is clearly not biblical as the Bible does not teach that we are all children of God. Instead, it teaches that we are all God's creation. Because of sin, we have fallen from God's Grace, and we need to repent and be adopted into God's family as a child of God. How do we do this? Jesus spoke these words to a Jewish priest named Nicodemus: *"Verily, verily, I say unto you, Except a man be born again, he cannot see the Kingdom of God"* (John 3:3).

Clearly, the Pope does not know what the Bible teaches on how one is to be saved and brought into the family of God. If he did, he would have to resign from being the Pope of the Catholic Church since Roman Catholicism teaches a completely different salvation message than the writers of the Bible penned.

When Kenneth Copeland stated that Pope Francis is a man of God and is filled with the love of Jesus, he completely shows how mislead he really is. I would describe Pope Francis as a "wolf in sheep's clothing" and I know this statement will make some people mad, but the truth is that the Pope is a Globalist who is trying to unite all the major religions of the world together into a one-world Religion which is prophesied in the Bible that this will happen in end times. The terms used by scripture for a man who does this in the end times is a "Beast" and a "False Prophet." By the look of things, is it pointing to and shaping up to be this very person.

For Kenneth Copeland to state that he was moved in his meeting with the presence of Pope, clearly shows that Kenneth Copeland doesn't understand the difference between biblical Christianity and Roman Catholicism. For the sake of unity, he is ignoring the historical and scriptural differences of the two. This is very dangerous! Jesus said, *"Take heed that no man deceive you. For many shall come in My Name, saying, I am Christ; and deceive many"* (Matthew 24:4-5).

THE PROSPERITY CHURCH

Over the past 40 to 50 years, many American churches moved away from orthodox Christianity that focuses on Christ, the Cross, and the teaching that *"in this world you shall have tribulation, but be of good cheer, I have overcome the world"* (John 16:33). Many have abandoned the traditional Christian mindset that this world is not our home and that we are just passing through. Instead, the church has promoted a materialistic mindset of building a financial kingdom right here and now.

The modern church brought in a new line of teaching and mindset. You can prosper in this world and be blessed and advance in this life; physically, financially, socially, and intellectually because Abraham was wealthy, so can you (Genesis 13:2). They teach that God wants every one of His children to be wealthy because Abraham is the father of us all (Romans 4:16).

There is a problem with this teaching or thought process as they fail to realize, Jesus (who came as an example to us all), left the riches of Heaven, and came to this earth to be born in a dirty stable, owned nothing in the 33½ years of His life and He even said: *"Foxes have holes, and birds of the air have nests; but the Son of Man has nowhere to lay His Head"* (Luke 9:58).

In fact, all the disciples and true followers of Jesus did not look to possess materials things in this world but forsook all things to be followers of Jesus. I once heard the statement, "to come to Christ costs you nothing, but to follow Christ will cost you everything." The modern false teacher twists this and says, "if you come to Jesus and live by faith, God will give you back what Adam had before he fell, and you will have dominion over the earth and have much financial blessings."

Now let's be balanced here because the Word of God says, *"A false balance is abomination to the LORD, but a just weight is His delight"* (Proverbs 11:1). God is a God of blessings and He rewards faith, which the Bible teaches (Hebrews 11:6). However, financial blessings is not to be our motive for living for God. Jesus said, *"But seek you first the Kingdom of God, and His Righteousness; and all these things shall be added unto you"* (Matthew 5:33).

Some time ago, my wife and I attended a Christian Leadership conference where a speaker said that God wanted Christians to be millionaires. The speaker asked the audience the question, "who wants to be a millionaire?" Many hands went up; however, mine did not. In fact, I raised my voice and said out loud, "I don't;" to which my wife gave me a shot in the ribs because she was embarrassed because of my boldness since we were sitting right in the front row. So, I turned to her and said even louder a second time, "I don't." Why was I so emphatic? Because I knew that the man was in the wrong spirit to even ask such a question. For the Bible says, *"But they who will be rich fall into temptation and a snare, and unto many foolish and hurtful lusts, which drown men in destruction and perdition. For the love of money is the root of all evil: which while some coveted after, they have erred from the faith, and pierced themselves through with many sorrows"* (I Timothy 6:9-10).

The above verse speaks of believers who lost sight of the true faith, which is the Cross, and instead ventured into a false faith that is used to garner much money." (Expositors Study Notes, page 2104).

This prosperity movement has built large churches as seen by Joel Osteen who pastors the largest church in America in Houston, Texas. He has written books entitled "Your Best life Now," *"The Power of I Am,"* "You Are Stronger," "Your Greater is Coming," "Rule Your Day," etc. You can see by these books titles, which by the way have earned Osteen millions of dollars in sales, that they all have one common theme "You." The bottom-line is a self-centered book about prosperity sells well in America and a self-centered church can also build a pretty big church if it has a charismatic leader to go with it.

Some years ago, I was visiting a prosperity church with my son Andrew who was about 12 years old at the time (if I remember correctly). When the pastor took the offering, he asked the people to hold up their offering envelope and repeat after him, "Increase, Increase" as he was teaching his church that the more you give, the more you will get. It has been labeled as "seed faith" by the prosperity preachers. As the service went on my son handed me a slip of paper that he had written on that read: "Dad, I thought the Bible says, "He must increase, and we must decrease" (John 3:30). I thought to myself our 12 year old son possesses more discernment than the preacher up there does.

There is much more I could say about the "greed gospel" but let me just tell you what Jesus said to the church at Smyrna: *"I know your works, and tribulation, and poverty, (but you are rich)."* The Church of Smyrna, although poverty stricken outwardly, the Lord Himself declared them as spiritually rich. The truth is if you have Jesus, no matter how much money you have in the bank, or don't have in the bank, you are rich.

Jesus spoke to the Laodicean Church which is the last church in the book of Revelation, symbolizing the modern church today. He said: *"Because you say, I am rich, and increased with goods, and have need of nothing; and knowest not that you are wretched, and miserable, and poor, and blind, and naked"* (Revelation 3:17). My friend I would rather be poor in this world and have Jesus, then to be rich and be deceived. The church must come back to the Word of God, make the focus leading souls into the Kingdom, and not seeking financial blessings.

THE DOMINIONISM/NEW APOSTALIC REFORMATION CHURCH

One of the major movements today in the Evangelical Church, particularly in the Pentecostal and charismatic churches world, is a movement called, "New Apostolic Reformation" (NAR). This movement began by a man named C Peter Wagner and is also referred to as the "Third Wave of the Holy Spirit." This movement differs from the traditional Protestant belief and teaching. Wagner lists the differences between the NAR and other Protestant denominations as follows:.

- **Apostolic Governance:** The restoration of church government led by appointed apostles within his church.

- **The Office of the Prophet:** A belief in present-day prophets as there were in the Old Testament.

- **Dominionism:** "When Jesus came, He brought the kingdom of God, and He expects His kingdom-minded people to take whatever action is needed to push back the long-standing kingdom of Satan and bring in the peace and prosperity of His kingdom here on earth." (Quote from C Peter Wagner)

- **Theocracy:** Not to be confused with theocratic government but rather the goal is to have kingdom-minded people in all areas of society. There are seven areas identified specifically: religion, family, education, government, media, arts and entertainment, and business.

- **Relational structures:** Church governance has no formal structure but rather is by relational and voluntary alignment to apostles.
[(https://en.wikipedia.org/wiki/New_Apostolic_Reformation)

KINGDOM NOW

Dominion teaching or "Kingdom Now" as it has been called is the idea that conservative Christians have the right and the responsibility to take dominion over all aspects of life, including the government. This term is taken from Genesis 1:26-28, which God instructs Adam and Eve to *"have dominion"* over every living thing on Earth. This "dominion mandate" has remained popular in certain fundamental circles for decades. This theological teaching is focused on bringing the Kingdom of God to earth through the church invading the culture to bring "Kingdom principles" to seven different segments of society. The Dominion teachers call this the "Seven Mountains" of influence, which are:

- Family
- Government/Military
- Religion
- Education
- Media
- Arts and Entertainment
- Business

The goal is to install "change agents" (i.e., dominion-minded Christians) at every level of society to gain influence and to use that influence to Christianize the nation, and eventually create a world-wide theocracy. The way in which they hope to accomplish this is by purging all aspects of society of secularism and anything deemed "not Christian" since these things are the work of the Anti-Christ and possessed by Satan's demonic agents. This world-wide dominion by Christians is necessary to create the Kingdom of Heaven on earth and prepare the world for the return of Jesus Christ. (Dominionism in America Part 5: The Seven Mountains Mandate, by Jack Matirk, Feb.20, 2019 https:...www.patheos.com/blogs/infernal2019/02/dominion-ism-in-america-part-5-the-seven-mountains-mandate)

This seven-mountain prophecy is an extra biblical teaching that has gained a following in Charismatic and Pentecostal churches. Those who follow this seven-mountain mandate believe that for Christ to return to earth, the church must take control of these seven major spheres of influence in society. They teach that once the world has been made subject to the kingdom of God, Jesus will return and rule the world.

These seven sectors of society are thought to be what molds the way everyone thinks and behaves. So, to tackle societal change, these seven "mountains" must be transformed. The mountains are also referred to as "pillars," "shapers," "molders," and "spheres." Those who follow the seven-mountain mandate speak of "occupying" the mountains, "invading" the culture, and "transforming" society.

The seven-mountain mandate has its roots in dominion theology that started in the early 1970's with a goal of "taking dominion" of the earth, twisting Genesis 1:28 to include a mandate for Christians to control civil affairs and all other aspects of society. The New Apostolic Reformation, with its self-appointed prophets and apostles, has also influenced the seven-mountain movement lending dreams and visions and other extra-biblical revelations to the mandate.

This movement states that it is the duty of all Christians to create a world-wide kingdom for the glory of Christ. Teachers in the movement will use Isaiah 2:2, which mentions mountains, to support their view, not realizing that the verse clearly says: *"And it shall come pass in the last days"* and is speaking of the Kingdom Age when Jesus is back on the Earth ruling and reigning.

The principal goal of dominion theology and the seven-mountain mandate is political and religious domination of the world through the implementation of the moral laws—and subsequent punishments—of the Old Testament.

Lance P. Wallnau coined the phrase "seven-mountain mandate" and is one of its most prominent teachers of the movement today. Wallnau adapts the missionary mandate of Jesus to His disciples to "go and make disciples" of all the nations into a mandate to effect social transformation. He reasons that, since churches already have a presence in every nation in the world, we need to now concentrate on influencing the systems (the "mountains") within these nations. The problem, according to Wallnau, is that Christians are not currently influencing society outside the church. Christians have left the mountains susceptible to the "gates of hell," which are spiritual portals over the "kings" (influence-shapers) of those mountains.

Wallnau's teaching is loosely based on the Abrahamic Covenant, which promised Abraham a seed and a lasting inheritance. Also, Israel was promised in Deuteronomy 28:12 to be the *"head and not the tail"* among the nations. Proponents of the seven-mountain mandate infer that the church, not Israel is the entity to claim that promise and it is now up to believers to move in proximity to the "gates of hell" and position themselves to exert the greatest amount of influence.

They teach the church then needs to be dissected into "micro components" and infiltrate the mountains and they go on to teach since every Christian can't position himself at the top of every mountain, everyone is to find his particular smaller peak and be a leader in that realm.

The leading edge of the seven-mountain mandate is the New Apostolic Reformation (NAR), which teaches that the church of the 21st century will be ruled by apostles and prophets. The movement is not governed by a specific denomination, but by the alleged apostles and prophets who, of course, claim to receive direct revelation from God. In lending credence to modern-day prophets and apostles, the NAR denigrates the Bible and sola scriptura, emphasizes experience-oriented theology, and promotes mysticism. The NAR and proponents of the seven-mountain mandate abandoned biblical teaching on the end times, choosing to believe that Christians must set the stage for Jesus' second coming by achieving dominion over the world's systems. According to seven-mountain theology, Jesus will only return to a world that mirrors the kingdom of God. This idea parallels the New Age teaching that anticipates a cosmic spiritual shift when man becomes a co-redeemer of Planet Earth. (https://en.wikipedia.org/wiki/New Apostolic Reformation)

This movement was generally supportive of Donald Trump's presidency with Paula White becoming the president's spiritual advisor. White claimed that Trump "will play a critical role in Armageddon as the United States stands alongside Israel in the battle against Islam." In 2020, Charlie Kirk said finally we have a president that understands the seven mountains of cultural influence during a speech at the Conservative Political Action Conference. (n.wikipedia.org/wiki/Seven Mountain Mandate)

Christians are called to be lights in the world (Matthew 5:14). However, there is no biblical requirement to take the helm of all the world systems and to usher in Christ's kingdom. The Bible says that the world will grow worse, not better, in the last days (2 Timothy 3:1, 13:2, Peter 3:3).

The theology associated with the seven-mountain mandate is dangerous as it's teaching puts a tremendous burden on believers to perform, make progress in their relative spheres of influence. Little emphasis is placed on the gospel message of salvation by grace through faith in Jesus Christ. The movement is more about staking claims and taking control. The seven mountain mandate is a movement that should be avoided and exposed whenever Bible-believing Christians encounter it.

DOMINION LEADERS

This growing movement among evangelicals started taking root in the late nineties. Peter Wagner of Global Harvest Ministries considered the year 2001 to be the beginning of the second apostolic age, for the movement holds that the lost offices of prophet and apostle were restored in that year.

After being named as part of the NAR, and critics believing that Bethel Church was instrumental in leading some Christians to embrace tenets of NAR, Pastor Bill Johnson of Bethel became regularly listed as an NAR leader. Johnson admitting that he does believe in the apostolic and prophetic ministries, he denied however in an official statement that his church had any official ties to the NAR.

Chuck Colson once said that Christians are "to take command and dominion over every aspect of life, whether it's music, science, law, politics, communities, families; to bring Christianity to bear in every single area of life." This is the same spirit that was in Israel in Jesus' day. The Jews were being oppressed by the Romans and wanted to overthrow the oppression and rule in their nation. In other words, they wanted dominion over their land and their people. When Jesus came, they hoped that He would overthrow the gentile rule of the Roman government and bring in the Kingdom Age. However, Jesus did not come to rule the nations in His first advent, but instead came to die on the Cross for the nations. Israel had their chronology wrong, just like many in the Church today have their chronology wrong.

The Jews wanted Jesus to fight for their nation and bring down the evil Roman Empire; however, this was not the mission of His first coming. He will one day come again, and then He will defeat the revised Roman Empire and the Antichrist empire. When Jesus comes back to the earth, He will usher in the Millennial Kingdom and rule and reign from Jerusalem. At that time, He will put Satan in the bottomless pit and lock him away for one thousand years. That is when man, under Christ's rule, will have dominion again and we will rule the nations as Kings and Priests. But only when King Jesus has full dominion over the earth will man have dominion again over society, only then, and not before (Revelation 1:6).

Israel, not understanding the prophets of old nor understanding their own sin and wickedness and the need for a Savior, were misguided in their mission. The same could be said of much of the Church today. Dominion teachers are trying to usher in the Kingdom Age, not realizing that we are not living in that dispensation yet and will not until King Jesus comes riding on a white horse to save all of Israel.

Dominion teachers reject or ignore the true mission of the Church Age, which is to preach the message of the Cross and see people saved and delivered. They fail to recognize or live out the truth that this world is not their home. They are deceived by their own pride and selfishness, and may I add the love of money and power with their hearts loving this world rather than the one to come. We must realize although the church preserves society by being salt and light, and holding back the Antichrist temporarily, our mission is not to save or to take over society, it is simples to pluck souls out of this fallen and sinful society.

THE POWERLESS CHURCH

There is a large segment in the church that believes in cessation (the ceasing of the gifts of the Holy Spirit) who are not necessarily 5-point Calvinists (although it includes them as well). The cessation doctrine teaches that the gifts of the Spirit are no longer in effect. Pastors teach their congregations that when the canon of scripture became complete, God did away with the gifts of the Spirit. Therefore, speaking in other tongues, gifts of healing, words of knowledge, words of wisdom, etc., have ceased.

They teach that the baptism with the Holy Spirit and Salvation are the same event, unlike in the Book of Acts where Salvation and being filled with the Spirit is seen over and over as two separate events (Acts 2:1-4, 8:14-17 9:17, 10:44-46, 19:1-6). This belief strips the church of understanding how the Holy Spirit works in supernatural power after one comes to Jesus. This produces a church that is limited in faith, and therefore, limited in seeing the miracles which the early church saw.

When I first came to know Christ, I was attending an independent church, which was Baptist in doctrine. They taught the gifts had ceased. They taught that Salvation and the Baptism with the Holy Spirit was the same event. However, in my studies from Pentecostals/Charismatic authors I learned that Salvation and being filled with the Holy Spirit were subsequent events. So as a new believer I was confused. Who was right?

One day after many hours and days of study and frustration on this topic I finally cried out to God and said: "Lord, this should not be that the church is divided over such an important issue as the Holy Spirit. Which side Lord is right? Then I heard the Lord speak to me and He simply spoke these words to my heart. He said: *"You shall know them by their fruits"* (Matthew 7:16). It was then that the lights went on in my mind. I saw for the first time the difference. In my Baptist church they were more subdued and less expressive in worship not because of personality, but because of what they believed. In turn the Pentecostal churches were not more expressive because of personality, or a chosen style of worship, they were bold with their faith because the Spirit had filled them. My church didn't have the same assurance as to God's ability to do miracles today as the Pentecostal church, and my church didn't have the same joy. I knew the Lord had showed me that the Pentecostals had this right, even though people in my church were saved and loved God, they did not have the Baptism with the Holy Spirit and the fruit proved it.

The truth is that all throughout church history, the Lord has continued to baptize believers with the Holy Spirit with the evidence of speaking with other tongues just like He did in the Book of Acts. The truth is He still heals the sick and delivers the possessed and oppressed who come to Him in faith (according to His Will).

The last words of Jesus Christ before His ascension were, *"But you shall receive power, after that the Holy Spirit is come upon you: and you shall be witnesses both in Jerusalem, and in all Judaea, and in Samaria, and unto the uttermost part of the earth"* (Acts 1:8).

Jesus never wanted His church to be powerless. If the Lord was going to stop filling believers with the Holy Spirit like He did in the early church, and if the gifts were no longer going to be in operation after we had the Bible, then why would an all-knowing God put I Corinthians chapters 12-14, in the Bible to teach us about gifts that were no longer to be in operation?

The Bible says that *"For God is not the Author of confusion, but of peace, as in all churches of the Saints"* (I Corinthians 14:33). People in the church have said how confusing it is to have half of the churches saying that there are no gifts of the Spirit operating today as it was with the early church, and the other half saying the gifts are still for today.

Remember, the Bible says, *"For the Gifts and Calling of God are without Repentance"* (Romans 11:29). I don't think God can make it any clearer than that! He is not going to give the early church gifts and then take them away. Also, the Bible says that *"Jesus Christ the same yesterday, and today, and forever"* (Hebrews 13:8). The truth is that the same Jesus who performed miracles and worked through the gifts of the Spirit in the early church still does the same today in the Church. The question is, does the church believe that, and do they have the faith that God still works in the same power as He did in the Book of Acts?

The Bible teaches us that God works through faith. If the church doesn't have faith that Jesus works in the same way today as He worked during the early church, then they will not be able to see it. James said, *"If any of you lack wisdom, let him ask of God, Who gives to all men liberally, and upbraideth not, and it shall be given him. But let him ask in Faith, nothing wavering. For he who wavers is like a wave of the sea driven with the wind and tossed. For let not that man think that he shall receive any thing of the Lord"* (James 1:6-8).

A powerless church is no threat to Satan, and Satan knows that he is no match for the Holy Spirit. Therefore, he does his best to deceive the church into embracing the idea that the Holy Spirit no longer does what He used to do. Satan knows if he can get the church to believe in cessation, he will then easily keep the church from being all she can be. The church that believes in cessation largely stays in this mindset when viewing the extremism of Pentecostal and Charismatic churches. These extremes allows them to be even more deceived that God no longer works in the gifts of the Spirit. How sad it all is! The saying is true the devil wouldn't be a bad devil if he wasn't a good devil. He is a master at deception.

THE BIZARRE (HYPER CHARISMATIC) CHURCH

There is yet another movement that I will refer to as the "Bizarre" church. Due to Pentecostal and Charismatic churches leaving the message of the Cross and going into what I would call hyper-charismania they become strange in the things in which they partake in. Whenever false doctrine creeps into a church under the disguise of the power of the Holy Spirit, things will begin to get odd and unusual in the church.

The church in the last 20 years has seen some of the most foolish and bizarre things labeled as "manifestations" of the Spirit. Things such as gold dust, angel feathers, animal sounds, grave sucking, laughing in the spirit uncontrollably, birthing, drunk in the spirit, toking the ghost, glory tunnel, etc.

If I had not witnessed some of these things with my own eyes, I would never have believed the church would participate in such foolishness. But preachers in the Pentecostal and Charismatic circles in our nation and other nations around the world have allowed this "strange fire" into their churches and have label it as "supernatural" or "being free in the spirit." It all goes on even though no scripture exists for these strange occurrences and so called manifestations. There is not even an inkling of evidence in the Bible for most of these bizarre things taking place in the church today, which is nothing more than blasphemy.

I once heard a preacher say that "if a Christian has the Word but not the Spirit, they will dry up. If they have the Spirit but not the Word, they will blow up. But, if they have the Word and the Spirit, they will grow up."

Every believer must worship the Lord in "spirit and in truth" (John 4:24). To have one without the other is an imbalance.

The message of the Cross is the central message of the Bible, and Jesus Christ and Him Crucified is the foundational truth of all Bible doctrine. In other words, the Cross of Christ is the foundation for every teaching. That is why the Apostle Paul said in I Corinthians 2:2: *"For I determined not to know anything among you, save Jesus Christ, and Him Crucified."*

The church that is dry and dead filled with formalism has denied the working and operation of the Holy Spirit and the church that is into fanaticism is trying to conjure up the Spirit, because it has left the Cross and has lost its vision, and it now is focused on manifestations rather than on the truth. The true church must guard itself against both extremes.

THE HYPER GRACE MOVEMENT

As does most false teaching the Grace movement today as it has been called takes a certain truth and takes it too far. The Grace movement teaches that since the church today is under Grace, we do not have to repent because we have been already forgiven from all of our sins, past, present, and future. Well friend, even though it is true that all believers are forgiven in terms of the penalty of sin, (for everyone who is truly born again), we as believers still sin and grieve the Holy Spirit and we still need to repent. When a sin is committed by a believer it breaks the sweet fellowship we have with the Holy Spirit.

We see in Romans 6:1 Paul asked the question, *"Shall we continue in sin, that Grace may abound?"* In other words, Paul is asking the question that now that we are saved by Grace, is sin no longer a big deal? He answered his own question and said: *"God forbid."* When we come to Jesus by Grace through faith we are not saved in our sin, we are saved from our sin. When a person is lost, sin is not really a big deal, we sin and think nothing of it. But whenever a person is truly saved, they now hate sin and the Grace of God doesn't give them a license to sin, but the Grace of God gives them the desire and freedom to no longer sin.

So, to say that now that we are under Grace, we no longer need to repent is simply a lie and false interpretation of what true grace is. In the 7 letters to the 7 churches in the Book of Revelation chapter two and three, Jesus repeatedly says to the church to repent or else. So, the Grace of God doesn't remove the importance of repentance, but it only enhances it. You will find that those who are pushing this Grace message today over television and radio are not teaching or preaching the Baptism with the Holy Spirit, with the evidence of speaking with other tongues. John said that when one is baptized with the Holy Spirit the Lord will begin to remove the chaff from the wheat, in other words God the Holy Spirit will make the believer more conscious of sin in their life and the need to repent (Luke 3:16-17).

THE CHURCH HAS MOVED AWAY FROM THE POWER OF THE HOLY SPIRIT

In the Book of Acts when someone was filled with the Holy Spirit, God granted them the gift of speaking with other tongues (Acts 2:1-4, 10:4446, 19:1-6). The doctrine of Baptism of the Holy Spirit is one of the most neglected, abused and ignored doctrine in the New Testament Church.

Make no mistake, the devil is afraid of the power of the Holy Spirit like nothing else. Therefore, he tries to abuse, counterfeit, and deceive this truth. Why? Because he wants to cut off the power source of the Church.

The Book of Acts church witnessed miracles with salvation being the greatest miracle of all. However, they also saw healings and believers being filled with the Holy Spirit and operating in the spiritual gifts. The Spirit of God is the One Who transforms the church from a human organization to a genuine house of miracles that has transformed countless lives, towns, cities, and nations.

There is an important and simple truth that we should all follow and that is if it is in the Bible, then the church should believe it, and follow it if it is in this dispensation (i.e. New Testament). Unfortunately, the modern church in America teaches that Jesus changed the way in which He does church, and He no longer performs the miracles He once did in the Book of Acts. Unfortunately, most in the modern church have bought into this lie. This ultimately is a failure of faith and results in a powerless church.

When someone got saved in the early church, that person was then water baptized and then the disciples went onto teach them about the Holy Spirit and His power. They would lay hands on them to receive the infilling of the Spirit. Then the new believers would be filled with the Spirit with the evidence of speaking in tongues (Acts 8:14-17, 19:1-6). This was the normal Christian experience of the early church.

The Book of Acts shows that God is personal, He speaks, He leads, and He still performs signs and wonders (i.e. miracles). However, through a lack of faith, the modern church is deceived into believing that God doesn't still move like He did in the early church. The result is we have a church that treats the book of Acts as a history book rather than a blueprint for what the church is supposed to look like. So, the church of today instead of following the book of Acts, as a blueprint for the church, ignores it, and instead follows a man-made church led by intellect (i.e., clever ideas and human talent).

When we look at all the evil happening in America today, we must face the fact that the lifeless, miracle-less, and even counterfeit church is the main reason behind why America is swiftly and surely going downward both spiritually and morally.

The only hope for the United States is that God would send a true-blue, red-hot, devil-chasing, Jesus' loving, book of Acts revival again. Without it, I believe there is no hope for America. The church must come back to the Bible, back to the Cross of Christ, back to the Book of Acts and believe that Jesus is the same today as He was in the early church. It is only then that the church will look like the church that Jesus died for.

CHAPTER 8

WOLVES IN SHEEP'S CLOTHING

God was going to deal with the faithless civil leaders (i.e., kings) and the faithless prophets. God, who is the Great Shepherd of the people, will judge the under shepherds (i.e., pastors, ministers) because they had not fed the sheep but instead, they have scattered them. The Bible tells us that God holds leaders to a higher judgment than the common man.

Woe unto the Pastors who destroy and scatter the sheep of My pasture! Says the LORD (Jeremiah 23:1).

God promises one day to restore and regather Israel and the sheep will then be properly fed. He will set up Shepherds over them during the Kingdom Age, when Christ comes again. Many in the modern church, particularly the charismatic church, teach Christians they are to take dominion over the earth during this dispensation of Grace and we are to set up the Kingdom. This is erroneous teaching and will only lead the church in the wrong direction.

The Scripture teaches that one day all of Judah will be saved and God will execute judgment and justice. It will be only when the "*Righteous Branch*" (speaking of Christ Himself) comes back to rule and reign (Jeremiah 23:5) will this occur and not before. The days of the Messiah, which will be during the Millennial reign of 1000 years (after the Great Tribulation) is the time, and only the time, when Israel will dwell safely in their own land. That is why we are to pray, *"thy Kingdom come, thy will be done."*

The false prophets did not have the mind of the Lord, and therefore, were not given anything from the Lord; however, they said what the people wanted to hear and, therefore, they were paid well! (JSESB, PAGE 1279).

God was about to send a whirlwind of judgment on the false prophets and the people. God called them "wicked" as there is no other description that can be given for those who do not follow the true Word of God (verse 19). God said, *"I have not sent these Prophets, yet they ran: I have not spoken to them, yet they prophesied"* (Jeremiah 23:21).

It is a very serious thing to say "Thus saith the LORD" when God has not said anything to you. God holds the one who acts in this function in high contempt. Why? Because a false prophet is falsely representing the Lord of Glory, the God of Heaven in a deceptive manner and gives the people a different message than what is true. It is a very serious thing when one becomes a leader of deception.

The Apostle Paul said, *"Now the Spirit speaks expressly, that in the latter times some shall depart from the faith, giving heed to seducing spirits, and doctrines of devils; speaking lies in hypocrisy; having their conscience seared with a hot iron "* (I Timothy 4:1-2). These seducing spirits are religious spirits, and to be frank they are demonic spirits working through false teachers to present lies to pull the believer, the church, and the nation away from the truth. The Word of God warns us:

> *"But there were false Prophets also among the people, even as there shall be, who privily shall bring in damnable heresies, even denying the Lord Who bought them, and bring upon themselves swift destruction. And many shall follow their pernicious ways; by reason of whom the way of Truth shall be evil spoken of. And through covetousness shall they with feigned words make merchandise of you: whose judgment now of a long time lingers not, and their damnation slumbers not "* (II Peter 2:1-3).

The false teachers' errors because of his or her spiritual ignorance, most of the time, which comes out of a heart of spiritual greed (Jeremiah 29:23). They exploit the people for the cause of money and, even though the judgment seems to be delayed, it ultimately comes to pass and slumbers not on these who mislead the people.

God is not afar off, for He has seen and heard what they say and do. He has heard their prophesies of lies in His Name and they claim that they had a dream from God when it was not from God at all. God says that they prophesy these lies from their own heart. These dreams of the false prophets pull the people away from the truth and cause the people's eyes to be put on wrong things.

God compares the false prophet as one who has a *"dream as chaff and the True Prophet who has God's Word as the wheat."* God said, *"Is not my Word like as a fire? And like a hammer that breaks the rock in pieces?"* (Jeremiah 23:28-29). This tells us that preachers who leave out the wrath of

God to come are false teachers, which is what many preachers in America have done throughout the past 40 years. Such preachers who does this may be popular by man's standards and they may even build "mega" churches, but God considers them as one whose teaching is but chaff.

God says three times in Jeremiah 23:30-32, that He is against these false prophets. They tell these false dreams, and it causes God's people to error. God says He commanded them not, nor did He send them; therefore, it will not profit the people at all to listen to or follow them. Many believers who have been caught up in these churches and have followed these ministries of false teachers and many of them end up shipwrecked in their faith and walk away from church and the Lord. Many of their children who grew up in these churches walk away from God when they go off to college and become an adult. The parents of these wayward children are responsible for bringing their children up in a worthless apostate church that was none other than sinking sand. In other words, they did not build their faith on the Rock, which Jesus Christ and Him Crucified.

The people of Jeremiah's day, just like today, were bent on believing the softer and more pleasant message of the false prophets and not the burden of the Lord spoken by Jeremiah. God would reject these prophets as the scripture says: *"Therefore, behold, I, even I, will utterly forget you, and I will forsake you, and the city that I gave you and your fathers, and cast you out of My Presence. And I will bring an everlasting reproach upon you, and a perpetual shame, which shall not be forgotten"* (Jeremiah 23:39).

This *"everlasting reproach"* is resting on Israel until the coming of the Messiah and is there due to their rejection of Jesus as their Messiah. They have suffered this *"everlasting reproach"* for some 2,500 years. (JSESB. Page 1281).

SIMPLE WAYS TO DISCERN TRUTH

There are three simple ways to discern truth from error. Understanding how to discern properly may mean the difference between a life of heartache, pain, confusion or a life of blessing and peace. It may also mean the difference between heaven and hell. So, there can be no more important subject than how to discern truth from error. The 3 main ways of Godly discernment is:

You must understand and know what the true Gospel message is, and you must test every teaching you hear against it. In other words, you must know the truth first (I John 4:1-6).

Is the teaching you are hearing focused on Christ and Him Crucified or on self? All false teaching changes the object of faith from Christ and the Cross to something else, usually "self."

Look at the fruits of the one who is teaching you God's Word. If his or her lifestyle does not display the fruits of the Spirit, turn away. No one can live a perfect sinless life; however, you should see in that pastor, Bible teacher, minister, etc., consecration and holiness, not worldliness and carnality.

THE TRUE GOSPEL

The word "Gospel" means "good news." The Gospel is good news because it tells the sinner how to be saved and how to be delivered from sin's controlling power. The Gospel is plain and simple, it is the death, burial, and resurrection of Jesus Christ. This is good news to a world who is lost and dying.

Notice the words of the Apostle Paul, as he wrote them to the early church in Corinth. He said,

"Moreover, Brethren, I declare unto you the Gospel which I preached unto you, which also you have received, and wherein you stand; By which also you are saved, if ye keep in memory what I preached unto you, unless you have believed in vain. For I delivered unto you first of all that which I also received, how that Christ died for our sins according to the Scriptures, and that He was buried, and that He rose again the third day according to the scriptures" (I Cor. 15:4).

As you can see, the Gospel message is simple. Jesus died, Jesus was buried, and Jesus rose again. This is the Gospel, the good news, and it is the power of God that when believed will saved the sinner and set the captive free. We must not tamper with that message in any way because if we do, it then loses its power. The simplicity of the Gospel has profoundly confounded the scholars for hundreds of years. They wonder how a dead man hanging on a tree can set the captives free. But what they miss is that He is no ordinary man hanging on that Cross, that was Jesus, the Prince of Life, the Creator of the Universe, God in the flesh, and through His death comes life everlasting, and only through what He did on the Cross.

THE CHURCH OF APOSTASY

The Bible says,

> *"Now the Spirit speaks expressly, that in the latter times some shall depart from the Faith, giving heed to seducing spirits, and doctrines of devils. Speaking lies in hypocrisy; having their conscience seared with a hot iron; forbidding marriage, and commending to abstain from meats, which God has created to be received with thanksgiving of them which believe and know the Truth"* (I Tim. 4:1-3).

The Holy Spirit was warning us that as we get closer to the end the Church will experience a great apostasy. The word "apostasy" means "a departure from the true faith." The Holy Spirit tells us that seducing spirts will come into the church and attempt to move people away from the truth of the Cross of Christ, the only place where Grace can be found.

Religion is a rule-based philosophy made up by man who attempts to add or take away from the Word of God. In other words, Religion puts the people under Law (i.e., rules). For example, Catholicism is a works-based salvation, and it has deceived literally millions and millions of people. If you want to be a priest in the Catholic church, you are forbidden to marry even though I Timothy 4:3 clearly commands against such a Law in the Church. Being under an unscriptural law has caused many priests (and nuns) to fall into sexual immorality and perversion that has decimated and shamed the Roman Catholic Church.

However, these seducing spirts are not limited to the Catholic church but can be seen in every other religion of the world. They teach the erroneous idea that one is saved by works, and one is sanctified (made holy) by their own works (i.e., through the "thou shall nots").

True Christianity is the only teaching in the world that teaches all one must do to be saved and delivered from hell and sin is to "Believe." One must properly understand and believe that they are a sinner and that they can't be saved or delivered through their own works. They must believe that they are only saved through the blood of Jesus, which was shed on the Cross as the ramson for their soul and they can be forgiven, and set free, through repentance and faith in the Gospel of Jesus Christ (Mark 1:15).

Satan attempts to deceives the true Church and tries to pull believers away from the Gospel truth. He attempts to move people into believing that "human" works is necessary to bring Salvation and victory over sin. But the Bible teaches "works" do not proceed proper faith, they follow it. The Bible says, *"Be sober, be vigilant; because your adversary the Devil, as a roaring lion, walks about, seeking whom he may devour"* (I Peter 5:8).

Today, Satan has come into the modern church and successfully moved many churches and people away from the simple Gospel message, making it about something else other than the Cross of Christ. Many churches today have chosen one fad after another to try to hype up the Gospel to build bigger churches. The modern church has become about church growth, speaking numerically. The modern pastor wants to grow his numbers larger so he does anything he can to make the people feel comfortable. The ministry of Jesus Christ was the direct opposite.

What I have seen happen in the church over the past 40 years of being a Christian, is shocking. I have watched and experienced first-hand the fads that come into the church to try to move believers away from the simplicity that is in Christ. I have personally witnessed the laughing revival where supposedly Christians start to experience some uncontrolled spirit of laughter where they cannot stop laughing right in the middle of the service, even falling to the ground while the minister is preaching. This was started by a man they called the "laughing evangelist Rodney Howard-Browne. In his services one would see "manifestations" of people acting drunk where they stagger around and fall over. They even called it "Joel's bar." This was all called the "anointing" of the Holy Spirit.

Then there was the fire wall where Christian's line up forming two rows with their arms stretched up. Then people walk or run through the line up. Supposedly the believer will receive and experience God's glory. It has been labeled as the "glory wall" or the "glory tunnel." I have seen ministers blowing on the congregation and the people literally (sometimes hundreds even thousands of people at one time) fall to the ground and act like they are in some subconscious state for minutes or sometimes even hours. I have even witnessed what has been labeled as "Grave Sucking" where believers go to a cemetery and find the gravesite of a great man or women of God who is buried there, some of which have been dead for hundreds of years. They lay on their graves prostrate wanting and believing they are going to receive their anointing.

I have been in services where people claim they have found "angel feathers." These so-called angel feathers have been found in the church during a service or after a service where it is said they belong to angels who supposedly are visiting their church. My question is where in the Bible do we see that angels have feathers and that the feathers are actually falling out? This sound more like fallen angels to me!

There are those in the charismatic churches who have said that they have experienced what is called "Gold Dust" all over their body. This gold like substance is supposed to be a manifestation where people are accumulating gold particles all over their bodies, in their hair, on their clothing, or on their hands. I was in a service where a preacher had me open up my hands and he told me I had gold dust in my hands, which really was only sweat particles which is normal when one's hand is a little sweaty.

How sad all this is, but wait it only gets worse. There was a movement in the Church sometime back where people in services would start to make animal sounds or even carrying out animal gyrations. They would claim that the spirit was making them meow like a cat or bark like a dog or walk like a chicken or go charging across the room like a buffalo. That was called the "Buffalo anointing." How ridiculous and very sad is all this absurdity. If I had not seen these things with my own eyes and heard it with my own ears, I don't think I would have believed it.

These are not some small, isolated churches oh no, this has happened in major Pentecostal and Charismatic churches across America. It is a reproach, it is offensive, and I believe much of it is demon inspired. It is the devil who comes to highjack the true moving and operation of the Spirit. His main purpose is to try to move the church away from the message of Jesus Christ and the Cross.

Many of these same churches are a part of the Apostolic Faith Movement that was brought in or revived by C Peter Wagner who teach and believe that the Kingdom Age is now. They don't preach the soon coming of the Rapture of the Church, in fact they even mock it. This group of churches are today dominating the Pentecostal movement and it is a sham, and it is false doctrine. This is a bad tree that continues to produce bad fruit, in other words this is not the Jesus of the Bible, it is not the Holy Spirit, and it is not the Gospel (II Corinthians 11:3-4).

My friend, the real Holy Spirit will not make the church look like freaks and make you do something that you have no control over. God's Holy Spirit never controls people or forces them (unless He is judging one), but He guides and directs them. He works within the surrendered will of the person.

ON THE OTHER SIDE OF THE TRACKS

The other extreme in Christendom today which really picked up momentum in the seeker sensitive moment is where Pastors are developing services to accommodate the people. They build their churches around shorter church services to please the congregation. They want to get the crowds in and out, sort like a fast-food restaurant. Coffee bars and bagel shops are put in the church where people sometimes are even allowed to have breakfast while they listen and watch the service in the sanctuary or outside the sanctuary on a big screen.

Today churches are turning their sanctuaries into looking like night clubs with dim lights, using flashing lights and stage smoke, and hanging up black curtains to give it a theater look. They give no altar calls because they do not want the people to feel uncomfortable.

Churches today take down their crosses and no longer sing songs about the blood of Jesus. The pastors preach from watered-down translations of the Bible, sometimes even using paraphrased versions instead of translations (i.e., The Message Bible). The pastor preaches in series about people's felt needs. Everything is planned and scripted. Very little mention of sin and repentance. The messages focus on self rather than on Christ and the Cross. It is about your destiny, your purpose, your prosperity, and your blessings. These types of churches are a dime a dozen in these end times.

Many pastors in these churches want to look hip preaching in jeans and casual wear on a Sunday morning. This is the way they come to church, to make others feel comfortable. Preachers sit at a table with their coffee mug and a nice throw rug under their feet. This is all to present that laid back atmosphere for the people. Their churches only meet once a week with no weekly prayer meeting. These kinds of churches are the norm today in America and have become even more popular than the weird Pentecostal and Charismatic churches. Why? Because lower standard preaching, making people comfortable, and ear tickling messages, have proven to grow bigger churches, and bigger churches means more money. So, this has now become the church model of choice for not only non-charismatic churches, but many Pentecostal and Charismatic churches as well.

I once asked a prominent and influential Pentecostal pastor who was beginning to follow the model of the Purpose Driven Church, started by Rick Warren, who pastored a mega church in California called Saddleback, why he was following his model? I told him Rick Warren is not a Pentecostal Pastor, and he does not preach or believe in the mighty baptism with the Holy Spirit, nor does he teach the gifts of the Spirit are for today. The pastor's answer troubled me greatly. He said, "Have you not seen that Rick Warren pastors one of the biggest churches in America?" To which I replied, "big doesn't mean healthy, the Roman Catholic churches teaches us that." Then I said to the Pastor: "A 400-pound man might be big, but he certainly is not healthy." The pastor had no response to my statements.

What we have seen in the churches of America and Canada over the past 40 to 50 years is an obsession for church growth strategies. It appears the modern preachers are more about building mega churches than they are about seeing the power of the Holy Spirit fall on the people of their church.

When one studies the church in the book of Acts you see that the great power of the Holy Spirit being experienced as the Gospel was preached under the anointing of the Holy Spirit. The truth is that the message of the Cross is the only message that draws the true Holy Spirit. The Apostle Paul penned these words:

> *"For the preaching of the Cross is to them who perish foolishness; but unto us who are Saved it is the Power of God"*
> (I Corinthians 1:18).

THE BOOK OF ACTS CHURCH

What one learns when studying the early church in the Book of Acts was that the early church was on fire for God. This is the blueprint model which every church should follow. The Book of Acts church was not a "Purpose Driven Church" or a "Prosperity Church" nor was it a fanatical or weird church. It was a Spirit-led and Spirit-empowered church that preached the Cross and the Resurrection of the Lord Jesus Christ. The gospel message was the central message preached- Jesus Christ crucified and has risen from the dead. They preached Jesus to the people, who He was, and what He did on Calvary to save their soul (Acts 2:22-24, 8:4-5, 10:36-43). They preached the baptism with the Holy Spirit, and they laid hands on the new believers to receive it (Acts 2:14-17, 4:33, 10:44-46, 19:1-6). They preached the soon coming of the Lord Jesus Christ, followed by the judgment of God on the world which is the Great Tribulation (Acts 2:19-20).

They preached repentance and faith to be saved (Acts 2:38, 3:19, 20:21). They offered water baptized to new believers (Acts 2:38, 9:18, 19:5). They were a soul-winning church (Acts 2:21,41,47, 4:32, 5:14). They were a church that continuously studied the Apostles Doctrine (Acts 2:42). They were a church that had a close fellowship together (Acts 2:42, 46). They held church services every day; not just once a week (Acts 2:46). They were a praying church. They had daily prayer meetings and even all-night prayer meetings when there were special needs (2:42, 3:1, 12:5). They were a very generous church, selling houses and lands and giving the money to the church so that every person's needs were taken care of (Acts 2:45, 4:32, 34-35). They experienced the power of God seen in the healing of the sick and even the raising of the dead (Acts 3:1-11, 9:36-42, 14:6-10, 28:9). They were seeing the Lord do great miracles (Acts 4:31, 12:7-11, 16:25-34, 19:11, 28:3-9).

People were being delivered from demonic possession (Acts 8:7, 16:16-18). God's judgment was falling on the people who were deceiving and opposing the church (Acts 5:1-10, 13:8-12). God was speaking to the leaders of the church through dreams and visions (Acts 9:1-7, 10:1-8, 16:9-10). The gifts of the Spirit, tongues, prophesy, etc. were all in operation (Acts 2:1-4, 10:44-46, 19:1-6). They were experiencing many signs and wonders (Acts 2:43) and the fear of God was on the church (Acts 2:43, 5:11). They saw great unity in the church, and they all believed the same thing (Acts 2:44, 4:32). The joy of the Lord was in the church (Acts 2:46-47).

When you take a closer examination of the above qualities of the early church you can see how far the modern church has fallen. Jesus said of the last church right before the Rapture would be "lukewarm." He said He was going to spit them out of His mouth (Revelation 3:16).

The Great Deception is all over the church today, but thank God there is still a remnant who will not bow their knees to the gods of this world, and who remain faithful to the preaching and teaching of the Gospel message.

The message of the Gospel is simple to understand, but the results of the Gospel when one believes it are profound and life changing.

The Apostle Paul wrote,

"And my speech and my preaching was not with enticing words of man's wisdom, but in demonstration of the Spirit and of power; That your faith should not stand in the wisdom of men, but in the Power of God" (I Corinthains 2:4-5).

We need to get back to preaching of the Cross and believing for a genuine move of the Holy Spirit that will revive the Bride of Christ and get us ALL READY for the coming of the Bridegroom. His return is imminent!

CHAPTER 9

FIGHTING THE WRONG BATTLE

The great deception in the time of Christ belongs to the Nation of Israel. During Jesus' ministry the religious leaders became envious of the popularity of Jesus, and they were worried that the Romans were feeling threatened by the huge crowds that were gathering to hear and see the miracles of Jesus. The Bible says: *"Then gathered the Chief Priests and the Pharisees a Council, and said, What do we? For this Man (speaking of Jesus) does many miracles. If we let Him thus alone, all men will believe on Him: and the Romans shall come and take away both our place and nation"* (John 11:47-48).

Sinful man is always more concerned about his own personal freedoms than the spiritual freedoms of others. The Jewish leaders in the time of Christ were more concentrated on the political climate of Israel then they were the spiritual condition of the souls of the people. This deceptive mindset led to the greatest deception that Israel ever fell for.

The Jewish High Priest of that day was a man named Caiaphas and one day he received a prophecy regarding Jesus. The Bible says he *"prophesied that Jesus should die for that nation; and not for that Nation only, but that also He should gather together in one, the Children of God who were scattered abroad"* (John 11:51-52).

Now this prophecy no doubt from God, but Caiaphas and the Jewish leaders due to their heart not being right with God misinterpreted it. They interpreted the prophecy to mean that if they turned Jesus over to the Romans to be crucified it would appease the Romans, and instead of the entire nation being destroyed, only one would have to die, namely Jesus, thus the Nation would be saved. But the prophecy given by God wasn't speaking politically, it was speaking spiritually. The prophecy was that Jesus was to die for the sins not only of the Nation of Israel but for the sins of the whole world.

The Bible says that from that day (the day Caiaphas gave the prophecy) the religious leaders took council on how to put Jesus to death. (John 11:53). Wow, what was meant to be a prophecy of the Revelation of the Cross, the true purpose of why Jesus came into the world, became a justification for the Jewish Sanhedrin to turn the King of Kings and Lord of Lords over to the Romans to be murdered by the cruelest of deaths, crucifixion. That my friend could be classified as the greatest deception of all time and Israel, and the Jewish people have paid a great price the past 2,000 years for this great deception.

We see today in America so many Christians who are more concerned about the political world, then they are of the spiritual condition of the church and our nation. Most are more afraid about losing their freedoms than they are concerned for the souls of men and women losing their souls for all eternity.

Most people in our churches today are fighting the wrong battle, they see the anti-God liberal agenda pouring into our Nation and they are watching how globalism is moving at a fast pace to set up a one world government and they want to protest and fight against this. Why? Because they don't want to lose their freedoms in this life. They are more afraid losing their freedoms like having their guns taken away, or their gas prices going up, then they are about lost souls in this nation going to hell.

You see nothing has really changed in 2,000 years. Israel was deceived in the days of Jesus and most American Christians are deceived today. And all because we don't study and discern the Word of God properly concerning end time prophecy.

Most believed the words of former President Trump who said on January 6, 2021, "if we don't fight like hell, we are going to lose this Nation." My friend, this is the same spirit that was in Israel during Jesus' day. However, fighting for freedom whether physically or politically was not the way Jesus treated the problems of His day and the last time I checked Jesus is the role model of Christianity, such as the Name "Christian" means "Christ-Like."

KINGDOM NOW, OR KINGDOM LATER?

When Jesus stood before Pontius Pilate, the Roman Governor said to Jesus, *"Am I a Jew? Your own nation and the Chief Priest have delivered you unto me: what have you done? Jesus answered, My Kingdom is not of this world: if My Kingdom were of this world, then would My servants fight, that I should not be delivered to the Jews: but now is My Kingdom not from hence"* (John 18:35-36).

Jesus was clearly saying that the Kingdom of God had not yet come, so His disciples should not fight for political dominance in this world. Remember in the Garden of Gethsemane when Peter drew the sword and cut off the ear of the High Priest's servant named Malchus. Jesus told Peter:

> *Put up your sword into the sheath: the cup which My Father has given Me, shall I not drink it? (John 18:12). Then Jesus said to Peter, "Thinkest thou that I cannot now pray to My Father, and He shall presently give Me more than twelve legions of Angels"* (Matthew 26:53).

One legion is 6,000 men, so Jesus was saying that He could have asked for 72,000 angels to come and defeat the Roman soldiers who came to arrest Him that night. But He didn't, and why? Because it was not time yet for His literal Kingdom to come.

When Jesus taught us to pray, He said for us to pray this way: *"Your Kingdom come, Your will be done in earth, as it is in Heaven"* (Matthew 6:10). This is not a prayer of bringing His Kingdom now; but it was a prayer for His Second Coming when He will set up His Millennial Kingdom. The modern church has this confused. We are not called to personally set up the Kingdom of God now, Jesus will do that at His Second Coming. One day, Jesus will come with ten thousands of His Saints to execute Judgment on the Earth (Jude 14). But that time is not yet here; not now and not until after the Rapture of the Church and the seven years of Daniel 70th Week has been completed.

This does not mean that right now we do not pray for our Nation and ask God to hold back the forces of evil that are trying to take this Nation down the wrong path. It does not mean we don't participate in our elections or pray that God will raise Godly leaders in our Nation to lead us politically. But the only way to change a nation ultimately is not through political means, if it were, Jesus would have taught and demonstrated this.

THE WAY TO CHANGE A NATION

The way to change a nation is the way that Jesus did it through the preaching of the Gospel, so that lost souls can be saved. When you reach a soul, you begin to change a culture one person at a time. The Bible says that the heart of a man is desperately wicked, and it cannot be changed politically by debate or protest. We saw this in the last election. When Former President Trump called out the sin and the sinner on the liberal left. They didn't change, they got worse. People came out in droves to vote for Joe Biden, but many were not voting for Joe Biden, they were voting against Donald Trump. Why? Because they didn't like the man who was calling out the sins of the democratic far left party. In other words, he poked the bear, and the bear woke up.

Some still do not think Joe Biden won the election, but say it was stolen. Well rather than get into that argument, let me just say one thing that will end that debate right from the get-go. The Bible says it is God *"who removes Kings, and set up Kings"* (Daniel 2:21). So, if we believe the Word of God, we must admit it is God Who removed Donald Trump and set up Joe Biden to be the next President of the United States. I know that is a hard pill for many on the right to swallow but remember God's Will is not always a good thing for man. The Will of God is sometimes the judgment of God and I believe this is what is happening right now in our country. In other words, we are getting what we deserve.

THE CAIAPHAS PROPHECY

Caiaphas and the Jewish leaders of Israel were concerned that the thousands of enthusiastic, messianic zealots who were following Jesus were going to worry the Roman Government and they would be threatened by the popularity of Jesus. Caiaphas and his religious leaders feared that Rome would think the people might mount up an insurrection against Rome, so they would send their legions of armies in to crush the rebellion and remove the existing religious authorities from power. In other words, the Jewish leaders (and the people) feared their freedoms, (the little they had) would be taken away. In essence, they feared man instead of fearing God.

The misunderstanding of the prophecy of Caiaphas invoked the ideal that it was better for one person to die for the Nation than for all to die. The prophecy of the High Priest was clear (so they thought); kill Jesus now before He gets us all killed. The irony was that Caiaphas unwittingly uttered the Gospel message in his prophecy, but yet he and the people didn't have the spiritual discernment to understand the true meaning and one must ask the question why? Because their heart was not right, and because they didn't understand what the prophets had long prophesied of the coming of the Messiah. Jesus was not just going to die for only the Jews, but He was going to die for the entire world.

So, the Jewish High Priest and the other religious leaders convinced the people to follow a prophesy that was falsely interpreted. They in fact led the

Jewish people down a road that has caused the Jewish people and the nation of Israel more heartache and pain for the past 2,000 years than any other people and nation has ever suffered in the history of the world.

The key lesson to learn here is that the Jewish people were more concerned about an evil government taking away their freedoms than they were about their own sins and need to repent and get right before a trice Holy God. The people in essence missed the entire meaning of why Jesus came because their eyes were more on this world, then the Kingdom to come. Jesus came to deal with sin and die on a cruel Cross to save humanity from the eternal penalty of their sins. But a prideful religious spirit and a worldly mindset got it wrong, as it will always get it wrong, and the consequences have been devastating for the Nation of Israel ever since.

Almost 40 years to the day after they turned Christ over to be crucified their worst fears became reality. The Roman legions invaded Jerusalem, tore down the Temple, burned it, killing many of the Jews and taking many into captivity. So, what they feared the most regarding having their freedoms taken away, actually came to pass; all because they feared man rather than fearing God. If they had put the Kingdom of God first their Nation and their own personal prosperity and freedoms would not have been destroyed.

The Words of Jesus found in Matthew 6:33 were not followed: *"But seek first the Kingdom of God, and His Righteousness; and all these things shall be added unto you."*

Caiaphas was in fact a false prophet because he falsely interpreted his own prophecy. The Nation of Israel was destroyed, and the people were either killed, put into slavery, or running for their lives from the Roman army in 70 AD. All of the people were listening to and following a false prophet and a false prophesy. This is so sad, and it could have been so different.

ELECTION 2020

The false prophets in our nation prophesied in the last Election year that Donald Trump would win. They did not say that they thought he would win or that they believed he would win, they said, *"Thus saith the LORD"* Donald Trump would be reelected. They not only spoke that to the church, but they spoke that to the world, and they spoke that directly over the President as they laid hands on him and prayed over him.

Now when you say that you think something is going to happen or you believe something is going to happen and it doesn't, that is just called bad judgment which many of us are guilty of. But when you say that God told you something is going to happen, and it doesn't happen than that is something altogether different. When it doesn't happen as you said God said it would, you are now what the Bible calls a "false prophet."

It is a very serious thing to say, "*Thus saith the Lord.*" The reality is that Donald Trump did not win reelection. Not only did he not win, but the Republican party lost all three branches of government (the Senate, the House and the Presidency) in the 2020 election. In other words, it could not have gone any worse for the false prophets. They were completely wrong in what they prophesied.

Then on January 6, 2021, there was a siege on the U.S. Capitol building following a rally that was in protest to the election results. Five people died as a result, and the world called it an "Insurrection." Many have been indicted and found guilty and gone to prison for their actions on that disturbing and very troublesome day.

The fact that they use the word "Insurrection" is very interesting. Talk about the Bible reliving itself right before our very eyes. I believe God through all of this is trying to reveal to us the deception that is in the Church today. He is exposing the false prophets in our land even as He did in Jeremiah's day.

The truth is the Great Deception of the end times is right before our eyes; however, most Christians can't see it or just don't want to see it. Why? I believe that it is because of three main reasons:

Most Christians don't study their Bibles today.

Christians spend hours and hours on the internet, reading and listening to conspiracy ideas that claim to be "true news." They trust in the words of man more than they trust in the Word of God.

Pride. Many Christians believed in a lie even when evidence stares them right in the face and proves them to be wrong. They still refuse to admit they were wrong due to spiritual pride. God said through the prophet Hosea, "*My people are destroyed for lack of knowledge: because you have rejected knowledge*" (Hosea 4:6). This verse proclaims not only do God's people spiritually die because of not having the true knowledge of God's Word, but even when it is clearly presented to them, they still chose to not believe it. This is what the Bible calls "Willful sin" and it is all due to the pride of man.

THE CHURCH IN THE LAST DAYS

The Bible says,

> *"But chiefly them who walk after the flesh in the lust of uncleanness, and despise Government. Presumptuous are they, self-willed, they are not afraid to speak evil of dignities. Whereas Angels, which are greater in power and might, bring not railing accusation against them before the Lord. But these, as natural brute beasts, made to be taken and destroyed, speak evil of the things that they understand not; and shall utterly perish in their own corruption. And shall receive the reward of unrighteousness, as they who count it pleasure to riot in the day time. Spots they are and blemishes, sporting themselves with their own deceiving while they feast with you. Having eyes full of Adultery, and that cannot cease from sin; beguiling unstable souls: an heart they have exercised with covetous practices; cursed children: Which have forsaken the right way, and are gone astray, following the way of Balaam the son of Bosor, who loved the wages of unrighteousness"* (II Peter 2:10-15).

Notice the characteristics of false teachers revealed in the above verses: They walk after the lust of the flesh and go into sinful impurities. They despise government. Matthew Henry said, "They also pour contempt on those whom God has set in authority over them and requires them to honor."

They are presumptuous in their faith (their faith is not rooted in the True Word of God).

- They are self-willed (led by their own spirit).
- They are not afraid to speak evil of dignities (condemning others).
- They take pleasure in riots (i.e., insurrection).
- They have eyes full of adultery (immoral hearts).
- They cannot stop from sinning (hypocrites)
- They are unstable souls (not of the right mind).
- They have covetous practices (care more about possessions, i.e. money, than winning souls).
- They have forsaken the right way and gone astray (not preaching and understanding the message of the Cross).
- They have gone the way of Balaam (most interested in money than following God).

I think this describes the spirit that is leading many in our Churches and Nation today. The Word of God called these false teachers *"cursed children."*

THE FALSE PROPHECY OF HANANIAH

Israel had a King in Jeremiah's day named Zedekiah and he listened to and followed the false prophecies of Hananiah. This false prophet confronted Jeremiah. Hananiah seemed to be the leader of those who opposed Jeremiah. Most probably, he was a Priest, just as was Jeremiah (JSESB, page 1289).

The word blasphemy in the Greek means "evil speaking, slander, insult, and irreverence. It is the act of insulting God and His name or showing a lack of reverence toward God. It includes slandering His Holy Name or spreading malicious lies that harm God's reputation.

Hananiah went against Jeremiah's word (that was given to him by God) and told King Zedekiah that God broke the yoke of the King of Babylon. And what makes this a blasphemous statement is that Hananiah said, *"Thus speaks the LORD of Hosts, the God of Israel."* Both prophets, Jeremiah and Hananiah, were saying *"Thus saith the LORD of Hosts."* But what they were saying was in direct contradiction to one another, meaning only one of them could be right! So in essence, one was speaking for God and the other was slandering God's reputation. To say *"Thus saith the Lord"* which is to say that God said something when in truth He had not, is a very serious sin indeed. This was the case; in fact, God was saying the direct opposite of what Hananiah, and the false prophets of Israel were saying.

Hananiah prophesied that within two years, Nebuchadnezzar would return to the Temple and give back everything that he previously had stolen from the Temple. Jeremiah said that Nebuchadnezzar was not going to return what he stole, but in fact was going to take the rest of the vessels from the Temple to add to his collection and he was going to invade and destroy the Temple all together and burn the city of Jerusalem. It happened exactly as Jeremiah said it would happen.

LIES OF THE FALSE PROPHETS

Jeremiah says to God, *"Ah, Lord GOD! Behold, the Prophets say unto them, you shall not see the sword, neither shall you have famine; but I will give you assured peace in this place"* (Jeremiah 14:13). You can clearly see the false prophets were saying the exact opposite of what Jeremiah was saying, and Jeremiah was standing alone in his pronouncements of Judgment coming to Israel.

The Lord told Jeremiah that the prophets were prophesying lies to the people in His Name. God said that He had not sent them, and He did not speak to them. God said that they speak *"false vision"* and *"divination,"* and a *"thing of nought"* and it all comes out of their hearts of deceit (Jeremiah 14:14). It is here that you see the root problem of these false prophets, it was that their hearts were not right with God. In other words, they were deceived because they were not in a right relationship with God.

The word "*divination*" in the Hebrew means, witchcraft, to foresee, to foretell, to predict, to prophesy, or to be inspired by a god. It is the attempt to gain insight into a question or situation by way of an occultic, standardized process or ritual. This word describes a cultic practice that is considered a GREAT SIN. False prophets use divination to prophesy in God's name, but God identified them as false and pledged to remove such practices.

God said that the false prophet would promise life, speaking lies and strengthening the hands of the wicked and they would not repent of their wicked ways. God called it vanity and divine divination. It is a very serious thing for a preacher to promise something in the Name of Jesus when God had not said it, and in fact, has said the very opposite (Ezekiel 13:22-23).

AMERICA IS WORSHIPPING OTHER GODS

U.S. Presidents in recent years have shown a lack of spiritual wisdom, discernment, moving our country away from worshipping the One True God, and into worshipping many different gods. One example of this was on May 7, 2020, at the National Day of Prayer. President Trump led an interfaith prayer service at the Rose Garden in Washington D.C where five different religions were represented. The leaders who President Trump invited to pray are as follows:

- A Hindu Champlain
- A Muslim Cleric
- A Jewish Rabbi
- A Catholic Nun
- A False Prophetess

All of this violated the first Commandment that God gave to Moses on Mount Sinai that says, *"You shall have no other gods before Me"* (Exodus 20:3). The shocking part of this prayer gathering was that most of the evangelical world had no problem with it. In their eyes, Donald Trump could do no wrong. I wonder where was the Evangelical Advisory team that President Trump set up? That should have been their last day serving on that committee. (We will deal with this Advisory Board later in the book)

On May 7, 2020, Paula White (President Trump's appointed Pastor) falsely prophesied from the Rose Garden in Washington D.C., regarding the future of President Trump. I want you to see the underlining errors in her words. But first understand that Paula White (like many in the charismatic movement) believes that she can "decree" things that are not and by her words she believes that she can call things forth into being. She believes that we have the same spiritual authority as God Himself. This is a very dangerous belief. She gets this idea from misinterpreting the verse in Scripture that says: *"As it is written, I have made you a father of many nations before Him Whom he believed, even God, who quickens the dead, and calls those things which are not as though they were"* (Romans 4:17). As you look closer at Romans 4:17, it is clearly stating that God, and God alone, has the power to decree as the scriptures clearly says, *"even God, Who quickens the dead, and call those things which are not as they were."*

Sinful man does not possess creative power, only God alone has that attribute. Whenever a preacher or so-called prophet takes on this authority, they then are acting beyond the attributes that God has given us. To call those things that are not as though they are, is rooted in the teaching that says Christians are "little gods." This erroneous belief that God has given Christians unlimited power and dominion with the exact same power that Jesus possessed comes out of the Word of Faith camp. That teaching elevates man and lowers Jesus to man's level, which is always considered to be blasphemy.

The Word of Faith movement teaches that we now have dominion over the earth, and what Adam lost in the Garden is now totally restored through Christ. They believe that God has given the body of Christ dominion to rule the earth in the here and now. However, this is not Biblical and will not be true until King Jesus has returns and He is ruling and reigning in His Millennial Kingdom. A believer can and should confess the Word of God and believe for God's Will to be done, however, we cannot create our own by our words.

I was in a pastors and leaders meeting a short time ago and I heard the Archbishop of the Anglican Church make a statement that Christian can create their own reality. That is clearly Dominion Teaching and is completely false. My question is if he is thinking that is true, how is that working out for you? The world is not getting better, it is getting worse. We cannot save society, but we can pluck people of this sinful world through the preaching of the Gospel of Jesus Christ.

On the National Day of Prayer in the Rose Garden Paula White, Donld Trump self-proclaimed pastor spoke in front of President Trump, Vice President Mike Pence, and the entire world. (This is from the exact transcript of her words- I will comment in those places in her speech where I believe that she falsely prophesies and takes scripture out of context).

Paula White's Transcript:
> "What an honor to be here with you, President and First Lady, Vice President, Second Lady. It's a beautiful day to lift up our Lord and Savior. He is a certain God in uncertain times. And the Bible says, if two or three of us agree as touching anything, it will be done. Job 22:28 says: If you decree a thing and declare a thing, it will be established."

Paula White, interestingly, right away gets into trouble as she quotes Eliphaz who was one of Job's friends who came to him in his suffering and falsely judged Job. He claimed to be speaking for God when he was not speaking for God at all.

Eliphaz said that Job's suffering was due to his sin, which was not the case. He placed the entirety of his theology on riches and poverty, which is what many do in the prosperity gospel movement which is where Paula White comes out of. How ironic it was that Paula White quoted this verse using it in the positive sense rather than the negative which is how it was given to us in the Bible.

Paula White's Transcript:
> "So, God, we come in agreement with your word and with your name — the name of Jesus. Psalm 40, verse 17 says: You are my help and my deliverer. Do not delay, Oh God. I declare no more delays to the deliverance of COVID-19. No more delays to healing and a vaccination. No more delays to restoration of this great Nation, the United States of America."

After she *"declared no more delays"* the Coronavirus got worse in our Nation and not better. Now the vaccination did come out in record speed, but the question that everyone wanted to know was that good or bad? If it was not thoroughly tested the vaccine could cause more problems than it solved. We are seeing now in 2024, that the vaccines have caused many illnesses and even deaths.

Paula White's Transcript:
"For Psalm 71:2 says: *In your righteousness, deliver us and rescue us, incline your ear, and save us. Psalm 107 says: You deliver us out of stress and out of destruction. Your word will not return void, according to Isaiah* chapter 55, verse 11. *So, I declare your word (no she declares her word), I declare divine intervention and supernatural turnaround.*"

Without repentance from our national leaders and the people, there can be no turnaround which Paula White fails to mention. Our Nation will not be restored without a turning back to the God of the Bible. God never promises divine intervention without the condition of confession of sin and turning from sin first (II Chronicles 7:14). Our nation has become much worse since Paula "declared divine intervention and supernatural turnaround."

Paula White's Transcript:
"According to Psalm 118:25: *Save our Nation, oh Lord, and send prosperity now.*"

Here you can see what Paula White's theology is centered on. It is financial blessings rather than our Nation being spiritually healed through the blood of Jesus. This is exactly as it was in Jeremiah's day, the false prophets wanted financial prosperity rather than being right with God spiritually and walking in obedience to His Word. "Send prosperity now" is the mindset of most of America's preachers. How sad that most can't discern this.

Paula White's Transcript:
"For Deuteronomy chapter 28:8 says: *Command your blessing upon this land. You said in Deuteronomy 8:9 to bring us into good land without any lack.*"

If you turn to Deuteronomy 28, you will see that God will only command the blessing on the land if the people in the land walk in obedience to His Word. Paula White failed to mention that!

Paula White's Transcript:
"For your word declares in Psalm 33:2: *Blessed is the nation whose God is Lord.*"

Now this is interesting that she quotes this verse when she is involved with a prayer meeting on the White House lawn, with leaders from the Hindu god, the Islamic religion, Roman Catholicism, and Judaism all praying to their own separate gods. All of which are all false gods, except for Judaism. But the majority of Jews deny Jesus as the Messiah, so they too are spiritually separated from the One True God. How hypocritical and spiritually blind for Paula White to think that God would bless this Nation, with all that is going on right before her eyes on the White House lawn, on the National Day of Prayer.

Paula White's Transcript:

> "So, I declare to you right now to be Lord over this Nation, over the United States of America, and we receive your blessing over any plague, over any economic distress."

If God were truly the Lord over our Nation Miss White, do you think we would have had a law on our books for over 50 years that has permitted the killing of over 60 million babies in their mother's womb? Or, how about a law that promotes the sin of homosexuality and gives marital blessings for that sin. God calls all this an abomination in His Eyes. It's true God is sovereign over the whole earth, but He is not Lord over the United States right now, and to declare that, is a lie. Just because the President's Pastors says it, doesn't make it so. Paula White says we receive your blessing over any plague, over any economic distress, but again she fails to give God's condition for that blessing, which is, REPENTANCE!

Paula White's Transcript:

> "You will stay the hand of the enemy, (here we have Paula White commanding God on what He is to do) according to Second Samuel chapter 21, verse 16: When 70,000 men died by a plague, David cried out as he covered himself in prayer. And the Lord answered and said, "It is enough."

President Trump's Pastor misquotes the reference of this verse, as it is found in II Samuel 24:15-16 which reads:

> *"So the LORD sent a pestilence upon Israel from the morning event to the time appointed and there died of the people of Dan even to Beersheba seventy thousand men. And when the Angel stretched out his hand upon Jerusalem to destroy it, the LORD repented Him of the evil, and said to the Angel that destroyed the people, It is enough: stay now your hand. And the Angel of the LORD was by the threshing place of Araunah the Jebusite. And David spoke unto the LORD when he saw the Angel who smote the people, and said, Lo, I*

have sinned, and I have done wickedly: but these sheep, what have they done? Let Your Hand, I pray you be against me, and against my father's house. And Gad came that day to David, and said unto him, Go up, rear an altar unto the LORD in the threshing floor of Araunah the Jebusite." Then Verse 25 says: "And David built there an Altar unto the LORD, and offered Burnt Offerings and Peace Offerings. So the LORD was intreated for the land, and the plague was stayed from Israel."

The altar in the above verse that David built is symbolic of the Cross and this alone is what God will recognize as the only means through which He forgives and restores a person or a nation. Throughout her entire speech, Paula White fails to mention the Cross once, where Jesus died. She fails to mention that it is only through Jesus' shed blood that we can be forgiven and spiritually restored individually and as a nation. In other words, we must repent of following other gods and come back to Jesus Christ and what He did on the Cross to save us.

Paula White's Transcript:

"Stay now thine hand. Lord, let that be the cry today, and let that be your answer. Lord, enough Coronavirus, enough to death, enough to fear, enough to poverty. Stay thine your hand."

What Mrs. White should have said was, "enough rebellion, enough sin America, enough wickedness, enough abortion, enough same sex marriages, enough Gay Parades, and enough abominations, repent or the judgment will be even greater in the future." That is what Jeremiah, a true prophet, would have said.

Paula White's Transcript:

"We pray over President Trump and First Lady, Vice President and Second Lady, and this administration. I declare Psalm 89, verse 21: Let your hand establish President Trump, and let your arm strengthen him. I declare Psalm 98:1 that your right hand and your holy arm will give Him victory. We declare victory in the name of Jesus. Isaiah 58:11 says: Guide him continually. And you said in Psalm 78:72 that you would guide him by the skillfulness of your hand." The later verse is Psalms 78:73, which reads: *"So he fed them according to the integrity of his heart; and guided them by the skillfulness of his hands."*

Pastor White quoted only half of the verse and failed to quote that God was really speaking about King David who He would guide by the skillfulness of his hand according to the integrity of David's heart. This means that the Lord fed Israel through David because David had "integrity of heart." By now, I think you can see what false prophets do. They quote or misquote verses from the Bible, taking them out of context, and mention them only as blessings of God without stating the conditions by which those blessing come. They misrepresent verses and give false meanings without understanding the entire counsel of God.

The devil did this with Jesus in the wilderness when he tried to tempt the Lord. The devil quoted Psalms 91:11-12 by saying, *"If you be the Son of God, cast Yourself down: for it is written, He shall give His angels charge concerning You: and in their hands they shall bear you up, lest at any time you dash your foot against a stone."* A closer look at Psalms 91:11-12 reveals that the devil took out the words *"in all your ways,"* and added the words "at any time."

This is how the devil deceives by mixing truth with error. A deceptive plan is never in absence of truth, but instead is a mixture of truth and error. This is exactly how the process of a good counterfeit is accomplished. Satan is the master of counterfeit and Jesus replied to him, *"It is written again, you shall not tempt the Lord your God"* (Matthew 4:6-7).

When listening to a false teacher or prophet, you must know your Bible to discern where the errors of their teachings are or where the false prophesy is. The main problem in the modern church is that most Christians do not study their Bibles anymore and cannot discern if what they are hearing is from God or not.

Paula White's Transcript:
> "And in conclusion, I declare Isaiah chapter 43, verse 19: I ask the Lord to do a new thing in our Nation by giving waters in the wilderness and streams in the desert. Malachi 4:2 says, "Jesus, arise over the nation with healing in your wings."

The above verses that Pastor Paula White quotes, is God speaking about what He will do in the Kingdom Age, during the one-thousand-year Millennial reign of Christ. This happens when Christ rules supreme from Jerusalem and from Israel, when all accept Him as Lord and Savior. In fact, Malachi 4:2 is proceeded by: "*For, Behold, the day comes, that shall burn as an oven; and all the proud, yes, and all who do wickedly, shall be stubble: and the day that comes shall burn them up, says the LORD of Hosts, that it shall leave them neither root nor branch*" (Malachi 4:1).

Can you stomach one more thing from Paula White? If it wasn't bad enough, she left the worst for last. Listen to her exact words:

Paula White's Transcript:

"Mr. President, one last word: Like David, who had victory, after victory, after victory, after victory, would face his biggest battle — it was called Ziklag. And they would take his wives and his children, and the city would be burned down. And he cried and he wept, and he began to pray out to God. And God gave him a word. And through fasting and praying, I believe this is the word for you and for this Nation: The Lord spoke to him and said: Pursue and go after them, and you shall, without fail, recover all. Sir, the word of the Lord, I believe, for this Nation and for this Administration is: You will recover all."

Notice how this "word' from Donald Trump's Pastor worked out. He did not recover all, but six months later, lost the presidency to Joe Biden. However, President Trump still believes it was stolen from him. So, the prophetic Word that his Pastor, Paula White, gave him, did not come to pass. I don't know if Paula White knew what she was talking about when she said, "Pursue and go after them," but that is exactly what President Trump did. Maybe his obsession that the election was stolen is due to this false prophetic word given by his pastor (and by many others)?

But the truth is, not only did President Trump lose the presidency, but he was impeached a second time, and the end of his presidency was not the way he thought it would end; especially if he truly believed his Pastor's words, "you will recover all."

Will this word come to pass in 2024? That remains to be seen, but in the context of what Paula White prophesied, it was completely wrong and clearly not from the Lord. Again, all her words promised blessings without repentance. What does God do in situations like this when false words are given to national leaders in His Name? Let's look at what He did in Jeremiah's day.

> *"Therefore thus says the LORD concerning the Prophets who prophesy in MY Name, and I sent them not, yet they say, Sword and famine shall not be in this land; By sword and famine those prophets be consumed. And the people to whom they prophesy shall be cast out in the streets of Jerusalem because of the famine and the sword; and they shall have none to bury them, their wives, nor their sons, nor their daughters: for I will pour their wickedness upon them"* (Jeremiah 14:15-16).

The pronouncement by the Lord in this verse is chilling! *"Those prophets"* then and the false prophets now will be consumed by the false message they proclaim. Not only will the false preacher be consumed, but those who listen to him will be consumed as well. This is the tragedy and horror of this Truth (notes taken from the Jimmy Swaggart Expositors Study Bible, page 1261).

The Lord went onto say,

> *"Therefore, you shall say this Word unto them; Let my eyes run down with tears night and day, and let them not cease: for the virgin daughter of My People is broken with a great breach, with a very grievous blow"* (Jeremiah 14:17).

Jeremiah's words jump forward to when the Nation will be judged. The false prophets in his day were shown that they were false, and they were liars who deceived the nation. God's Judgment was cast down on the nation and the slain were killed with the sword and the people of the land were "sick with famine."

God will do the same even in our day when He judges this Nation severely, and those who prophesied peace and safety are exposed. Judah would be utterly rejected and smitten by God. They looked for peace that was promised by their false prophets, but they could not find it. They only found trouble, sickness, and death.

The true prophet, Christ Himself, faithfully told men of their sins and the wrath to come; but He did so with sobs and tears. Every preacher controlled by the Holy Spirit in like manner warns men with tears (Acts 20:31), either secret or public. (Notes taken from the Jimmy Swaggart Expositors Study Bible, page 1261).

Jeremiah, the true prophet, says these words:

> *"We acknowledge, O LORD, our wickedness, and the iniquity of our fathers: for we have sinned against You"* (Jeremiah 14:20). *"Do not abhor us, for Your Name's sake, do not disgrace the Throne of Your Glory: remember, break not Your Covenant with us. Are there any among the vanities of the Gentiles who can cause rain? Or can the heavens give showers? Are not You He, O LORD our God? Therefore, we will wait upon You: for You have made all these things"* (Jeremiah 14:21-22).

CONCLUSION

On May 7, 2020, Paula White declared the White House to be Holy Ground and compared President Trump to the prophet Jeremiah. She said, *"Now we lift up our president, you declared in Jeremiah chapter 1:5 that before he was ever formed in his mother's womb, that you had set him apart and you have ordained him."*

After Donald Trump lost the Election on November 6th, Paula White held a prayer service the following day at her church she pastors, declaring that angels were *"dispatched"* to help the 45th President remain in the White House. She said, "I hear a sound of victory. The Lord says it is done. For I hear victory, victory, victory!" White proclaimed, *"Angels are being dispatched right now."*

In the days that followed the election, a political controversy broke out in our Nation that the election was stolen from Donald Trump and illegally given to Joe Biden. Then, on January 6, 2021, eight months from when Paula White decreed Donald Trump would receive everything back that he lost, President Trump held a rally in Washington D.C. where tens of thousands came to protest the election. Maybe it was his pastor's prophecy spoken on the National Day of Prayer that was fueling his hopes of overturning the election. I mean in Trump's mind he could have been thinking "God said I would win and recover all." He may have just been following the words of the prophesy his Pastor Paula White was giving him. This could be why he believe the election was stolen, because he couldn't have lost fairly because God said he would win. In fact Pastor Paula White told him on the National Day of Prayer in front of the whole world:

> "Pursue and go after them, and you shall, without fail, recover all. Sir, the word of the Lord, I believe, for this Nation and for this administration is: You will recover all."

Following the rally on January 6th, a riot broke out at the Capitol Building where hundreds of people poured onto the Capitol steps. Some broke down doors and windows and committed a siege on the Capitol. This, stopping a congressional meeting in process and causing Vice President Pence and Congress members to go into hiding from the violent intruders. Five people died because of that day, many injured and many arrested in the days that followed as our democracy was interrupted. President Trump was impeached by the House of Representatives several days later, only to be acquitted soon after. What a fire storm it was, and a terrible way for President Trump to end his presidency. It was a far cry from "Victory" as President's Trump's pastor Paula White had declared, and a far cry from all the false prophecies from the many false prophets who declared, *"Thus saith the Lord"* Donald Trump would win the election over Joe Biden. What a political and spiritual mess! Maybe Paula White should be called to testify before a Senate hearing?

HANANIAH'S IN THE LAND

In Jeremiah's day Hananiah, the false prophet, told the Kings what they wanted to hear. But it wasn't the truth, it was a lie. This was exactly what Paula White did while speaking and praying on the White House lawn in front of former President Donald Trump. Hananiah the false prophet said that all the captives would be returned, but God said the opposite, that they would die in a foreign land.

The false prophet, Hananiah, claimed that all would be returned to Judah, when the opposite was going to happen. The false prophets of America are saying "Peace, Prosperity, Restoration, when the true prophets are saying, Sword, Famine, Pestilence and Judgment if America doesn't repent and turn back to God. You see nothing has really changed in over 2,600 years. History is repeating itself right before our eyes. This is all so tragic. Judah and Jerusalem were about to be judged as they were being led by blind and misguided false prophets. So it is at this moment, that the exact same thing is happening to America today.

Jeremiah confronted Hananiah right in front of the Priests and in the presence of all the people who stood in the House of God. The prophet of God was not afraid to confront this error, no matter who liked it or didn't like it. This is what the true preachers of the Gospel must do today. Be assured it won't please most of the people in the modern church who only want to hear positive messages.

In modern times, I wonder what the unity crowd would think of Jeremiah! Virtually all of Judah and Jerusalem are in unity, except for this lone Prophet Jeremiah. He alone disturbs this unity! However, unity at the expense of compromise is man's way and not God's Way. (Words taken from the Jimmy Swaggart Expositor's Study Bible, page 1289.)

No true prophet of God wants to see judgment come to their nation or to the people, so I'm sure that Jeremiah wished that the words of Hananiah were true. However, he knew better, in fact Jeremiah said these words:

> *"Nevertheless, hear you this word that I speak in your ears, and in the ears of all the people; The Prophets who have been before me and before You of old prophesied both against many countries, and against great Kingdoms, of war, and of evil, and of pestilence. The prophet which prophesies of peace, when the word of the prophet shall come to pass, then shall the Prophet be known, that the LORD has truly sent him"* (Jeremiah 28:7-9).

A litmus test as to whether a prophet is a prophet of God is that if what they say actually comes to pass or not. If so, they are a real prophet of God. If what they said does not come to pass, then they were not sent by God.

In the 2020 presidential election, the prophets who stated a *"Thus saith the Lord"* prophesy that President Trump would be re-elected, have been exposed as being false prophets and they were not sent from the Lord. The question is whether Christians will turn away from these prophets now that they have been exposed? Will the church turn away from these supposed prophets who committed such blasphemy? I would like to say yes, but I'm afraid most will continue to follow and believe their lies.

A good question is, why would people continue to follow them after they clearly prophesied wrong? I believe it is because their pride does not allow them to admit that they were wrong. The people are in spiritual bondage and cannot see the errors of their ways. Even worse, they do not want to see it because they want blessings and prosperity more than they want repentance and truth.

HANANIAH BREAKS JEREMIAH'S YOKE

In a display of anger, Hananiah the false prophet, takes the yoke from around Jeremiah's neck right in front of the people to show them that he does not believe in the prophecies of Jeremiah made against Judah. It was probably done with much favor by the people at the House of God (i.e., the Temple) as the kings just stood watching the entire confrontation.

In his continual defilement of the Word of God, Hananiah said this in front of all the people, "Thus says the LORD; *Even so will I break the yoke of Nebuchadnezzar king of Babylon from the neck of all nations within the space of two full years"* (Jeremiah 28:11).

In essence, Hananiah was saying that God was going to continue to bless and protect Israel. However, the Lord had not said any such thing, it was all lies! The Bible says, *"And the prophet Jeremiah went his way,"* which probably means that he went out alone. He must have felt a sense of loneliness that day. This reminds me of the song I learned when I was first saved. The lyrics are as follows: "I have decided to follow Jesus, no turning back, no turning back, though none go with me, still I will follow, though none go with me, still I will follow, no turning back, no turning back!"

Jesus said the road that leads to life is narrow and few are those who find it. Jeremiah was willing to walk that narrow road, and this narrow road can indeed feel very lonely at times. But at the end of the road, there is a great reward for men and women who do not bow their knees to the gods of this world. The question is are you and I willing to walk that same narrow road today?

JEREMIAH GIVES ANOTHER PROPHECY

After this encounter with Hananiah, the Lord came to Jeremiah and said: *"Go and tell Hananiah, saying, Thus says the LORD; You have broken the yokes of wood; but you shall make for them yokes of iron. For thus says the LORD of Hosts, the God of Israel; I have put a yoke of iron upon the neck of all these nations, that they may serve Nebuchadnezzar king of Babylon; and they shall serve him: and I have given him the beast of the field also"* (Jeremiah 28:12-14).

It is obvious that the Holy Spirit was grieved that Hananiah forcibly took the yoke off Jeremiah's neck. This false prophet set himself against the true Prophet and against the Word of God, and God Himself, which is always a dangerous thing to do.

Because the people listened to Hananiah's prophesies, they were now not going to have "yokes of wood" but now God would give them "yokes of iron." Iron is heavier than wood, so their judgment would now be even greater and more severe due to the way they treated the true prophet of God, namely Jeremiah. If they would have listened to Jeremiah, the true prophet of God, everything could have been so different.

Jeremiah then had a direct prophesy to give the false prophet Hananiah as follows: *"Hear now, Hananiah; the LORD has not sent you; but you make this people to trust a lie. Therefore thus says the LORD; Behold, I will cast you from off the face of the Earth: this year you shall die, because you have taught rebellion against the LORD"* (Jeremiah 28:15-16).

The true prophet pulled no punches but confronted the false prophet directly. We must understand that if the men of God do not confront error, many will perish as they will never know that they are following a false way.

The Word of God came to pass as it always does, and Hananiah died in the seventh month that same year (Jeremiah 28:17). The Word of God is strong against those who falsely speak in the Name of the LORD.

Remember that God is a merciful God, and Hananiah could have repented of his false ways and turned to God. But his arrogance did not allow him to do that, which is most often the case.

The Bible is very clear in its instruction on what to do with false teachers and false prophets, as stated in the book of Philippians:

> *"Brethren, be followers together of me, and mark them which walk so as you have us for an example. (for many walk, of whom I have told you often, and now tell you even weeping, that they are the enemies of the Cross of Christ: whose end is destruction, whose god is their belly, and whose glory is in their shame, who mind earthly things)"* (Phil. 3:17-19).

"This year you shall die" are words said by God and should be a reminder to all that one better be careful how one treats a True Prophet and True Man of God. Hananiah should have never touched Jeremiah nor taken God's yoke off his neck and broke it. Even though there was ample time for him to repent, there is no record that Hananiah did so. Notice that God said his rebellion was against Him and not Jeremiah.

The word "rebellion" in the Hebrew means a defection, revolt, and an apostasy. This term refers to God's people turning away from Him to follow false gods. Frequently, this describes those who choose to rebel against God. This is what is happening in America right now. We see it in churches, and we see it in the political arena. Those in the church want to demonize one party over the other and cannot see that both parties have departed from the truth.

When Joshua was at the eve of the battle of Jericho, he encountered a pre-incarnate appearance of the Lord Jesus Christ. The Lord Himself stood before him with a drawn sword. Not knowing it was the Lord, Joshua said to him, "Are you for us, or for our adversaries?" (Joshua 5:13). Jesus said, *"No; but as Captain of the Host of the LORD am I now come."* (Joshua 5:14).

You see, Joshua asked the Lord the wrong question like many today ask the wrong question. The question shouldn't be what side is God on (e.g., Republican or Democrat), but the question should be: "What side is America on?"

Hananiah's life ended just as the prophet Jeremiah said it would. He touched God's anointed one, that being Jeremiah. When a person touches God's anointed, scripture supports that you have touched God. Therefore, one must be careful how they treat a true man or woman of God. Even more important is how we handle God's Holy Word. Israel touched the "Anointed One" through misinterpreting the Caiaphas Prophecy and they as a nation has been suffering greatly ever since.

CHAPTER 10

GOD IS OUR ONLY HOPE

Trusting in political and spiritual leaders was one of Israel's biggest deceptions. They did not seek the Lord personally for their answers, but listened and followed the words of man. And when man spoke for God in the Name of God, the inhabitants of Jerusalem and Judah had no spiritual discernment to know if these men were in fact speaking for God or if they were false prophets. So, the result was the sheep were easily led to the slaughter.

Just like ancient Israel, the United States of America is on the brink of judgment because of the many abominations that have occurred in our country over the past 60 years. The true prophets of our nation, although they are few, have given continual warnings, but our nation fails to listen to them, and instead chooses to follow the false prophets who promise peace and prosperity.

In 2020-21, we saw our nation heading in the wrong direction and under a world-wide pandemic that crushed the American economy. Today there is political turmoil between the two political parties that is dividing our nation in such a deep way. We have not seen such division and hostility between two parties since the Civil War.

There is violence in the streets as citizens disrespect authority, and most of the Church looks towards man instead of God to solve the many social ills. The Church does not recognize that the problems in America are not political, but spiritual. The political problems in this nation are merely the fruit of the real problem. The Bible says, *"the axe is laid unto the root of the trees"* (Matthew 3:10). Until America tends to the root of the problem, there will be no healing in our nation.

The way I see it, the main reason why America is spiritually failing is because the preaching and teaching from behind most pulpits today does not include the Gospel of Christ but mostly consists of the foolishness of man. The Bible says, *"For the preaching of the Cross is to them who perish foolishness; but unto us who are Saved it is the Power of God. For it is written, I will destroy the wisdom of the wise, and will bring to nothing the understanding of the prudent."* (I Corinthians 1:18-19).

The message of the Cross is the only message that can save this nation, everything else is the wisdom of man and it will produce nothing in the way of understanding and deliverance. Paul said: *"And I, Brethren, I yet preach Circumcision, why do I yet suffer persecution? Then is the offense of the Cross ceased"* (Galatians 5:11).

It is the message of the Cross that offends the world and even the people inside of our churches today. If a pastor/preacher proclaim the message of the Cross as the only answer for sin, they will be called narrow minded, and he or she will suffer persecution and most don't like that. But if they avoid telling their congregations that they are sinners and they will be judged for their sins and spend eternity in hell unless they go to the Cross of Christ, and repent, and believe in the blood of Jesus that was shed for their forgiveness, then that preacher will one day have to answer to God.

The Bible declares that God is a just God. His just anger burns forever, which means that God will conduct Himself accordingly towards willful rebellion and disobedience. Man can create a god of his own liking and believe that his god will never get angry and will never judge sin, but that is not the God of the Bible. It is only the Cross of Christ that appeases the anger of God for the sins of man. God's anger is only appeased when the sinner comes to the Cross, cries out in repentance, and trusts in Jesus to save and deliver them from their sinful lifestyle.

Many people in the church of America in 2021 believed that a man, i.e., Donald Trump was the hope for our nation, which is the same mistake that Israel made in 600 B.C, putting their trust in man. Most of the church looked the other way at Donald Trump's mean, hostile, arrogant, profane and self-centered antics. They would just give him a pass by saying, *"he's not my pastor, he's a businessman."*

Why was the church so quick to give Donald Trump a pass on issues such as character, integrity and treating his fellow man with love and forgiveness? I will tell you why, because the left was so far gone and away from scripture, people felt that there was no other alternative but to back Donald Trump and look the other way when he was showing a lack of character and good grace.

Many even in the church like when he was like a battling ram confronting the liberal agenda in our nation. They like the fact that the former president was willing to call out the sin and evil of the left like few ever had in politics. People identified with his straightforward and bold appraisal of our country's leadership. His "drain the swamp" statement resonated with people and their frustrations with this country's leadership that is mostly ungodly and demonic in nature. However, what the people couldn't see was the man calling it out, had such a checkered past of immorality, failure both in business and in his home life, he was just like the one in the Bible described when He said: *"Judge not, that you be not judged. For with what judgment, you shall be judged: and with what measure you mete, it shall be measured to you again. And why do you behold the mote that is in your brother's eye, but consider not the beam that is in your eye?"* (Matthew 7:1-3).

I guess there are people who only believe that applies to some, and not the political people they like and who call out sin. I think where former President Trump failed in his approach to "draining the swamp" is that he not only showed hatred for the sin, but also to the sinner. As in most of his political speeches he would make it personal in his name calling of his political rivals, and he made personal attacks, rather than sticking with the issues of our nation that are clearly evil. He developed a strong base of evangelicals that supported him for his stance and even after everything that has occurred in his presidency and after he has been in office, they still support him.

President Trump once bragged that he could get away with murder on 5th avenue. Maybe based on everything that has occurred and he is still the front runner of the GOP right now (February, 2024) he may be right about that after all. There is one thing for sure Donald Trump has helped create a hatred and divide in our nation that has not been seen in over 150 years in our nation.

When Adam and Eve fell, they disobeyed God and ate from the one forbidden tree in the Garden. What was the forbidden tree called? It was called the *"tree of the knowledge of good and evil."* (Genesis 2:17). Notice that the tree was both good and evil. Most people don't realize that a sinner must repent not only from the evil things they have done, but also from the good things. You may say, "I don't understand what this means. Why do I have to repent of the good things I have done? Doesn't God want me to do good?" The answer is yes He does, but when you are depending on those good things or get puffed up by what you have done, then you become self-righteous and you think you can sanctify yourself. But the Bible teaches us that God looks at our works as but *"filthy rags"* (Isaiah 64:6).

The only thing God accepts is His Son Jesus Christ, who was perfect in Word, Deed and Motive. You see, our good works are lined with selfish pride and judgment against those who don't do or believe as we do. This is called self-righteousness and the Bible says, *"the heart is deceitful above all things, and desperately wicked: who can know it?"* (Jeremiah 17:9)

The devil likes to trick us by giving us two choices; one clearly being evil and the other one looks and sounds "good" and "righteous." The truth is both are evil. However, it is always harder to discern when the so-called "good choices", are lined with poison as well.

TRUSTING IN MAN

"IN GOD WE TRUST" is written on our American currency. The question is whether this statement is true in the year 2024? Sadly, the answer to that question is no, because most Americans are putting their trust in man.

Similarly, the people of Judah formed an alliance with the Egyptians as a protection from the Chaldeans (i.e., the Babylonians) instead of trusting in God to provide their protection. They looked to man for the answers to their problems. Likewise, today, America is committing this same sin as Israel did by not trusting in God for their current issues and situations.

In the last presidential election, I believe many American evangelicals were deceived and looked to man rather than calling for national repentance for the sins of our country that offended a thrice Holy God.

I believe the false prophesy of a Trump victory, given by many of the so-called prophets, revealed an even bigger problem than the false prophesy itself. The five main errors that I see that was made in the Trump Presidency that were mainly ignored in many evangelical's circles.

Many in the church trusted in a man to solve America's problems and even looked the other way when President Trump led an interfaith prayer gathering in the Rose Garden on the National Day of Prayer. He clearly violated the Word of God that says: *"Thou shall have no other gods before Me."* (Exodus 20:3). This is a very serious sin in God's eyes for a nation to make, since it is the very first of the 10 Commandments that God gave Moses on Mount Sinai.

The church looked the other way when President Trump arrogantly praised himself for the nation's successes during his first three years in office, and then in the fourth year of his presidency the entire nation fell apart during the outbreak of COVID 19 as President Trump shut down the country and launch "Operation Warp Speed" to create a vaccine. The Bible declares: *"Pride goes before destruction, and an haughty spirit before a fall"* (Proverbs 16:18).

Many overlooked when President Trump cursed Israel by creating what he called the "Peace Deal of the Century," which called on Israel to stop building settlements in certain areas of their land to try to create peace with the Palestinians.

Many people made excuses for President Trump when he made crude and insulting remarks about people's looks, character, or political position and they gave him a pass when he used insulting and graphic and lewd language. A common response from evangelicals and even spiritual leaders was to say, "he is not my pastor, he is my president." The problem with this line of thinking is God did not give this same pass to the political leaders, (i.e., kings and governors) in Jeremiah's day. He held all leaders both political and spiritual leaders to the same moral standards.

The false prophets who prophesied that Trump would win were from evangelical churches who backed Trump. When they falsely prophesied that Trump would win, most of them never repented after he lost the election. And most of the evangelical world who follow those false prophets did not hold them accountable. What these same false prophets do is they fail to preach and teach the soon coming rapture of the Church, followed by the seven-year tribulation. This does not seem to be in their theology as most of them are dominion teachers. This belief teaches that Christians are going to take over the seven mountains of influence (i.e., business, education, entertainment, etc.) and usher in the Kingdom Age. False teaching in America today is where the root of the problem lies. Simply said, they are not hearing from the Holy Spirit, but are listening to another spirit, following another Jesus and preaching another gospel that does not emphasize the Cross.

> *The Apostle Paul said, "But though we, or an Angel from Heaven, preach any other gospel unto you than that which we have preached unto you, let him be accursed. As we said before, so say I now again, If any man preach any other gospel unto you than that you have received, let him be accursed. For do I now persuade men, or God? Or do I seek to please men? For if I yet pleased men, I should not be the Servant of Christ"* (Galatians 1:8-10)

TRUST IN THE LORD

The Bible says that God is a jealous God. Jesus said, *"Apart from Me you can do nothing"* (John 15:5). Those who trust in the Lord will be like a tree firmly planted by the waters (Psalm 1) and fruit from the tree will grow. The fruit of the Spirit will be present in all who trust in the Lord. To trust in man is to be cursed by the Lord. The modern church should make note of this in her acceptance of humanistic psychology in the place of the Word of God.

God knows the human heart and how wicked it is and what it can do without Him. All the problems of violence, seduction and civil disobedience in the earth is due to the corrupted sinful heart that lies in all of humanity that is living without a personal relationship with God. That is why man needs to be *"Born Again"* (John 3:3). When one is born again, they receive a new nature and a new heart, which is called the *"Divine Nature"* (II Peter 1:4).

Man will be judged according to the fruit of what he does. The fruit of his life proves the attitude of his heart. God said that whoever trusts in wealth is a fool. The Lord is the hope of Israel and all those who forsake Him shall be ashamed. He is the fountain of Living Waters (Jeremiah 17:13).

Jeremiah says,

> *"Heal me, O LORD, and I shall be saved: for You are my praise. Behold, they say unto me, Where is the Word of the LORD? Let it come now"* (Jeremiah 17:14-15).

The prophet Jeremiah was pleading on behalf of the people as their representative, identifying himself as one of them also. He prays for their healing, speaking of their sick hearts and souls. Only God can save, and this is what the prophet was saying in his prayer. The people who Jeremiah was warning ridiculed him for proclaiming judgment on the nation of Israel and the surrounding nations. These arrogant leaders opposed the warnings of Jeremiah and even taunted Jeremiah's warnings with their skeptical comment that tempted God by saying, "Let it come now." The people showed no fear of God.

Jeremiah did not choose to become a preacher, but God assigned him that calling. What came out of his lips was not his own words, but God's words. Jeremiah feared God, unlike most of the people of his day, and he said to God, *"Be not a terror unto me: You are my hope in the day of evil"* (Jeremiah 17:17).

The only hope for every American is the Lord Jesus Christ. Outside of Him there is no hope for our nation. The truth is that every individual person on the earth today is on the brink of seeing the coming judgment of God in these last days unless they personally come to Christ and know Him personally. When God's judgment comes, it will come quickly and will come on this nation and the nations of the world like it has never been seen before, not since the days of Noah.

Jeremiah asked God to confound them who persecuted him. He asked that they would be dismayed, but that God would not let him be personally confounded or dismayed. Jeremiah saw the need for them to see the day of evil and destruction. They had reached the point of no return, there was nothing else that could be done as they were bent on going their own way, which was living a life away from God.

HONORING THE SABBATH

God tells Jeremiah to go and stand in the gate of the city where the kings of Judah came in, and go out and say unto them, *"Hear you the Word of the LORD, you kings of Judah, and all Judah, and all the inhabitants of Jerusalem, who enter in by these gates: Thus says the LORD; Take heed to yourselves, and bear no burden on the sabbath day, nor bring it in by the gates of Jerusalem. Neither carry forth a burden out of your houses on the sabbath day, neither do you any work, but hallow you the sabbath day, as I commanded your fathers."* (Verses 20-22).

The people would not receive the message God gave to Jeremiah to speak to the kings and people passing by the gate. God told Jeremiah to tell the people to honor the Sabbath. The Sabbath represented what Christ would one day do on the Cross for all of humanity. The Sabbath rest represented a rest from the penalty of sin and a deliverance from sin. The spiritual meaning of the Sabbath Rest is that Salvation was all of God, and none of man. All that men had to do to be saved was to believe in God's sacrifice, His Blood. The Blood of the Lord Jesus Christ shed on the Cross, and through the Cross alone one is saved.

Therefore, breaking the Sabbath and working on this day symbolically spoke of religion; man working to obtain his own salvation, which is impossible to do. To God, this sin was the most insulting sin of all. In essence, a works-based salvation is a slap in God the Father and God the Son's face! It is like saying that Jesus' blood is not enough, and a person must add to it.

Remember that God did not accept Cain's work from his hands when he brought God a planted crop from his field where he worked it, watered it, and harvested it himself. The Lord in fact rejected it. However, God did receive Abel's sacrifice, as it was from the first fruits of his flock. It was the sacrifice of a lamb, representing the Lamb of Glory, Jesus of Nazareth. God declared Abel as being righteous and Cain unrighteous (Hebrews 11:4). The works of religion can never take away sin, but only the blood of Christ.

Cain became angry at the rejection of his "religious" offering, as self-righteous men do. He then went out and committed the first murder recorded in the Bible and killed his brother in cold blood. It has been said that "religion" has caused more bloodshed than any other thing in the history of man. (Genesis 4:3-11)

Israel would not take heed to Jeremiah's warning to honor God's Sabbath; not only the weekly Sabbath, but they also refused to honor the yearly Sabbath that God commanded them to let their fields rest every seventh year. For 490 years, Israel did not follow God's Word and they did not honor the yearly Sabbath of resting the land from planting their crops every seventh year, which was called the Sabbatical year.

Therefore, God took His 70 Sabbaths that His people would not obey (490 years divided by 7 years equals 70 years) and caused the children of Israel to be removed from the promise land by the Babylonians. This removal from their land lasted for 70 years which was the consequence of not obeying the Sabbatical commandment, (not to mention many other abominations) so God allowed them to be held captive in Babylon for 70 years.

Therefore, the land of Israel did rest with no crops being planted and no people working on the land for 70 years, and the land became a wilderness. This was the penalty for the sins of the people of Israel for not following and honoring God's commandments regarding the Sabbatical Rest, etc., Man must realize that God is going to get what He commands, one way or another.

The Bible declares that Christ is God's Sabbath. To burden that Sabbath with sacerdotalism and its ceremonies and doctrines is to desecrate and destroy it. In other words, under the New Covenant, serving Christ, who is the True Sabbath, constitutes "keeping the Sabbath." (JSM Notes, page 1268).

THE FALL OF AMERICA

I am 61 years old at the writing of this book and I can still remember as a little boy that Sunday was a special day, a day of rest in America. It was not a day that you could played ball, as all youth sports were shut down. My parents could not even buy gas for their automobile or go shopping at a grocery store or shop in the malls. Everything was closed. Sunday was the Lord's Day and a day of rest. It was a day you were to go to church.

Back in 2003, our ministry (Joshua Revolution) held a big Youth Conference in Birmingham, Alabama. Once a month for a year leading up to the event, some of my staff and I would travel to Birmingham and hold meetings with youth pastors and leaders to promote and prepare for the conference. One thing I learned about Birmingham right away, which is known as the Bible belt, is that you do not plan anything on Wednesday nights or on Sundays. Those two times and day belongs to the church. Public schools would not even hold any events during these two days.

However, in most places in America today Sundays are just another day. There is no difference between Sunday and any other day of the week anymore. What was once a day that belonged to the Lord is now a day that belongs to man to watch football, cut his grass, shop, work, go to his children's sporting event, or any other gathering. Even the church has reduced the Lord's Day to being the Lord's hour; and God forbid if the church service goes longer than that one hour. Also, most churches do not hold Sunday night services anymore because they cannot get the people to come back after being in church Sunday morning.

In America most Christians have no problem sitting in front of a television set on Sunday watching their favorite hometown football team for 3 hours, but they won't sit for more than an hour or so for the King of Kings and Lord of Lords.

I remember when our son Drew was younger, and he played youth football and I was one of the assistant coaches. Our team made it to the playoffs, and we were playing on a Saturday, which was our normal day to play all of our games. We won the game and advanced to the Semi-Final game. This was exciting for our boys and their families because the Semi-final game was going to be played at the Buffalo Bills stadium. This professional team had recently built a youth football field right next to the NFL stadium in Orchard Park, New York, and we were going to be the very first team to play on that field, with other games in the older divisions to follow our game. But we would be the first ones to use this beautiful new field.

After we won the quarter-final game, our head coach announced to the players, coaches, and parents that we would be playing the following Sunday at 10:00 am at the Buffalo Bills Stadium. I could not believe my ears as I turned and look at my wife and whispered the words: "I can't go to that game." After our head coach dismissed everyone, I stayed behind to speak with him. I tried to explain to him that I would not be able to be at the game next week since it conflicted with our church service. He said to me, "Coach, you must be at that game, you are the one that calls all the offensive plays. We cannot win without you." I looked at our team's head coach right in the eye and said these words with a deep conviction: "Coach, if I skip church next Sunday for our football game, out team won't win that game." This man who was not overly religious looked at me and totally understood what I was saying. He responded by asking if I would allow our son to play in the game which I said, my wife and I will have to think about that, and I will let you know.

My wife and I later that week after much pondering decided to let our son play in the big game. We just didn't think at his young age (9 years old) that he would understand the spiritual conviction of us not letting him play in the big game. Also, we did not want his absence to affect the team in anyway, so we made an exception. Looking back, I am not sure that we made the right decision before the Lord.

Sunday arrived and I went to our church and Drew and his mother drove out to Orchard Park, New York to the Buffalo Bills stadium to play in the Big Game. If the team were to win the game, we would go onto to play in the championship game which was to be held the next week, right back at the Buffalo Bills brand new youth football field.

I told my wife and our son not to call me after the game and tell me what happened because I did not want to hear the results of the game over the phone. I had pre-arranged with our team's videographer to pick up a copy of the video of the game from his mailbox after church and I intended to drive to an area coffee shop and watch the game by myself without knowing the outcome.

The day of the game came and after our church service ended, I was greeting people from our church when one of my staff members came up to me and said "Pastor, you have a call, it's your son." I could not believe that he disobeyed my orders to not call me. I went to the phone and before he could say anything I said "Drew, I told you I did not want to hear the results of the game until I watched it first on video."

My nine-year-old son interrupted me and said, "But Dad, wait something happened." I was quickly concerned that maybe he got hurt in the game, so I responded and said, "What happened?" He said, "Dad, we were playing the game and then it started raining and there was lightning, and thunder and they stopped the game. They waited for the weather system to blow over, but when it didn't, they made an announcement that they were postponing our game to Tuesday night at our home field." I replied, "What! Put your mother on."

With joy and shock in her voice, my wife reaffirmed what my son had told me. She said that it was incredible; the dark clouds came out of nowhere with lightning. They stopped our game and they waited for about 20 minutes and then made the announcement that they were postponing our game. She then continued to say that as soon as our team began to get into their cars to leave the field, the weather cleared up and they made the announcement that they were going to start the next game that was scheduled to follow our game. All the other games played, except for ours.

I was so amazed by what happened that day. I knew that God honored my decision to put him first on His day. On a side note, I believe that we spell the word Sunday wrong; it should be spelled 'Sonday" because it is a day that we should all set aside our own activities for the Son of God who died on a cruel Cross to save us from our sins, and He rose from the dead on a Sunday morning to give us life everlasting.

When I went to football practice the next day to prepare our team for the rescheduled game that would be played on our field the following night, I walked onto the field and one of our assistant coaches saw me coming. This African American man was grinning at me from ear-to-ear as he walked up to me and said, "Coach, you're a bad man, I want to start going to your church." We both had a big laugh at his comment.

The next night we won the game and went on to play in the Championship game the next week at the Buffalo Bills Field which was held on Saturday (thank God). Unfortunately, we lost the Championship game by a score of 13-0 but what a thrill it was to be with our boys and see them play on that new field. I should point out that our team returned to the Championship Game the following year and won the big game on a beautiful Saturday afternoon in Lancaster, New York on the same field that I coached high school football for 10 years. God's Ways are so much higher and greater than our ways. Glory to God!

In this nation, we used to honor the Lord's Day; but today it is just treated as any other ordinary day. Personally, I believe that what a nation does with Sunday (the Christian Sabbath) tells you where a nation is at spiritually. If a nation honors the day set aside for remembering Jesus coming out of the grave, that nation (whomever they are) will be blessed.

On the other hand, if they ignore the Lord's Day, they will reap curses and consequences. For the Bible says, *"for them that honor Me I will honor, and they that despise me shall be lightly esteemed"* (II Samuel 2:30).

The weekly Sabbath for Jews is the "day of rest," which they still strictly observe to this day. When the sun sets on Friday, Israel goes into the day of rest from their weekly labors, which was commanded to them in the Law of Moses.

But the Mosaic Law also spoke of the Sabbatical Year. God told Moses to tell the people, *"When you come into the land which I give you, then shall the land keep a Sabbath unto the LORD. Six years you shall sow your field, and six years you shall prune your vineyard, and gather in the fruit thereof: But in the seventh year shall be a Sabbath of rest unto the land, a Sabbath for the LORD: you shall neither sow your field, nor prune your vineyard. That which grows of its own accord of your harvest you shall not reap, neither gather the grapes of your vine undressed: for it is a year of rest unto the land"* (Leviticus 25:2-5).

You might ask the question of what they would eat during that seventh year in which God commanded them not to plant any crops? You see, God promised that He would provide for them. Therefore, the command of taking a Sabbatical "year of rest" required faith to believe what God promised, He would fulfill and indeed He did. The Bible says, *"But without faith it is impossible to please Him: for he who comes to God must believe that He is, and that He is a rewarder of them who diligently seek Him"* (Hebrews 11:6).

The Lord sentenced Judah to *"seventy years"* of service to the king of Babylon for their failure to honor the Sabbath year. Because the nation of Israel would not honor God with the Sabbatical year, He judged them and removed them from their land. In other words, for every Sabbatical year they missed, they were placed in slavery. This reveals that God will judge His people and His nation when we fail to obey and honor His Word.

70 AD

After the nation of Israel spent 70 years in captivity in Babylon, the grace and mercy of the Lord brought the Jewish people back and they rebuilt their Temple in Jerusalem and return to their land. However, in 70 A.D., it happened again, and the Temple was burned down, and they were again removed from their land. Then nearly 1900 years later the Jews returned to the land and become a nation again. The land of Israel has been restored again exactly as prophesied by Jesus.

What is interesting is that the destruction of the Temple and the dispersion of the Jews was for the same sin that caused God to remove them from the land in 586 BC. In 70 A.D., it was again for the rejection of God's plan of Salvation. In 586 BC, it was the sin of not keeping the Sabbatical year (among other sins) which symbolically pointed to the Cross of Calvary when Jesus would finish the work of our salvation (John 19:30).

In 70 A.D., when the Romans were used as the arm of judgment against the Jews, it was for the sin of the rejection of Jesus and the blood He shed as the Lamb of God for their sins and the sins of the world. The Jewish religious leaders continued the sacrificial system to cover sin instead of embracing and trusting that Jesus Christ, Who was the sacrificial Lamb, once and for all, had removed our sin. God gave Israel 40 years to repent of that sin and believe in "God's Sabbath," but they would not believe. So, God judged them and used the Romans, like He used the Babylonians approximately 650 years earlier, to destroy the Temple and remove the Jewish people from their land.

I believe that America's downfall is just like ancient Israel's downfall, as we today treat God's Day of rest (i.e., Sabbath) as an ordinary day of doing anything we want (i.e., work, shop, play). Even though there is much more to the downfall of America, I believe this is where it all starts. Just take a drive around your neighborhood on a Sunday morning and observe most of the American activity on this day. The markets are packed, the ball diamonds in the summer are full of young people playing baseball, malls are filled with shoppers, etc. Sunday has become just another work and play day in America.

Today in America only 20% of the people go to church on Sunday. Even Christians are quick to miss Church on a Sunday morning if their son or daughter has a secular sporting event. Fifty years ago, it was not this way, oh how we have fallen.

The reality is that America no longer honors the Lord's Sabbath and just like ancient Israel, it does not fear God, nor follow the Word of God any longer. If God doesn't judge America soon, He will have to apologize to ancient Israel and guess what, He is not going to apologize to ancient Israel for all His Judgments are right and just!

CHAPTER 11

THE REMOVAL OF THE HEDGE

Jeremiah was told by God to tell the captives in Babylon to build houses and dwell in them, and plant gardens and eat the fruit of it. Why? Because they were going to be there for a while (Jeremiah 29:5). Jeremiah told them to pray for peace while they lived under Babylonian rule in a strange land. God warned them of the false prophets who prophesy to them falsely. Here is what he said:

"Thus says the LORD of Hosts, the God of Israel; let not your prophets and your diviners, who be in the midst of you, deceive you, neither hearken to your dreams which you cause to be dreamed. For they prophesy falsely unto you in My Name: I have not sent them, says the LORD" (Jeremiah 29:8-9).

Notice that false prophets were still around, even though they got it wrong about how the Babylonians would come and siege their land. They did find themselves in Babylon and continue to falsely represent God. You would think that the people would have rejected them for their lies, but that was obviously not the case.

God told Jeremiah to tell the people that the captivity would last 70 years and then God would bring them back to their land (Jeremiah 29:10). The following reveals how the timing of this all occurred:

- 605 BC was the first Babylonian siege.
- 597 BC was the second siege.
- 586 BC was the final destruction of the Temple.

But God promised the Jewish people that He would restore them after 70 years of captivity and they would rebuild their Temple. God said through the prophet Jeremiah: *"For I know the thoughts that I think towards you, says the LORD, thoughts of peace, and not of evil, to give you an expected end."* (Jeremiah 29: 11).

When one obeys the Lord and follows His ways, he finds peace and a good ending. But to rebel against Him and His ways produces the opposite result. There was a coming restoration for Israel after their 70 years of captivity and God said so through the prophet Jeremiah. He said that when the people called on Him, He would listen to their cries. God promised that when they seek Him, they will find Him, if they would search for Him with all their heart. (Jeremiah 29:12-13). What a wonderful promise for us all!

God promised Israel that He would restore them and bring them back to their land. The nation of Israel experienced this great miracle on two different occasions: once around the year 538 BC and then again in 1948. After the Romans invaded Israel, burned the city, and destroyed their Temple in 70 A.D. (there is the number 70 again), God miraculously brought them back to their land a second time. There has been no nation in the history of the world that ever experienced the return to their land once, but it has miraculously happened to Israel twice. Why did God do this for the nation of Israel? Because He is a Promise Keeper. The Bible says that all His promises are yes, and in Christ, Amen (II Corinthians 2:20). What He promised to Abraham eventually will come to pass.

God told the Jewish people that He would persecute them with the sword, with famine and with pestilence. He would deliver them over to all the kingdoms of the earth to be accursed. They would be an astonishment and a hissing, a reproach among all the nations to where He had driven them. He said He would do so because they did not listen to His words, which He sent by way of the prophets (i.e., Jeremiah, Ezekiel, etc.). But He also said that He would restore them.

It must be remembered that God's judgment is not so much for the purpose of God getting back at His people, but it is for getting His people back to Him. God tries to bring His rebellious people back to Him in every way possible; but when all else fails, He uses judgment as His last resort.

JUDGMENT ON THE FALSE PROPHETS IN BABYLON

From Jerusalem, Jeremiah sent a letter to those in Babylonian captivity saying that the false prophets, namely Ahab and Zedekiah were prophesizing lies. Through Jeremiah, God said He would deliver these two false prophets into the hand of Nebuchadnezzar, and they would be killed before their eyes.

So, the Holy Spirit through the prophet Jeremiah named the false prophets and pronounced doom on them for their false prophesies. This should put to rest any thought that we are not to name the names of persons when it comes to those who falsely prophesy or teach in error. If God said to do it back then, then it is not wrong to do now. It is never a pleasant thing to Name a person's name, but for the attempted rescue of the blind and spiritually undiscerning, it must be done.

It appears that these false prophets were put into a fiery furnace. It says that the king of Babylon roasted them in the fire because they committed wicked criminal behavior, adultery with their neighbors' wives, and spoke lying words that God had not commanded them (Jeremiah 29:22). God delivered the Hebrew children from the Babylonian fiery furnace but did not deliver these false prophets.

Then God said to speak to Shemaiah, who was believed to be the leader of the false prophets. Again, Jeremiah publicly called out the name of another false prophet. Shemaiah sent letters to Jerusalem, to all the people and all the Priests and to Jehoiada the Priest. Zephaniah the Priest read the letter to Jeremiah. In the letter, Shemaiah called Jeremiah a mad man and a self-proclaimed prophet. (Jeremiah 29:24-26). But then came the Word of the LORD to Jeremiah saying:

> *"Send to all them of the captivity, saying, Thus says the LORD concerning Shemaiah the Nehelamite; Because that Shemaiah has prophesied unto you, and I sent him not and he caused you to trust in a lie. Therefore, thus says the LORD; Behold I will punish Shemaiah the Nehelamite, and his seed: he shall not have a man to dwell among this People; neither shall he behold the good that I will do for My People, says the LORD, because he has taught rebellion against the LORD"* (Jeremiah 29:31-32).

These verses proclaim that the preacher of the Gospel must proclaim the Word of God without fear or favor. How many hundreds, if not thousands, of preachers currently *"cause people to trust in a lie"* and, thereby, cause them to be eternally lost? Judah and Jerusalem would suffer terror at least in part because of these false prophets.

The Gospel of Jesus Christ is the most important truth in all the world, and true preachers must not only preach truth, but they must serve as watchmen and point out error. At times, they must even call out the names of those who preach false messages, which is exactly what Jeremiah did. To be sure, such will not be met with acceptance, but anger and rebuke from much of the Church; nevertheless, it must be done!

To proclaim another gospel is the work of Satan. Paul was concerned that the Church would be pulled into believing in "*another Jesus.*" In the Second book of Corinthians 11:3-4, he said,

> "*But I fear, lest by any means, as the serpent beguiled Eve through his subtilty, so your minds should be corrupted from the simplicity that is in Christ. For if he who comes preaching another Jesus, whom we have not preached, or if you receive another spirit which you have not received, or another gospel, which you have not accepted, you might well bear with him.*"

There are 3 concerns that Paul had regarding how the devil will try to deceive and corrupt the Church:

- "Another Jesus" would be preached to you.
- You would receive "another spirit" that is not the Holy Spirit (i.e. demonic spirits).
- "Another gospel" would be accepted, which is not the true Gospel.

What we see here is that Satan presents to the believer and the church a different "Jesus" and claims to be the "Holy Spirit," but is a counterfeit. Remember that in the counterfeit business, the goal is to make the fake look as close to the original as possible, so that the untrained eye does not even know that what is being offered is phony.

When you use a $50 or $100 bill at a drug store or in the market, many times the cashier will take that bill and hold it up to a light which can show if it is counterfeit or not. This is exactly what we are to do with all things that are preached or taught in Jesus Name. We must lift it up into the Light of the Gospel, the Word of God, to make sure it is not a counterfeit. Most in the modern church do not do this.

The Bible says that the false apostles are deceitful workers, transforming themselves into the Apostles of Christ. But the Bible says do not be surprised by this, for even Satan himself is transformed into an Angel of light. Therefore, just as Satan appears to look good and commits acts of goodness, so are his ministers transformed to look like ministers of righteousness. But underneath, they are anything but righteous, whose end shall be according to their works (II Cor. 11:13-15).

Remember Jesus warned that the false prophets would come in sheep's clothing, meaning that they would look and sound innocent but underneath this façade, were ravening wolves. How then does one spot them? Jesus said that you will know them by their fruits (Matt. 7:15-16).

The Word of God tells us that in the last days there would be those who claim to be Christians, but the fruit will not match their testimony. Whenever a person falls away from the truth, they begin to produce bad fruit.

Paul said in the last days:

"For men shall be lovers of their own selves, covetous, boasters, proud, blasphemers, disobedient to parents, unthankful, unholy, without natural affection, trucebreakers, false accusers, incontinent, fierce, despisers of those who are good, Traitors, heady, high-minded, lovers of pleasures more than lovers of God. Having a form of Godliness, but denying the power thereof" (II Timothy 3:2-5).

The word **"form"** means "mask." In other words, in the last days the church will resemble the church in an outward form; meaning they claim to be believers, however their lifestyle will not be surrendered to Christ. They are not willing to be persecuted for their faith and die as a martyr if God required it. Instead, they love this world and the things of this world more than they love God. This is what the scriptures say will happen in the last days of the church. This is the apostasy in which we are living right now, and the cause is that Christians have accepted "another Jesus." They follow *"another spirit"* and believe in "another gospel."

The Apostle Paul dealt strongly with this by saying, *"But though we, or an Angel from Heaven, preach any other gospel unto you than that which we have preached unto you, let him be accursed"* (Galatians 1:8). This word accursed means to be eternally condemned, cut off from the faith forever.

A LESSON FROM THE POTTER

God told Jeremiah to arise and go down to the potter's house and there He will speak to Jeremiah. When Jeremiah went down to the potter's house, the Potter showed him a work on the wheel. The vessel that the potter made was marred in the potter's hand, so he had to make it again to suffice what seemed good to the potter. This was all a picture of what God would do with the House of Israel (Jeremiah 18:1-6). The lesson here tells us that God never rehabilitates someone, which is what the world tries to do and always fails. But God rejuvenates; in other words, He creates something new. Such is the term *"born again"* (John 3:3).

When a person asks Jesus to become the Lord of their life, the "born again" miracle happens, which is when the Spirit of God comes into the life of that person. From that point on, the individual becomes a "new creation." The Bible says, *"Therefore if any man be in Christ, he is a new creature: old things are passed away; behold, all things are become new"* (II Corinthians 5:17).

God told Jeremiah that if the nation of Israel turned from their evil ways and repented of their sins against Him, He would repent of the evil He thought to bring unto them (Jeremiah 18:7-8). True heart-felt repentance is the only thing that can stop the judgment of God. Without repentance, judgment comes, and that judgment continues. The question must be, are the leaders listening and discerning what is really going on in our nation? The sad answer is that I don't believe they are.

God blessed the United States of America like no other nation in the modern world. It is the greatest country on the face of the earth; however, over the past 50-60 years it has lost its way. The blessings of God on this nation existed because of its acceptance of the Lord Jesus Christ; this and this alone is why America was blessed by God.

But God said that if that nation does evil in His sight and does not obey His Voice, then He will repent (change His mind) of the good that He planned for that nation. America ought to read this and take heed to this instruction, which God gave to Jeremiah a long time ago. It still rings true today or else God's Word is not true. In fact, God and His Word is the only thing we can trust today (Jeremiah 17:7).

God sent Jeremiah to the men of Judah to speak to them and to the inhabitants of Jerusalem, as He said to them, *"Thus says the LORD; Behold, I frame evil against you, and devise a device against you: return you now everyone from his evil ways, and make your ways and your doings good"* (Jeremiah 18:11).

This tells us that it is God who either frames good or evil against His children according to their obedience or disobedience. The sad truth is that most modern Christians have not been taught this by the modern preachers. Instead, they are told that because we are under Grace, God only frames good for His children. But God spoke through the prophet Malachi and said, *"And I will come near to you to Judgment; and I will be a swift witness against the sorcerers, and against the adulterers, and against the false swearers, and against those who oppress the hireling in his wages, the widow, and the fatherless, and that turn aside the stranger from his right, and fear not Me, say the LORD of Hosts. For I am the LORD, I change not; therefore you sons of Jacob are not consumed"* (Mal. 3:5-6).

In Malachi 2:17, the question was asked, "Where is the God of judgment?" God told them that in no uncertain terms that He would come near to them in Judgments because of their wickedness, immorality, false prophets, etc.

The reason people practice these sins, and many others is because they have no fear of God. The modern church has been taught that since we are now under Grace, God no longer judges sin the way He did in the Old Testament. I do not see this in scripture, but in fact, I see the following verses in the New Testament:

Jesus said,

> *"Or those eighteen, upon whom the tower in Siloam fell, and slew them, think ye that they were sinners above all men who dwelt in Jerusalem? I tell you, No: but except you repent, you shall all likewise perish"* (Luke 13:4-5).

> *"Remember Lot's wife. Whosoever shall seek to save his life shall lose it; and whosoever shall lose his life shall preserve it"* (Luke 17:32-33).

> *"So then because you are lukewarm, and neither cold nor hot, I will spue you out of My mouth"* (Revelation 3:16).

The truth is that God has not changed how He judges mankind. He was long-suffering in the Old Testament, and He is still long-suffering in the New Testament today. However, there is a limit for how long God will allow a person or a nation to continue in the direction of disobedience. Hebrews 13:8 reads, *"Jesus Christ the same yesterday, and today, and forever."*

The modern church has changed God into a God who looks the other way when it comes to sin. Modern preachers have said that God no longer is a God of judgment, but only a God of grace. But when you study the Bible, you see that this is not true, it is a deception and a lie; and a BIG ONE at that.

The New Testament states,

> *"What shall we say then? Shall we continue in sin, that grace may abound? God forbid, How shall we, that are dead to sin, live any longer therein"* (Romans 6:1-2)?

One of the big deceptions in the modern church is that it embraces a *"new image"* that God is only a God of love and blessing and not a God who punishes disobedience and rebellion. In Acts chapter 5, a couple in the early church named Ananias and Sapphira lied about money that they said they intended to give to the church as it related to a possession they sold.

Because they lied, the Holy Spirit immediately judged them on the spot and their lives were taken (Acts 5:1-10). The modern church has no idea what to do with this portion of scripture because it is under the New Covenant.

The Bible says that after this happened, *"great fear came upon all the Church, and upon as many as heard these things."* (Acts 5:11). The modern church, by and large, is missing the fear of God mainly due to the lie that God no longer judges sin. Today's church says that because we are under grace, God looks the other way when it comes to sin. However, this is simply not biblical and has, I'm afraid, created a church that no longer works out their salvation with *"fear and trembling"* (Phil. 2:12).

THE PEOPLE'S RESPONSE

The people of Israel said to Jeremiah, *"There is no hope: but we will walk after our own devices, and we will everyone do the imagination of his evil heart"* (Jeremiah 18:12). The deception of the people in Jeremiah's day was so great that they literally said to this prophet of God, "There is no hope in your preaching." You are a prophet of gloom and doom. They wanted prophets that offered them prosperity and peace, not judgment. They were saying to God's prophet, which means they were really speaking to God, your preaching is too depressing. In essence, they were rejecting all that was said about their evil hearts and their evil religious plans.

God was saying to Israel, *"The virgin of Israel has done a very horrible thing"* (Jeremiah 18:13). God was speaking about Israel forsaking Jehovah for Baal. Here, the word *"virgin"* speaks of Israel being the only nation in the world who knew the one true God, which is what makes their sin so serious. Because if Israel got it wrong, then the whole world will get it wrong. They were in fact God's light bearer to the other nations of the world. The same could be said of America today. Most of the world follows what America does, or doesn't do so the stakes are extremely high as it pertains to whether our nation follows the Lord.

Jesus Christ is compared to cool and pure waters that flow from the summit of Lebanon (Jeremiah 18:14-15). But man's religious ways are compared to the muddy waters of the trampled field. God's people had forgotten the Lord, and they burned incense to vanity (pointlessness) and their foreign gods caused them to spiritually stumble and leave the ancient paths. They instead chose to walk in paths to a new way that is not cast up but is instead cast down. For the most part, such is what the modern church is doing today in America.

By Israel leaving the God of the Bible, the people would be judged and forced to leave their land. God said that the world will be amazed at the desolation of their land. The LORD said, *"To make their land desolate, and a perpetual hissing; everyone who passes thereby shall be astonished, and wag his head"* (Jeremiah 18:16).

Israel's forsaking of the Bible *"made their land desolate,"* just as it will make America desolate as well if we do not repent! Jerusalem, which had been the city of God, would now be destroyed so completely that a passerby would be "astonished" and "wag their heads." (Jeremiah 18:16, Notes from JSESB, page 1270).

JEREMIAH'S PRAYER

"Give heed to me, O LORD, and hearken to the voice of them who contend with me" (Jeremiah 18:19). Jeremiah cried for a righteous God to righteously judge the evildoers in the interest of truth and society. If it is right for God to punish evildoers, then under the Law, it was right to pray for God to punish evil. However, this and similar prayers in the Bible belong to the past dispensation of Law and the future dispensation of Righteousness, and not to the present dispensation of Grace. (JSEBS, 1270).

Under Grace, we are to pray for our enemies. Jesus said, *"You have heard it has been said, An eye for an eye, and a tooth for a tooth: but I say unto you, that you resist not evil: but whosoever shall smite you on the right cheek, turn to him the other also"* (Matthew 5:38-39).

Jeremiah said to God, *"Yet, LORD, You know all their counsel against me to kill me: Forgive not their iniquity, neither blot out their sin from Your Sight, but let them be overthrown before You; deal thus with them in the time of Your Anger."*

The people of Jeremiah's day not only hated the message, but they hated the prophet who brought them this message and wanted to kill him. Not much has changed in 2600 years!

THE SYMBOL OF THE BROKEN POTTERY

God tells Jeremiah to go and get a potter's earthen bottle, a bottle made of clay, and take it to the people and the priests. He was to promise them that God's judgment was coming and then he was to break the pot of clay in front of them to symbolize the destruction of Judah and Jerusalem.

He was to do this in the valley of Hinnom, which was located by the entrance of the eastern gate towards the Temple. It was there that God told him to go and that He would give him the words to tell the people. God makes the statement *"I will bring evil upon this place,"* (Jeremiah 19:3) which spoke of His sovereignty. It is God Who controls the affairs of man, as it pertains to the consequences of sinful rebellion. Satan is only able to do to man what God gives him the liberty to do, and no more. Many people quote the scripture that reads, *"In whom the god of this world,"* (speaking of Satan) to suggest that the devil controls the world; however, this is not correct. In the context of this verse in II Corinthians 4:4, the Word of God is speaking about the spiritual deception currently in this world and not the control of the world.

If it were true that Satan was sovereign, which means having supreme power or authority over this world, then he would immediately kill, steal, and destroy every Jew and Christian who he vehemently hates. The reason he does not kill us is because he cannot kill as he is not sovereign over the earth, GOD IS!

Make no mistake, Satan is a vehement foe and has power. He has caused great deception and destruction since the fall in the garden of Eden; but he does not possess almighty power. God is the one who has total control over all things. The evil man and heathen monarch, King Nebuchadnezzar would think the plan was his; but yet he was only a tool in God's hand.

God proclaimed judgment was coming in the very place where the slaughter of little children were being offered up in sacrifice to Moloch (verse 4). This is chilling indeed.

THE SPREAD OF THE CORONAVIRUS

When the coronavirus first began to spread throughout our country in early 2020, the President of the United States, Donald Trump, gathered together a panel of scientists and health experts and He boldly declared that he would allow "science" to lead us. No offense to the those who work in science, but my Bible says that we are to let the Holy Spirit lead us. Unfortunately, America left that conviction a long time ago, and so has most of the modern church as well.

It wasn't long after that the U.S. became the number one country in the world with the most coronavirus cases and deaths. The number one city hit the hardest with this infectious disease was New York City. Many experts give scientific reasons why New York City was hit the hardest by this deadly disease, but I believe the answer is spiritual.

By January 21, 2021, the United States led the world in COVID-19 deaths with 407,919. The next closest country was Brazil who had 209,906 deaths. At the time, third place in the world was India where 152,588 people died. The next country was Mexico where 140,740 deaths occurred, with there being no other country in the world with over 100,000 deaths (at that time). By April of 2022, America still led all other nations in deaths with over one million.

In the U.S., the number one state with the most deaths was California, with 89,132. Second was Texas with 87,894 deaths and third was Florida with 73,290. Following was New York with 68,500 deaths.

I'm reminded of what occurred in the state of New York one year prior to the outbreak of the Coronavirus. The former Governor, Andrew Cuomo, signed into law the most aggressive Pro-Abortion Law ever made in the history of our country. It is called the Reproduction Health Law (RHL). It was signed into law on January 22, 2019, the very day of Roe vs. Wade's 46th anniversary. This, of course, was no accident but by arrogant choice. This new RHL law allows women to have an abortion throughout their entire pregnancy term without having to fear any criminal penalty.

On the day that Governor Andrew Cuomo signed this bill into law, he said "In the face of a federal government intent on rolling back Roe vs. Wade and women's reproductive rights, I promised that we would pass this critical legislation within the first 30 days of our new session. Today we are taking a giant step forward in the hard-fought battle to ensure women's rights to make their own decisions about their own personal health, including the ability to access an abortion. With the signing of this bill, we are sending a clear message that whatever happens in Washington, women in New York will always have the fundamental right to control their own body."

In other words, no matter what happens in our country, the former Governor of New York Andrew Cuomo wanted to make sure that New York State continued to be the capital of baby homicides. How incredibly sad, demented and evil is that new law. It should be pointed out that just a few years later, Governor Cuomo resigned from his office due to multiple sexual harassment charges being made against him. I believe God removed him from office.

Now, for all the feel-good preachers out there who do not want to tell people the truth that God still judges sin, I want to be clear that I believe what the Governor signed into Law is what has brought the judgment of God on New York City and New York State and on to the Governor himself. It is true that coronavirus affects every state in our union and the entire world, so in that matter, we are all under God's permissible judgment and chastisement for our sins. However, nowhere in our country did we see the kinds of deaths that New York City saw in the first year of this virus. No other place even came close!

Therefore, we could safely say that New York State, and particularly New York City, was "ground zero" for the onslaught of the coronavirus in this nation. There are many modern preachers who do not believe that the coronavirus is an end-time pestilence or the beginning of birth pang judgments from God but let me give you what the Word of God says so you can connect your own dots.

The Bible says that there are seven things that the Lord hates and that are an "abomination" to Him. The first one is *"A Proud Look"* (Proverbs 6:17).

Back on January 22, 2019, the state senate was cheering when the RHA was signed by Governor Cuomo, as it gave women a more liberal and viable access to murdering innocent babies in the womb. You can see in Governor Cuomo's bold and boastful statement that Washington D.C., the nation's capital from where the President runs the country, was not going to tell New York what to do in terms of abortion (i.e., murder).

Listen to the words of Lieutenant Governor Kathy Hochul (who is the current Governor of New York State following Cuomo's resignation). The same day that Governor Cuomo signed this abortion bill, Hochul said "As keepers of the torch for women's rights that was first ignited in New York State back in 1848, we have a moral responsibility to continue this fight today. Thanks to an election that saw record numbers of women elected to office, I presided over the State Senate, and we finally enacted the Reproduction Health Act to protect the rights of women across our great state. We act today on the anniversary of the groundbreaking decision of Roe vs. Wade and recognize the threat we face from a Supreme Court determined to overturn protections that have been in place for over four decades. Today is a historic day for women in New York, and I'm proud that we are working every day to ensure full equality and safety for women."

I wonder if Lieutenant Governor (now Governor) Hochul understood that her "moral responsibility" (as she called it) would bring the judgment of God on her state and the people? Her bold proclamation that this RHA Law will "ensure full equality and safety for women" would work to the contrary and not only put women in danger but put the whole state of New York in danger of God's judgment.

Another of the seven things listed in Proverbs, Chapter 6 that God hates is "hands that shed innocent blood." (Proverbs 6:17). This pertains to murder and there is no other way to spin the act of abortion other than the murder of an innocent baby, and God says it is "an abomination unto Him." The word "abomination" means disgusting in God's eyes.

God promised in His word, *"Be not deceived; God is not mocked: for whatsoever a man sows; that shall he also reap. For he who sows to the flesh shall of the flesh reap corruption; but he who sows to the Spirit shall of the Spirit reap life everlasting"* (Galatians 6:7-8).

Be assured that God watches the affairs of men and women. When we boldly disobey His Word with no repentance there will be a reaping for that unrepented sin or sins. I'm afraid that New York State and America is reaping what we have sown due to sin of abortion, not to mention a host of many other sins for which there is no repentance.

The most sobering part is that most preachers in the modern church have taught the people that God would never do such a thing, when speaking of judging a country for their repeated sins. But the Bible gives example after example in both the Old and New Testament, that God did and still does judge a person and a nation who repeatedly goes against God's Word with no remorse or idea of repentance. In fact, the Bible teaches that God still judges His own people under the New Covenant and chastens them. The Bible tells us to *"despise not the chastening of the Lord, nor faint when you are rebuked of Him"* (Hebrews 12:5).

GOD PULLS DOWN THE HEDGE

The year 2020, was a year of testing as many people and families endured great trials and tribulations with the Coronavirus. It was a year of great loss of precious loved ones, jobs, retirement funds, possessions, and even our own liberties. This was not necessarily caused by God directly, but He allowed it. If that were not true, then we would have to say that God has no control and every one of us would be dead since Satan's ultimate mission is to kill, steal and destroy (John 10:10).

Regarding Job, Satan returned to the Lord a second time and God again boasted of Job's faith. Satan then said to the Lord, *"if you will let me take his health than he will curse you."* (Job 2:5). God granted the devil permission to go after Job's health, but with the one restriction that he could not take his life (Job 2:6). So, God lowered the hedge of protection in Job's life.

There are many things in this old world that tests a person's faith, but there is nothing that tests us more than when our health fails. This is the greatest test of all. Job became very sick, sustaining open blisters on his skin and He was in great pain. The sores on his body disfigured him and brought him great shame, even to the point of his own wife suggesting he should just curse God and die (Job 2:9).

But Job's faith endured and finally God called Job out of the test. He healed and restored Job and gave him back twice as much as he had lost (Job 42:10). After the test was over, all of Job's relatives and friends came to his house to rejoice over his healing and being blessed again by the Lord.

There is an interesting statement given in Job 42:11, it reads: *"They came there unto him all his brethren, and all his acquaintance before, and did eat bread with him in his house: and they bemoaned him, and comforted him over all the evil that the LORD had brought upon him."*

Notice who the Word of God credits for what Job had gone through. The Bible credits the Lord, even though it was the devil who destroyed Job's health, family, and welfare. However, remember that Satan could not do anything to Job without God lifting the hedge of protection that was around him.

THE SIN OF ABORTION

I believe that God has started to bring down the hedge of protection that has been around America for quite some time, and this is why we see our country going through one of the most devastating times in the history of our nation. Now I believe that there are many reasons for this, but there is none bigger than the sin of abortion.

In the past 47 years, America averages over one million abortions a year, which brings the grand total to over 60 million babies lives ended since 1973. The highest rate of Abortion in our country happens in the District of Columbia, with the rate of 32.7 (this is based on every 1,000 pregnancies of women between the ages of 15-44). New York State has the second highest abortion rate in the nation, which has a rate of 29.6. New Jersey has the third-highest abortion rate of 25.8 and is one of the few states in America that lacks mandatory consent for minors to get abortions through parental notification or a judicial bypass. In addition, this state does not require a waiting period, nor does it prohibit state funding for abortions. (World Population Review, www.worldpopulationreview.com)

The states with the lowest abortion rates are Wyoming with a rate of 1.1, South Dakota with a rate of 3.5, Mississippi with a rate of 3.8 and in Kentucky as being the fourth lowest abortion rate at 4.1.

THE REMOVAL OF THE HEDGE

On March 15, 2019, Kentucky Governor Matt Bevin signed the "Fetal Heartbeat Bill," which was temporarily blocked in court by a federal judge on the same day. Before the Heartbeat Bill, abortions in Kentucky were banned after a 20-week gestation period.

So, let's compare the year 2017 abortion statistics with the Coronavirus Statistics as of May 2020. In 2017, there were 862,320 abortions in the U.S. (taken from the 2017 U.S. Statistics for Abortion- https://www.gutt-macher.org/statecenter/)

State Ranking	No. of Abortions	Abortion Rate per 1000	U.S. Ranking	Coronavirus Deaths	U.S.
New York	105,380	26.3	3	24,874	1
New Jersey	48,110	28.0	2	7,886	2
Mississippi	2,550	4.3	47	303	27
Kentucky	3200	3.8	48	253	36
South Dakota	500	3.1	49	21	41
Wyoming	140	1.3	50	7	49

(Coronavirus statistics as of May 8, 2020 - WorldOmeter.com)

Notice the parallel in the chart that compares the states with high abortion numbers to Coronavirus deaths. I believe the numbers could be connected, especially if you consider what the Word of God says in Joel 3:19, *"Egypt shall be a desolation, and Edom shall a desolate wilderness, for the violence against the children of Judah, because they have shed innocent blood in their land."*

The Bible says, *"for it written, Vengeance is mine; I will repay, saith the Lord"* (Romans 12:19). This speaks of God's wrath, and it means that God is the One who repays people and nations who go against His will.

However, most people today in America and even in the church think that when calamity comes, be it draught, fires, tornados, flooding, pestilence, plague, earthquakes, etc., it is not God who sends it. Instead, people believe that it is just a consequence or "Mother Nature" or it is "Climate Change" causing it. Or in the church they blame the devil most of the time never connecting it to the God judgement because of our sin. But the Word of God teaches that *"If I shut up heaven that there be no rain, or if I command the locusts to devour the land, or if I sent the pestilence among my people; If my people, who are called by My Name, shall humble themselves, and pray, and seek My Face, and turn from their wicked ways;*

then will I hear from Heaven, and will forgive their sin, and will heal their land." (II Chronicles 7:13-14).

My friend, if America never connects the dots of the sin of abortion, same-sex marriage, the removal of prayer from public schools, the pulling down of the 10 Commandments from our public squares, etc., nothing will ever change, and the judgment of God will keep coming until there is nothing left of our nation.

I believe the judgment of God that is behind the Coronavirus calamity and other disasters (i.e., the increase of storms, earthquakes, and economic downfalls) is God trying to open our eyes. Our churches and our Nation need to realize how evil sin is to God and unless we repent, there is no hope for the United States of America.

VALLEY OF SLAUGHTER

The *"valley of slaughter"* referred to is the same valley as Hinnom, where these awful human sacrifices were conducted. As they had made it a *"valley of slaughter"* of children now God would make it a "valley of slaughter," of His Judgment and even on a far greater scale! Jesus plainly said, *"With what measure you mete, it shall be measured to you again."* (Matt. 7:2). (Notes from the JSESB, page 1271).

God told them that the counsel of Judah was going to be void. This spoke of their plan to defeat the Chaldeans (i.e., Babylonians). They were looking to the Egyptians and their alliance to defeat their enemies. Jeremiah 17:5 says, *"Thus says the LORD; Cursed be the man who trusts in man, and makes flesh his arm, and whose heart departs from the LORD."* This is exactly what Judah and Jerusalem were doing, which is what America is doing today. The pride of man says that "I do not need God. I can defend myself without Him. We have the most powerful military in the world." O how foolish sinful mankind is!

Israel was going to be punished for allowing the very torture of children to be burned alive in the fire that worshipped Molech. Such cruelty to children, especially by God's chosen people, (i.e., the Jews) was unthinkable. God said that He was going to make the city desolate for their sin and everyone who passed by would be astonished by its plagues. He said that He would cause them to eat the flesh of their sons and daughters. Their plague would be so bad that when the Babylonians invaded, their food supply would be cut off. In other words, there would be a food shortage and the siege was going to be catastrophic. Man does not realize the seriousness of getting on the wrong side of God and how horrible it can be. Proverbs 1:7

says: *"The fear of the LORD is the beginning of knowledge: but fools despise wisdom and instruction."*

Back to Jeremiah and the clay bottle. He would break it to symbolize the destruction of Judah and Jerusalem that would soon come! God said that He would *"break this people and this city, as one breaks a potter's vessel, that cannot be made whole again."* (Jeremiah 18:11).

The destruction would be so great that God said they would not be able to ever be whole again. There would be so many who would die in the siege that they would not be able to even bury all the dead. The worship of other gods was the cause of this slaughter.

After Jeremiah prophesied in the Valley of Hinnom, he went up to the Temple where people were worshipping Jehovah. However, they were also pouring out drink offerings to other gods. This mixture was an abomination to God and because of the hardening of the people's hearts, Jeremiah's words fell on deaf ears and sadly the nation would have to face the evil that was pronounced against them.

CHAPTER 12

THE WEEPING PROPHET

There are 52 chapters in the book of Jeremiah and over half of these chapters begin with *"The Word of the Lord "* given to Jeremiah and this makes it one of greatest prophetic books in all of the Bible. In Jeremiah, chapter 22, the prophet was told by God to go down to the house of the King of Judah and speak the following words:

> *"Execute you judgment and righteousness, and deliver the spoiled out of the hand of the oppressor: and do no wrong, do no violence to the stranger, the fatherless, nor the widow, neither shed innocent blood in this place."*

The King whom Jeremiah addresses is King Jehoiakim, and the message was simple and to the point. The King was to execute judgment and righteousness in the following way:

- Deliver the spoiled out of the hand of the oppressor.
- Do no violence to the stranger.
- Do no violence to the fatherless.
- Do no violence to the widow.
- Do not shed innocent blood in this place.

If the King did what the Lord said, then all would go well. However, if he did not take heed to the Lord's instructions, the house would become desolate. God told the King that the land is Gilead unto Him and the head of Lebanon meaning it is beautiful; yet if the king did not follow the Lord's instructions, God would make the land a wilderness and their cities would not be inhabited, which is exactly what happened in the land of Israel.

God gave the warning, and it was carried out exactly as it was said to the kings, priests and prophets who were disobeying the Word of the Lord. God said that the other nations shall say of Jerusalem, *"Wherefore has the*

LORD done thus unto this great city?" (Jeremiah 22:8). They questioned why would God do this to His great city? The answer is found in Jeremiah 22:9: *"Because they have forsaken the Covenant of the LORD their God, and worshipped other gods, and served them."* Nothing has really changed in 2600 years.

Today in America, the nation that God birthed in 1776 and blessed like no other nation in the world, is now worshipping other gods. For example, on January 3, 2021, Congress started their 117th new year session in prayer.

That would seem to be a good sign, right? However, a Methodist pastor by the name of Rev. Emanuel Cleaver, ended his prayer with the following words:

> "We ask it in the name of the monotheistic God, Brahma (the Hindu god), and (the) God known by many names, many different faiths." He then concluded by saying "Amen and Awomen."

The United States of America today is a nation who no longer follows the first Commandment, *"You shall have no other gods before Me."* (Exodus 20:3). The same words that God said about Israel He could say about the United States of America today:

> *"Because they have forsaken the Covenant of the LORD their God, and Worshipped other gods and served them"* (Jeremiah 22:9).

The Covenant is the Bible and just as ancient Israel, we in America have forsaken it. The New Covenant which is the Cross of our Lord Jesus Christ. Just as there was no other Covenant in Jeremiah's day, there is no other Covenant today.

In Ancient Israel, the Temple was attacked by King Nebuchadnezzar, and they took the vessels from the Temple and placed them inside the Temple in Babylon (II Chronicles 36:7). No doubt, these vessels included items such as the "golden lampstands," which were put in the temple of the god Baal.

The Bible says that the "rest of the acts of Jehoiakim, and his abominations which he did, and that which was found in him, behold, they are written in the book of the Kings of Israel, and Judah: and Jehoiachin his son reigned in his stead " (II Chronicles 36:8). Notice the term "abominations," this is what God thought of King Jehoiakim's reign.

His son King Zedekiah was only 21 years old when he began his reign and lasted for 11 years in Jerusalem. He was also an evil King and did not humble himself nor listen to Jeremiah (II Chronicles 36:11-12). The Bible says that he rebelled against King Nebuchadnezzar and all the chief priests and the people, *"transgressed very much after all the abominations of the heathen; and polluted the House of the LORD which He had hallowed in Jerusalem"* (II Chronicles 36:14).

This could be called the final indictment of the people of Judah. The Word of God tells us that even the priests practiced abominations. God, in His mercy, sent messengers (i.e., prophets) because He had compassion on His people and on His dwelling place (i.e., Jerusalem). Who were those messengers? Their names are Isaiah, Jeremiah, Ezekiel, and Daniel. However, the people mocked these messengers of God and despised the Lord's words spoken through these prophets. They not only rejected their words, but they mistreated God's prophets. That is until God had enough, and the Wrath of the LORD arose against the people, till there was no turning back (II Chronicles 36:15-16).

When God sent the Babylonians as His judgment arm, the devastation was severe. Here is the description of II Chronicles:

> *"Therefore, he brought upon them the king of the Chaldees, who killed their young men with the sword in the House of their Sanctuary and had no compassion upon their young men or maiden, old man, or him who stooped for age: He (the Lord) gave them all into his hand. And all the Vessels of the House of God, great and small, and the treasures of the king, and of his princes; all these he brought to Babylon. And they burnt the House of God, and broke down the wall of Jerusalem, and burnt all the palaces thereof with fire, and destroyed all the goodly vessels thereof. And them who escaped from the sword carried he away to Babylon; where they were servants to him and his sons until the reign of the kingdom of Persia"* (II Chronicles 36:17-20).

The time of Israel's captivity in Babylon lasted 70 years. The Bible says that all of this was *"to fulfill the mouth of Jeremiah, until the land had enjoyed her Sabbaths: for as long as she lay desolate she kept Sabbath, to fulfill threescore and ten years"* (II Chronicles 36:21).

God prophesied through Jeremiah as follows: *"And I will cast you out, and your mother who bore you, into another country, where you were not born; and there shall you die"* (Jeremiah 22:26). All of this came to pass exactly as Jeremiah said it would. How sad to think that all of the destruction, misery, torture and death could have been avoided if only the leaders of Israel and the people would have listened to the true prophets and repented! Oh, how hard is the heart of sinful man!

THE BOOK OF LAMENTATIONS

Jeremiah, the weeping prophet, also authored the book of Lamentations that begins with the words; *"How does the city sit solitary, that was full of people!"* (Lamentations 1:1)

How could this have ever happened to Jerusalem, the city of God? The people and the nation were judged and the land that once thrived with people and activity now sat quiet and desolate. Recently we have seen what happened to the island Maui, Hawaii where the fires destroyed most of the people's home, many died and most of those who survived lost everything.

The Word of God says,

"She weeps sore in the night, and her tears are on her cheeks: among all her lovers she has none to comfort her: all her friends have dealt treacherously with her, they are become her enemies" (Lamentations 1:2).

How quickly it all changed for Israel. God's judgment was a long time coming; but once it came, it was complete and too late for the nation to change their lot. The weeping prophet who once wept in warning for his nation, now wept for his nation in captivity.

The result of Israel not heeding the prophetic warnings from Jeremiah cost them their freedom, the loss of loved ones and all their possessions and their land. The Word of God declares, *"Wherewith the LORD has afflicted me in the day of His fierce anger"* (Lamentations 1:12).

The question to ask today is not, will God judge America, but when will God judge America? I believe God's hourglass of His patience has been turned over and this nation is running out of time. This should put a chill down every true believer's spine, and it should put a call on every preacher of the Gospel and every born-again believer to weep before God like Jeremiah did. It says, *"For these things I weep; my eye runs down with water, because the comforter that should relieve my soul is far from me: my children are desolate, because the enemy prevail"* (Lamentations 1:16).

When we look around and see all the sickness and death caused by COVID-19, all the violence and destruction on our streets, poverty, homelessness, not to mention the escalated race issues and all the political dishonesty and corruption; and all the storms, floods, fires, etc., this should cause the church to be on their knees weeping before a Holy God.

But what has the church been doing ever since the pandemic and all the financial problems began? Some Christians believe that COVID-19 was just a hoax, or they blame China or the democrats or Bill Gates, George Soros or Dr. Fauci, etc. We are acting no better than the world as the blame game that once started in the Garden of Eden with Adam and Eve continues still today. Man does not like to take ownership for his own sin.

When Adam disobeyed God and ate from the forbidden tree, God confronted him and asked, "who told you that you were naked? *Have you eaten of the tree, whereof I commanded you that you should not eat?"* Adam responded to God and spoke. *"The woman who You gave to be with me, she gave me of the tree." (Genesis 3:11-12).*

Let me ask a simple question to all who are reading this book, has your church started corporate prayer gatherings since the COVID-19 virus broke out? Do you regularly attend prayer gatherings yourself if they exist at all? If your answer to each question is no, then your church and you are not in the right spiritual place. You may not like to hear this but the Word of God says if His people who are called by His Name will humble themselves and pray and seek His Face and repent then God would hear and heal our land (II Chronicles 7:14). The only place to go in times like this is on our knees, to weep for the souls of men and women. Our youth are suffering in many ways and they need our prayers and we must repent of our sins and the nation's sins that has put us in this spiritually dark place.

Our hearts should break for our young people and the world which they have been born into. What a terrible childhood they are experiencing right now, with all the restrictions and cancellations. They had to go to school (if they attend at all) for two years wearing a mask for most of the day. They were not allowed social interaction or only given little opportunity to do so. What kind of a world is that?

Church, do we care? Do we see this moment in American history as very dark? Do we really believe if this nation doesn't come back to the God of the Bible in a hurry, is it only going to get worse? Jeremiah wrote, *"Zion spreads forth her hands, and there is none to comfort her: the LORD has commanded concerning Jacob, that his adversaries should be round about him: Jerusalem is as a menstruous woman among them"* (Lamentations 1:17).

The nation of Israel became unclean, and God judged her. There was no one to comfort her. Do you and I understand that this is soon to be the fate of America if we do not turn back to God in a hurry? Jeremiah said the words that every person should say at this very moment as we experience so much death all around us. He said:

"The LORD is righteous; for I have rebelled against His Commandments: Hear, I pray you, all people, and behold my

sorrow: my virgins and my young Men are gone into captivity" (Lamentations 1:18).

The question I want to ask everyone is "Do we care that our nation is going to hell in a hand basket? Do you and I care that God is going to judge America like He judged ancient Israel if we don't repent?" Jeremiah felt such distress that he said his bowels were troubled and his heart turned inside of him. He said that there was none to comfort him. (Lamentations 1:20-21)

In the Spirit, can you see the trouble that is coming to America and the world? Can you see it, and can you feel it? Jeremiah said, *"The LORD was as an enemy: He has swallowed up all her palaces: He has destroyed His strongholds, and has increased in the daughter of Judah mourning and lamentation"* (Lamentation 2:5).

I don't know which is sadder and more pathetic, having to prepare for what is to come upon America and the world or seeing the incredible apathy found in today's church? How is it that we are not fasting and praying for God's mercy at a time like this?

God spoke through the prophet Joel regarding the time we are living in right now. God said for Joel to tell the people, *"Blow the trumpet in Zion, sanctify a fast, call a solemn assembly: Gather the people, sanctify the congregation, assemble the Elders, gather the children, and those who suck the breasts: let the bridegroom go forth of his chamber, and the bride out of her closet. Let the Priests, the Ministers of the LORD, weep between the porch and the Altar, and let them say, Spare your people, O LORD, and give not Your heritage to reproach, that the heathen should rule over them: wherefore should they say among the people, where is their God?"* (Joel 2:15-17).

It is time for the true church of Jesus Christ to blow the trumpet of warning of the soon wrath and judgment that is coming to the entire world. We are to call a weekly solemn prayer assembly, if not a daily one, and assemble the ministers of the church and all the people. This should include the elderly to the youth, to even the infants, and cry out to God in a broken heart of repentance. We are to cry for one last move of God before the Rapture of the Church.

The problem in America right now is that church ministers refuse to face the fact that we are experiencing the beginning of God's judgment right now. These ministers refuse to deal with the book of Revelation and the book of Daniel. They ignore teachings on the prophetic warnings of Isaiah, Jeremiah, or Ezekiel, to name a few. They want only to continue preaching and teaching about nice things that makes everyone feel good. To be blunt, the church at this present moment is being led mostly by a bunch of spiritual ostriches who are living with their heads in the sand.

Jeremiah declares in Lamentation 2:14, *"Your prophets have seen in vain and foolish things for you: and they have not discovered your iniquity, to turn away your captivity; but have seen for you false burdens and causes of banishment."*

"And they have not discovered your iniquity," means that these false prophets and teachers would not point out Israel's sins; they rather preach what Israel wanted to hear. The words *"false burdens"* refers to false prophecies. Here, the Holy Spirit says that the *"false prophets"* led this parade, which led to spiritual destruction." (JSESB, page 1353).

One must wonder what the final fate of the United States of America will be if we continue down the path we are presently on. The people of Jeremiah's day could not comprehend the destruction that was coming to their nation and the city of Jerusalem. Could it very well be what the people said of ancient Israel will soon be said of America? *"Is this the city that men call the perfection of beauty, the joy of the whole earth?"* (Jeremiah 2:15).

It would be completely foolish for us to think that God would not do to us today what He did with Israel of old because of their continual abominations and idolatries. His Word should ring loud in our ears today for what he said of ancient Israel. *"The LORD has done that which He had devised; He has fulfilled His Word, that He had commanded in the days of old: He has thrown down, and has not pitied: and He has caused your enemy to rejoice over you, He has set the horn of your adversaries"* (Lamentation 2:17).

JUDAH CALLED TO REPENTANCE

Judah erroneously thought that their idols would save them, or the Egyptians would deliver them from the Chaldeans (i.e., Babylonians). The truth is that they were not looking to God, but rather to man for their answers. One could say the same of America today! The Word of the Lord says: *"O Jerusalem, wash your heart from wickedness, that you may be saved. How long shall your vain thoughts lodge within you?"* (Jeremiah 4:14)

God told them that the calamities of Jerusalem was because of their own rebellious ways and their own evil doings. God said, *"this is your wickedness, because it is bitter, because it reaches unto your heart"* (Jeremiah 4:18). All of this would have been avoidable if they had only repented, but they did not.

THE WEEPING PROPHET

Jeremiah is called the weeping prophet due to verses like Jeremiah 4:19 which reads: *"My bowels, my bowels! I am pained at my very heart, my heart makes a noise in me; I cannot hold my peace, because you have heard, O my soul, the sound of the trumpet, the alarm of war."*

This one prophet of God understood and believed in the warnings of God. He proclaimed it to his nation, but it only fell on deaf ears. Jeremiah felt the judgment that was coming to the nation down into his inner-most bowels and felt the pain of destruction that was coming soon. Every true prophet of God is broken for the message that God gives him, particularly when it is a message of judgment.

In Israel one of the uses of the trumpet was to warn that an enemy was coming. I find it interesting that Donald Trump was our president in 2020 when the COVID-19 virus and racial riots invaded our nation. It was as if his last name, "Trump" was trying to warn us that something bad was coming.

When Jesus comes for His bride, there will be the sound of a trumpet, which is referred to as the LAST TRUMP, and the bride of Christ will be lifted off the earth and we will fly away (instantly vanish). Then the wrath of God will be poured out on a world that has rejected God and His Only Son.

In I Thessalonians 4:16-17, the Word of God says, *"For the Lord Himself shall descend from Heaven with a shout, with the voice of the Archangel, and the Trump of God: and the dead in Christ shall rise first: Then we which are alive and remain shall be caught up together with them in the clouds, to meet the Lord in the air: and so shall we ever be with the Lord."*

The Greek word for being *"caught up"* is harpazo, which means, "robbery, to seize, to pluck, to take by force." It means to snatch away suddenly. In essence, the Rapture of the Church is a rescue and the sound of the trumpet will not only be an alert of Jesus's coming to take His bride off of the earth, but it is **THE ALARM OF WAR**. Very soon after the Rapture of the Church the Judgment of God is going to begin.

I heard a prominent leader in Buffalo, New York the other day say something that grieved and even shocked me to hear someone who is responsible for leading many other pastors from the greater Buffalo area make such a foolish statement. She said: "The teaching of the Pre-Tribulation Rapture is nothing more than escapism." She went on to say that this teaching only came out about 200 years ago and it causes believers to stay in the four walls of the church and wait for the Rapture. She even went so far as to say she and her church would never sing the famous hymn "I'll fly away."

Well first, let me say there could be nothing more ignorant for a preacher or ministry leader to say than this. I would probably gather that this individual and her church are probably reaching very few souls for Christ. Secondly, the pretribulation Rapture doctrine is 2,000 years old. She was just missing a zero. And that doctrine is called the "Blessed Hope" (Titus 2:13) and is in fact the next event on God's prophetic calendar. In other words, He is coming soon friend to rescue His Bride from the Judgment of God that is about to be poured out on this old sin soaked world. The Rapture of the Church is a rescue, it is God's rescue. You can mock it, persecuted and deny it, but my Bible says: *"Watch ye therefore, and pray always, that you may be accounted worthy to escape all these things that shall come to pass"* (Luke 21:36). These are the Word of Jesus Christ!

Jeremiah could hear in his spirit the battle and literal screams of the people, and it pained him to the core of his being. He was such a true prophet or preacher of the Lord. He said:

> *"Destruction upon destruction is cried; for the whole land is spoiled: suddenly are my tents spoiled, and my curtains in a moment"* (Jeremiah 4:20).

The prophet saw such devastation in his spirit and knew that what was coming was going to be horrific. It was all going to be so terrible that it was without description. The Babylonians would go from house to house in their invasion, and they were going to do a complete destruction of the land. The people were very clever in doing evil, but very ignorant in doing good and discerning the judgment that was coming. Their lack of knowledge was due to their abandonment of the Word of God. The knowledge to do good is found in the Word of God and only found in the Word of God.

America is in the same position today as Israel was long ago; they do not even know when they hear the Word of God because they do not study their Bibles. Ancient Israel was God's chosen people, but they did not know the Word of God. We could make the same case for most of the modern church goers in America. In His Word, God said that His people die for lack of knowledge, and they reject knowledge. (Hosea 4:6).

WAR IS COMING

The whole city will flee for the noise of the horsemen and bowmen.

They shall go into the thickets and climb up upon the rocks.

Every city shall be forsaken and not a man will dwell therein (this speaks of Jerusalem).

What a sobering vision! No wonder Jeremiah's bowels pained him. None will come to help the Jews, God said, *"your lovers will despise you, they will seek your life"* (Jeremiah 4:30).

In this description, Jeremiah said that he heard a voice of a woman in travail, bringing forth her firstborn child in birth. The woman refers to Jerusalem who weeps over her destruction and the slaughter of her inhabitants. The Holy Spirit likens it to *"birth pangs,"* but in reality, it is "death pains." Her cry is *"woe is me now!"* How sad when you think of all the death and destruction that was avoidable if only the nation would have repented and turned back to the one true God. How incredibly wicked and stubborn is the heart of sinful man!

Let us all take example from Jeremiah, the infamous weeping prophet who cared so much for his people and his land that he shed tears that ran down his face like rivers of waters. We should be so broken for what breaks the heart of God. The church today needs some weeping intercessors and some weeping prophets and prophetesses and some weeping pastors.

> *"Fear and a snare is come upon us, desolate and destruction. My eye runs down with rivers of water for the destruction of the daughter of My people. My eye trickles down, and ceases not, without any intermission, till the LORD looks down, and behold from heaven. My eye affects my heart because of all the daughters of my city. My enemies chased me sore, like a bird without cause. They have cut off my life in the dungeon, and cast a stone upon me. Waters flowed over my head; then I said, I am cut off. I called upon Your Name, O LORD, out of the low dungeon. You have heard my voice: hide not Your ear at my breathing, at my cry. You drew near in the day that I called upon You: You said, Fear not."*
> (Lamentations 3:47-57).

CHAPTER 13

BARABBAS OR JESUS ....WHOM DO YOU WANT?

Even though today in America the President is seen mostly as a secular king and not a spiritual king, the truth is God did not see it that way with Israel, and I don't think He sees it that way now. The President of the United States should not get a pass for not being spiritual. He may not be your pastor, but He is the leader of the most powerful nation in the world. And Jesus said, *"To whom much is given, much is required."*

The Lord said that neither King Zedekiah, nor his servants, nor the people of the land did hearken unto the Words of the LORD, which He spoke by the prophet Jeremiah (Jeremiah 37:2). King Zedekiah and his cabinet ministers, like many today, were willing that God's Servants should pray for them (Jeremiah 37:3), but determined to continue to disobey the Word of the LORD. The Holy Spirit is emphatic that basically the entirety of the land of Judah would not heed Jeremiah. (JSESB page 1312).

Jeremiah was given access to the leaders until he was put into prison. So, if he had told the kings what they wanted to hear, he would have continued to be accepted, but when he spoke "thus saith the LORD" and it wasn't what the leaders wanted to hear, they eventually threw him into a prison. It has not changed much today!

Former President Donald Trump, while in office, set up a pastoral task force that he met with and prayed with during his presidential term in office. They were invited to meetings at the White House. They exchanged calls, texts, and emails with administration staffers. And they occasionally prayed with the former President. Now this would seem to be a very positive thing, right? But not if those who had access were not the right voices.

Here's a list of some of the key evangelical leaders — mostly men, and one woman — who were on President Donald Trump's hand-selected evangelical executive advisory board and/or served in an advisory role from his inauguration up until the end of his presidency. Now the naming of these leaders is not meant to condemn these particular leaders or their ministries but only to raise the question, where were these men and women when President Trump was acting in a very unscriptural manner and taking our country in the direction that did not line up with the Word of God? My question is did they try to warn him? And if they did, why did they stay on his advisory team when president Trump didn't listen to them, and why did they continue to praise him?

The President's Pastoral Advisory
consisted of the following people:

- Gary Bauer — president, American Values; former president of Family Research Council; former chief domestic policy adviser in the Reagan Administration.

- Mark Burns — co-founder and CEO of The NOW Television Network in Easley, SC; spoke at the 2016 Republican National Convention

- Tim Clinton — president, American Association of Christian Counselors

- James Dobson — author, psychologist, and host, Family Talk

- Jordan Easley — pastor of Englewood Baptist Church in Jackson, TN; chairs Southern Baptists' Young Leaders Advisory Council

- Jerry Falwell Jr. — president, Liberty University in Lynchburg, VA

- Ronnie Floyd — author and senior pastor, Cross Church northwest Arkansas; former Southern Baptist Convention president

- Jack Graham— author and pastor of Prestonwood Baptist Church in Plano, TX; former Southern Baptist Convention president

- Rodney Howard-Browne — co-founder of The River at Tampa Bay Church and Revival Ministries International in Florida

- Harry Jackson — senior pastor, Hope Christian Church in Beltsville, MD; co-founder of The Reconciled Church: Healing the Racial Divide

- Robert Jeffress — senior pastor, First Baptist Church of Dallas; hosted Fourth of July event at Kennedy Center featuring Trump as a speaker.

- Richard Land — president, Southern Evangelical Seminary in Matthews, NC; former president, Southern Baptist Convention Ethics and Religious Liberty Commission

- Greg Laurie — author and senior pastor of Harvest Christian Fellowship in Riverside, CA

- Eric Metaxas — author and host, The Eric Metaxas Show; speaker, 2012 National Prayer Breakfast.

- Johnnie Moore — author, religious freedom advocate and public relations executive; serves as unofficial spokesman for group of evangelicals who advised Trump administration.

- Frank Page — president and CEO, Southern Baptist Convention Executive Committee; former Southern Baptist Convention president; former member of President Obama's Advisory Council on Faith-based and Neighborhood Partnerships

- Tony Perkins — president, Family Research Council

- Ralph Reed — founder, Faith, and Freedom Coalition; former executive director, Christian Coalition

- Tony Suarez — executive vice president, National Hispanic Christian Leadership Conference

- Paula White — senior pastor, New Destiny Christian Center in Apopka, FL; first clergywoman to give an invocation at an inauguration. She was called by President Trump as his pastor. She was actually given an office in the Whitehouse!

I wonder what these men and woman were saying to President Trump when on January 28, 2020, President Trump held a press conference with Israeli Prime Minister Benjamin Netanyahu announcing a Peace Plan for Israel and the Palestinians that was officially entitled *Peace to Prosperity*, a Vision to improve the Lives of the Palestinian and Israeli People. President

Trump referred to it as the "Peace Deal of the Century." However, it violated Genesis 12:3, as it cursed Israel by restricting land settlements that goes against the Word of God. Whenever America has put pressure on Israel to give up land for peace, we always have paid a high price in our homeland. I wish every future president would learn this one simple truth.

In February 2020, it was President Trump who elected the first LGBTQ person to a cabinet position. Richard Grenell became the acting director of National Intelligence. This decision violated Leviticus 21:13, and Romans 1:26-28, and God promised that when a nation goes down this path of immorality, He will turn them over to a reprobate mind.

Then we saw on May 7, 2020- President Trump and Vice President Pence led an inter-faith prayer gathering of spiritual leaders from five different faiths, in the Rose Garden on the National Day of Prayer. This prayer gathering that occurred right in front of the White House violated Exodus 20:3, which says, *"You shall have no other gods before me."* Where was President Trump's Pastoral Advisory team on that day? Then if it couldn't get any worse on January 6, 2021, President Trump called for and planed a rally for his supporters to come to Washington D.C., three hours before Congress met to confirm the Electoral College vote of the Election. He told them before the date of the rally that it was going to be "wild." Then on the day of the rally, those words became prophetic. After the rally, a riot broke out at the Capitol Building as some of the Trump supporters stormed the Capitol forcing their way through security and into the building. Five people died as a result of that assault of the Capital grounds and hundreds of arrests were made that day, and the weeks and months that followed. President Trump was accused of inspiring an insurrection. This was followed with the House of Representatives impeaching the president.

The question must be asked, where were the men and women of the President's Pastoral Advisory team? How come we never heard from any of them on any of these issues? One of the few to speak out against the January 6th riot on the Capitol was Pastor Jeffries who condemned the violence. However, Pastor Jeffries has kept his support for Donald Trump even up to the date of this book's publication.

Just like in Jeremiah's day, the kings did not have the right spiritual men around them. They did not listen to the one true prophet Jeremiah but chose to listen to the "wrong voices" who continued to tell them what they wanted to hear.

THE CHALDEANS DEPART JERUSALEM; THEY WILL RETURN

Before the final Babylonian invasion, the army of Egypt assisted Judah and caused the Chaldeans to retreat. This caused ridicule to the prophet Jeremiah as it appeared his prophecy to be false concerning the Babylonians destroying Judah. It also appeared that the false prophets were right in their predictions concerning the salvation of Jerusalem. Jeremiah had constantly prophesied that no help from Egypt was going to prevent the coming destruction and that Judah and Jerusalem would not be spared. For a short time, it looked like Jeremiah was wrong as Egypt did help Israel.

But then the scriptures tell us that God spoke to the prophet Jeremiah. The Word of God reads: *"Then came the Word of the LORD unto the prophet Jeremiah, saying: Thus says the LORD, the God of Israel; Thus, shall you say to the king of Judah, who sent you unto Me to enquire of Me; Behold, Pharaoh's army, which is come forth to help you, shall return to Egypt into their own land. And the Chaldeans shall come again, and fight against this city, and take it, and burn it with fire. Thus says the LORD; Deceive not yourselves, saying, The Chaldeans shall surely depart from us: for they shall not depart"* (Jeremiah 37:6-9).

God was reassuring Jeremiah that what God said was still going to happen. One thing I have learned in my walk with God is, if God said it, you can be assured that it will come to pass. He was giving the King of Judah a clear warning and understanding of what was still to come. God was telling Israel that the Chaldeans were going to return and destroy the Temple and burn the city of Jerusalem.

JEREMIAH ARRESTED AND ACCUSED

After the Chaldeans were broken up from Jerusalem for fear of Pharaoh's army, Jeremiah went forth out of Jerusalem to go into the land of Benjamin (verse 11-12). No doubt Jeremiah was fleeing to separate himself from the persecution he was receiving from the people.

But Jeremiah was captured by Irijah, the grandson of Hananiah the false prophet. He falsely accused Jeremiah of defecting to the Chaldeans. Jeremiah said, *"it is false;"* however, Irijah did not listen to him and had Jeremiah arrested and brought to the princes (Jeremiah 37:14).

The princes were wroth with Jeremiah, and they smote him and put him in prison. The crime that they charged him with was being a traitor. Jeremiah remained in that prison for many days. The word used here for prison is "dungeon," which refers to an underground excavation, with the word "cabins" possibly referring to particular vaults or cells underground in this place.

After many days, the King of Judah took Jeremiah out of prison and secretly asked him if he had a Word from the LORD. Jeremiah said that he did, and he told him that the Lord had told him that the king was going to be delivered into the hand of King Nebuchadnezzar. This took great courage for Jeremiah to speak these words to the King, knowing he had control over his prison time. A true prophet of God must possess tremendous courage to deliver the Word from the Lord when they are clearly not popular as is warning of the judgment of God to come never is.

Jeremiah asked the prophet why he had been offended by his Words to put him in prison? He asked the King where his prophets were who prophesied unto him that the king of Babylon shall not invade the land? In essence, Jeremiah was saying that those are the "true false prophets" that deserved to be locked up (Jeremiah 37:18-19).

Jeremiah, in his humanity, pleads with the king to not put him back into the dungeon. But his plea failed as King Zedekiah returned Jeremiah to the dungeon. This is where Jeremiah would remain until the Babylonians laid siege to the city of Jerusalem.

BARABBAS OR JESUS

> *"But Pilate answered them, saying Will you that I release unto you the King of the Jews? But the Chief Priests moved the people, that he should rather release Barabbas unto them"*
> (Mark 15:9, 11).

Pontius Pilate, the governor of Rome over Judah, knew that Jesus was an innocent man and did not want to have Jesus crucified; but the religious leaders of Jerusalem demanded it. How could the so-called spiritual leaders of Israel be so blind? How did they get it so incredibly wrong that they literally cried out to Pilate, *"His blood be on us, and on our children?"* (Matthew 27:25).

It was this final cry of the Jewish people, led by the religious leaders, that caused Pilate to release Barabbas (a notorious prisoner) and have Jesus, the King of the world, scourged and crucified instead (Matthew 27:26). It is almost unthinkable how the Jewish leaders could be so oblivious to the truth. Let's examine closer how anybody, much less the spiritual leaders of Israel, could be so deceived and caught up in the Greatest Deception of all time.

The Romans had a custom that allowed the governor (i.e., Pilate at this time) to perform a "Passover Pardon" every year at the Feast of the Passover. This allowed the governor to release one Jewish prisoner, which was another feeble attempt by Rome to keep the Jewish people somewhat in check.

Pilate, who did not want anything to do with Jesus of Nazareth, presented to the Jewish people what he felt was a slam-dunk decision whereby Jesus would be pardoned due to the awful reputation of Barabbas. This man Barabbas was in prison because of murder.

The name Barabbas means "Son of the father" (bar abba) or "son of the teacher" (bar rabban), indicating that perhaps his father may have been a Jewish leader. It is believed that Barabbas's full name was in fact "Jesus Barabbas" and this name was found in the original text of Matthew's gospel, but later removed by the translators due to the feeling that it was not right to use the holy name of Jesus accompanied with such an evil man.

The name "Jesus" was a common first name for Jewish males in the time of Christ. That is why Jesus Christ was known as "Jesus of Nazareth" because the village of Nazareth was a small remote town that only had an estimated population of about 500 people in it during the time of Christ. So, Jesus was most likely the only Jesus from His hometown of Nazareth and when someone said Jesus of Nazareth, everyone knew exactly whom they were referring to. If Barabbas was indeed "Jesus Barabbas," how even more interesting does this governmental pardon become. The crowd was presented with two men, and they would have to decide which Jesus they wanted to set free and which Jesus they wanted executed. In a profound way, this was not only a decision Israel had to make almost 2,000 years ago, but it is a decision that the church still must make today.

Jesus Barabbas was a man who wanted to overthrow Rome. The oppressive evil workings of the government of Rome were just too much for him to bear. He was not going to just sit back and let these ruthless leaders dictate to the people of God on how they were going to live. He was going to rise up and fight back and try by every means possible to stop the ruthless evil-spirited system of Caesar to prevail against God's people. You could label Barabbas as a zealot, a "freedom fighter," or a "nationalist."

However, the Word of God called him a *"notorious prisoner"* who was in prison with other rebels who had committed acts of insurrection against the occupying Roman forces (Mark 15:7, Luke 23:19). The man Barabbas was part of the revolt, rebellion, or resistance against Rome. He was a rebel against civil authority or an established government. He was what the Bible called an "insurrectionist." The Greek word is "Stasis," which means a standing position, a division, or separation. It speaks of a popular uprising, controversy, dissention, or uproar. It is one who creates controversy with the idea of violence threatened.

Barabbas was involved in a riot, and probably one of the numerous insurrections against the Roman power and he had committed murder which he was in prison for. In the Gospel of John, it calls Barabbas a "robber" which in the Greek means he was a "bandit." This word is used by the Jewish historian Josephus always when talking about "Revolutionaries."

Barabbas lived during a time when the independent Jewish state established by the Hasmonean dynasty, had been ended by the unrivaled power of the Roman Empire. The Hasmoneans themselves had been considered corrupt by strict religious Jews, but puppet kings such as Herod the Great, who ruled on Rome's behalf, created an atmosphere of widespread resentment.

The two mainstream religious parties, the Sadducees and the Pharisees, came to represent opposing ideas; with the Sadducees generally controlling the Temple priesthood and the Pharisees appealing to a more popular piety. Consequently, the Sadducees came to be seen as Roman collaborators, while the Pharisees were divided in their attitude toward Roman rule. (The Pharisees, Sadducees, Essenes, and the Zealots https://hellerhigh.org/). During this time there were what was called "Jewish Zealots", a group of passionate Jews who were in opposition to Rome, willing to use violence against these foreign oppressors to hasten the coming of the Messiah. They believed that the Messiah, when He came, would provide liberation for the Jews from the evil Roman Empire.

Most of the Zealots led violent revolts to overthrow the Roman rule. There was another group known as the "Essenes" who were prepared for the day when the corrupt Temple priesthood would be replaced by their own purified priests and the Day of the Lord would bring about not only the kingly Davidic Messiah, but also the priestly Messiah, the Son of Aaron.

The Zealots were a political movement that sought to incite the people of Judah to rebel against the Roman Empire and to expel them from the Holy Land by force and they attempted to do that during first Jewish -Roman War (66 A.D.- 70 A.D.).

In the time of Jesus, Rome no longer ruled Judah through a client king, but directly through a Roman governor and of course this was none other than Pontius Pilate who ruled as governor from 26 A.D. to 36 A.D.

There was concern among the Jewish Sanhedrin (i.e., religious leaders) that messianic movements would create a serious threat to Rome, and they would in turn clamp down further on Jewish autonomy. In other words, the religious leaders of Jesus' day were more concerned with their freedoms, then they were about spiritual freedom which only the Messiah Jesus could give them.

Jesus went into the Temple and overturned the tables of the money-changers and said, *"It is written, My house shall be called the house of prayer; but you have made it a den of thieves"* (Matthew 21:13). It was considered in the minds of the Jewish Sanhedrin that this was an act of treason. This prompted the high priest's party to move against Jesus, bribing one of his disciples to betray him and arresting him at night in the Garden of Gethsemane. After a late-night religious leaders meeting at the home of Caiaphas' father-in-law, it was decided to hand Jesus over to Rome (John 18:13).

THE SPIRIT OF BARABBAS IS ALIVE IN 2020

The spirit of Barabbas is alive again in America and at no time did we see it more on display in our nation then in 2020. Today it just goes by different names than it did in Israel during the day of Christ. They are not called zealots today, but they are called "patriots" and they use movies like Braveheart as their inspiration. It should be of no surprise when the world fights governmental authorities and rebels against oppressive government restrictions; however, when it is the church leading the charge or joining in, we should be more concerned.

Nowhere in the New Testament did Jesus teach His followers to revolt and fight against Rome. In fact, this is what agitated many of the Jewish leaders and people because they wanted Jesus to fight. On one occasion, the Pharisees tried to entangle or trap Jesus on the issue of obeying government.

They said to Him, *"What do you think? Is it lawful to give tribute unto Caesar, or not?"* (Matthew 22:17). This was a trick question because if Jesus answered "Yes," He would be in essence denying His claim as Messiah, the King of Israel. But if He answered "No," this would put Him in opposition to human government and in violation to the Word of God.

God's Word teaches, *"Let every soul be subject unto the higher powers (i.e., Human Government). For there is no power but of God: the powers that be are ordained of God. Whosoever therefore resists the power, resists the Ordinance of God: and they who resist shall receive to themselves damnation"* (Romans 13:1-2).

God's Word even calls government a *"minister of God,"* a revenger to execute wrath upon him who does evil" (Romans 13:4). So, this movement towards "defund the police" and overthrow the government is not only of a Barabbas spirit, but it directly violates the Word of God.

The Word of God teaches it is God who ordains human government, and it is set up by God to regulate the affairs of men. When a people rebel against human government, the result is always anarchy. Therefore, every Christian should respect Civil Government and always obey the law of the land providing it does not go against the Word of God. The Word says, *"Will you not be afraid of the power? Do that which is good, and you shall have praise of the same: For he is the minister of God to you for good. But if you do that which is evil, be afraid; for he bears not the sword in vain: for his is a minister of God, a revenger to execute wrath upon him who does evil. Wherefore you must needs be subject, not only for wrath, but also for conscience's sake"* (Romans 13:3-5).

There should be a fear whenever one breaks the law assuming that the Law is right and good. God has given the state the right to enforce laws with force to stop evil, i.e., crime. They are even given authority by God to the point of using capital punishment. So, make no doubt that Christians are subject to the laws of the land.

How would Jesus respond to the Pharisees where He would not deny His Messianic person and at the same time not violate the Word of God? His answer to them was, *"Why tempt you Me, you hypocrites? Show Me the tribute money. And they brought unto Him a penny. And He said unto them, whose is this image and superscription? They say unto Him, Caesar's. Then said He unto them, Render therefore unto Caesar the things which are Caesar's and unto God the things that are God's"* (Matthew 22:18-21).

Jesus recognized and supported human government, and His example shows us there is a way to support government without violating the ways of God and thus we should endeavor to do that. But today in America, there is a move among evangelicals to fight against the liberal left who are in government and stand up against them.

I understand that America is changing and not for the better. The sins of this nation have gone on for far too long, and I believe that the Lord is turning this nation over to a reprobate mind, if He hasn't already done so. I'm afraid that in the next several years, we are going to see a lot of things not sitting well with the freedoms that we have enjoyed as Christians in this nation. But the question to be asked is, "what are we to do in times like these?"

TURN TO JESUS AND FOLLOW WHAT HE TAUGHT

It has been said that the greatest sermon ever preached was the Sermon on the Mount, which is recorded in Matthew's Gospel, chapters five to seven. I want to present just six "Golden Rules" taught by Jesus in this sermon that teaches us how to live in times like these.

- First, we are to be Salt and Light- We are to preserve society by our lifestyle, and we are to shine the light of the Jesus into a dark world (Matthew 5:13-16).

- We are not to be led by Anger- If we are angry and hate our brother, it is as if we murdered them (Matthew 5:21-22).

- We are not to live by Retaliation- We are not to live by an *"eye for eye or a tooth for a tooth"* (Matthew 5:38-41).

- We are to live by the Law of Love- We are to love unconditionally, even our enemies (Matthew 5:43-48).

- We are not to Judge others- If we judge (i.e., condemn the sinner), then we too will be judged (Matthew 7:1-2).

- We are to live by the Golden Rule- To do unto others as we would want them to do unto us (Matthew 7:12).

The spirit of Barabbas says to fight for your freedoms, but Jesus says to love your enemies and be a peacemaker. The Barabbas spirit says that if you don't fight for your nation, then you're going to lose it. If you do not resist evil, then they are going to take away all your freedoms.

Jesus said,

> *"That you resist not evil: but whosoever shall smite thee on your right cheek, turn to him the other also. And if any man will sue you at the law and take away your coat, let him have your cloak also. And whosoever shall compel you to go a mile, go with him two"* (Matthew 5:39-41).

It has been said that Jesus was the greatest revolutionary who ever lived, and you can see why. I mean the spirit of this world says that if someone tries to sue you, then get the best lawyer you can and sue them back (i.e., countersue them). But Jesus said whatever they are trying to get from you in the suit, materially speaking, not only are you to give it to them, but give them more on top of it.

How does a modern-day believer rationalize this teaching in a land (USA) where materialism is everything? One way you must repent and stop trying to protect and fight for your rights and surrender to Jesus and live for the lives of others. I know this is hard to hear, but I'm not the one who said it; it came from Jesus Himself. The modern Evangelical movement in America has to decide which spirit they want to follow, Barabbas or Jesus? Do they want to lead an insurrection against the government, or do they want to be a part of a spiritual revolution, where men and women are brought to Jesus?

Now that doesn't mean we shouldn't support political groups that are fighting to keep the freedoms that our nation was founded on. However, that doesn't mean we are to violate the Words of Jesus in doing so.

PRO-LIFE MOVEMENT IN BUFFALO

When I first went into the ministry, there was a movement in Buffalo, New York (my hometown) called the "Pro-Life" movement. It was a national movement across the country where Christians rose up to resist the law of abortion and it attempted to overturn Roe vs. Wade in order to save the lives of babies who were being given no chance to live.

Ministers in the Buffalo, New York, area headed up the charge to try to overturn the abortion law in our nation. It was national news as ministers in Buffalo were being arrested and sent to jail for blocking abortion clinics in order to try to prevent women from entering the facilities to have their abortions.

I would travel down to the abortion clinics and see hundreds of people gathered in front of these clinics, both from the Pro-Life side and the Pro-Choice side. The anger and hostility was clear for all to witness. Hundreds of Christians standing for life and praying, some holding signs to condemn the abortionists. The Pro-Choice advocates were very angry at the Pro-Life demonstrators, and it was only by the grace of God and the police presence that kept the situation from turning into a complete all-out riot.

One day while I was there outside a clinic in Buffalo, I saw a Pro-Choice man who had interlocked arms with other Pro-Choice advocates, blocking the way for Pro-Life people to get close to the abortion clinic. This man started pointing me out in the crowd and he started to persecute me by yelling profanities at me. I was not very far from where the man was standing, and he was relentless with his insults towards me. I then approached the man and began to speak personally to him. He said to me in a profane way, "You're a hypocrite." I asked the man why he felt that way towards me as I was not yelling or even responding back to his obscenities. He said, "If I were you and I really believed abortion was murder, and I don't, I would be down here 24-hours a day, seven days a week trying to save lives." Then he repeated his accusation again, "So, you are a hypocrite." I then said these words to this angry man. I said, "Sir, that is the reason I am here, because I feel so convicted about my inaction towards this issue. I do believe abortion is murder and I am feeling convicted that I am not doing enough to help save the babies; but you see, I am a husband and I have a family, and I have to go to work every day to support them. But I am here today because I do feel like a hypocrite and want to ask God to forgive me." (this is a paraphrase of what I said that day)

    I will never forget what the man did next. He let go of the interlocking grips he had with the person on his right and left. And he then walked up to me and said he had not met anyone like me from the Pro-Life movement. He said they all want to condemn us as baby killers and how God is going to judge us and send us all to hell if we don't repent (as I remember it).

    Then that man and I walked away from the crowd that was around the clinic to move to a quieter place. I remember sharing the Gospel of Jesus Christ with him. I remember telling him the story of Josh McDowell and how he was an atheist and started out to try to disprove the Bible, but then after many months of research, realized the Bible was in fact true and he made the decision to become a Born-Again Christian. I told the man that He authored the book, "More Than a Carpenter" and in that book, Josh McDowell shares how he became convinced Jesus was truly the Son of God. I encouraged the man to purchase a copy of that book.

    That day I became friends with someone who an hour earlier hated my guts. He did not become a Christian that day, but I felt that he did move a step closer to the Savior. The greatest memory I have of that moment is watching the man who had cussed me out, now was shaking my hand and telling me he had not met a Christian like me ever before. He then walked to his car, and he drove home. His protest was over! On that day I learned one of the most important lessons we can ever learn as a Christian as it pertains to reaching this lost world for Christ. First, we must not condemn the sinner. Remember when the Scribes and Pharisees (the religious leaders) brought the woman caught in adultery to Jesus. They said to Jesus, "Master, this woman was taken in adultery, in the very act. Now Moses in the Law commanded us, that such should be stoned: but what do you say" (John 8:4-5)? Jesus responded with these Words, "He who is without sin among you, let him first cast a stone at her" (John 8:7). The Bible says that when they heard Jesus say this, they were convicted by their own conscience. They all put down their stones and went home. Their protest was over!

What I see happening more and more in the evangelical churches is that we keep picking up the stones and hurling them at people, i.e., the liberal left. We want to condemn them and call them wicked and evil. Let me ask you a question: "If you were unsaved and not a believer and someone from the church kept calling you evil and wicked, do you think you would ever step foot into their churches or even want to hear what they have to say about Jesus?"

Paul said,

> "To the weak became I as weak, that I might gain the weak: I am made all things to all men, that I might by all means saved some" (I Corinthians 9:22).

I have some advice for the evangelical world, stop listening to people night after night over Television or your YouTube channels or spending hours and hours on social media with people who want to condemn others. Instead, open your Bibles and start listening to Jesus who told us to love our enemies and pray for them.

Former President Donald Trump was a man who stood for good policies and was sensitive to Christian concerns and values, but his own personal character was lacking. He ridiculed and dishonored those who did not agree with him, and most of the church laughed at it and loved it and most of us got all caught up in it (me included). Then the Church started doing it themselves, and before long they got caught up in the Make America Great Again (MAGA) movement instead of a movement of loving and not judging our enemies. The church got duped and most do not want to admit it and repent of it. Some even get angry at you when you point it out to them, which ought to tell you something right there.

We should point out that the word "MAGA" in Latin means "witch" which ought to tell you something right there. The Church of Jesus Christ must be careful that they are not "bewitched" by false doctrine or by following false movements that are not Biblical and are not of the Holy Spirit.

Even after January 6th, when it became crystal clear, what spirit was working at the Capitol riot that day, many evangelicals in this country still will not get off the "Trump Train."

January 6th was called an "Insurrection." Why can't many in the church see that it is not the Spirit of Christ? I personally think it is mainly because of our pride. We have trouble admitting when we are wrong and have shown poor judgment. But if we will humble ourselves and compare the current spirit in the church to that of Christ, we will then have to admit we are not operating in the spirit of Christ. I have had to repent of this myself.

But to those in the church who want to continue to fight in this movement, and continue to be loyal to Donald Trump, let me just challenge you in one area. Try to find one scripture in the Gospel where Jesus Christ condemns the government of Rome or spoke against Caesar. Go ahead, search the scriptures. Let me save you the time. Guess what; you will not find it! In fact, you will only find one verse where Jesus even mentioned Caesar, the evil god that the people worshiped. He said, *"Render to Caesar the things that are Caesar's, and to God the things that are God's"* (Mark 12:17).

Jesus of Nazareth is the role model of how we are to treat others. If He did not condemn Caesar or the Roman government, why are so many in the church condemning our government? Do you think our government has more evil in it than that of Rome? I don't think so! Let us repent and begin to follow the master's example because, He will be the only one to whom we are going to have to answer to one day.

Don't forget the slogan, WWJD, What Would Jesus Do? Ask yourself the question today, would Jesus protest the government, applaud, and cheer when a man uses obscenities and crude remarks regarding a person looks or their character? Or would Jesus preach the Gospel to the poor, feed the hungry, heal the sick, and stand against the hypocrisies in the Church? I think you know the answer to those questions, it is the latter and not the former.

So, it is time for the Church to repent of the Great Deception and instead of standing behind the "Make America Great Again" (MAGA) movement, let's start standing for our own movement "Make America Good Again." Only Jesus is Good and only He can help us to achieve this!

CHAPTER 14

ISRAEL'S GLORIOUS FUTURE

God tells Jeremiah to *"write you all the words that I have spoken unto you in a Book"* (Jeremiah 30:2). Of course, because Jeremiah was obedient to that command of the Lord, we have the great book of Jeremiah in our possession as one of the 66 books of the Holy Canon. Glory To God!

God gave Jeremiah the promise that He would bring His people out of captivity in Babylon and bring them back into the land of Israel. He said he would one day return to them what He gave to their fathers. While this would be done partially after their captivity in Babylon ended, its total fulfillment awaits them in the Kingdom Age.

I believe America is about to be judged if it does not turn back to the God of the Bible and follow Him as our forefathers once did. Let me ask the question, at this late hour, is it possible for America to turn back? I will answer that question without a national revival I don't think it will ever come back.

THE GREAT TRIBULATION

The Lord spoke through the Prophet that *"We have heard a voice of trembling, of fear, and not of peace"* (Jeremiah 30:5). During the Great Tribulation, Israel will be fooled into believing that the "Son of Perdition" (i.e., the Antichrist) is their Messiah. He will come onto the world stage with all power and signs and lying wonders to deceive the whole world, even the elect (II Thessalonians 2:9). Israel will believe that he is their knight in shining armor, their prince. However, at the mid-point of the Tribulation, their eyes will be opened as to who he really is.

They will see that he is Hamon, Herod, and Hitler all rolled into one. In other words, their worst nightmare. When the people understand who he really is, they will then run to the hills to try to escape him and his armies

(II Thessalonians 2:3-11, Revelation 6:1-2, Matthew 24:15-20).

It will be so bad for Israel at that time that God said, through the prophet Jeremiah, *"Ask you now, and see whether a man does travail with child? Wherefore do I see every man with his hands on his loins, as a woman in travail, and all faces are turned into paleness?"* (Jeremiah 30:6). In that day, Israel will know that they have been deceived and they will be faced with what looks like total annihilation. God said: *"Alas! For that day is great, so that none is like it: it is even the time of Jacob's trouble; but he shall be saved out of it"* (Jeremiah 30:7).

The time of horror for the Jews and the nation of Israel is just ahead. In fact, everything that we see happening in our world today is rushing towards that time. It is called "Jacob's Trouble" for a reason. Remember that in the Bible Jacob, the son of Isaac and grandson of Abraham, had his name changed by God to "Israel" (Genesis 32:28). From the loins of Jacob came twelve sons who became the twelve Tribes of Israel (Revelation 7:4-8).

Jacob's Trouble could also be called "Israel's Trouble," and this refers to the last three and one-half years of the Tribulation. Jesus said of this time, *"For then shall be great tribulation, such as was not since the beginning of the world to this time, no, nor ever shall be"* (Matthew 24:21).

THE REGATHERING OF ISRAEL UNDER THE MESSIAH

God promises that He will "break his yoke" from off the neck of Israel. The yoke that has been there a mighty long time ever since the time the Jewish leaders turned Christ over to be crucified. It has been a very hard journey, to say the least, for the Jewish people for rejecting their Messiah. This yoke speaks of slavery and Israel's bondage, slavery to the Babylonians for 70 years, and then God delivered them and brought them home, only to have history repeat itself again in 70 A.D. by the Romans.

The last king of Babylon that will enslave the Jews is the Antichrist, and God will break his yoke over the Jews at the end of the Great Tribulation when Jesus comes again. The LORD said, *"but they shall serve the LORD their God and David their King"* (Jeremiah 30:9). This is speaking of the Lord Jesus Christ and David being the man whom God originally called as the anointed king of Israel in which the linage of the Messiah Jesus came through.

David, who defeated Goliath, will receive his glorified body at the resurrection (i.e., the Rapture) with all the many saints. He will serve as King of Israel in the coming Kingdom Age, and do so under Christ, the King of Kings.

God told Israel to not fear nor be dismayed, for He will save them from afar. He tells them that their seed from the land of their captivity and Jacob shall return to the land of Promise. They will then have rest and be at peace and no one will be able to make them afraid again. This speaks of Israel's restoration at the beginning of the Kingdom Age.

The Words "and Jacob shall return" began to be fulfilled in 1948, when a part of the original Promised Land was declared by the United Nations as the recognized State of Israel. However, it will not be totally fulfilled until the Second Coming of the Lord Jesus Christ when all the Jews will return from all over the world.

God promised the Jewish people that He is with them, to save them. However, He will make a full end of all nations where He has scattered the Jews too, but He promises the Jewish people *"I will not make a full end of you: but I will correct you in measure and will not leave you altogether unpunished"* (Jeremiah 30:11).

God tells Israel that their wound is incurable and there is no one to plead their cause, and there are no healing medicines for them. In fact, the only healing medicine for this nation (or any nation) is the Cross of the Lord Jesus Christ. In terms of the world helping or healing Israel, their wound is incurable and there was no one to plead their cause.

God told His people that all their lovers have forgotten them, and they seek them not. God said these Words, *"For I have wounded you with the wound of an enemy, with the chastisement of a cruel one, for the multitude of your iniquity; because your sins were increased"* (Jeremiah 30: 14).

The *"cruel one"* was Nebuchadnezzar, but in the future, it will be the Antichrist. The key revelation to embrace is that even though God does not directly do the wounding, He does take responsibility for sending it and He is justified for doing it as He said, *"because your sins were increased."*

As we have written, most of the world and most of the modern church have been taught that God would never send evil to a person or to a nation. Due to this unscriptural truth, blindness has come over God's people, and the people of the world as they never connect the dots between their sin and the judgment of God. This is how Satan keeps the world deceived and in sin, with no fear of God, and no fear of the Judgment Day. The world creates a god of love only and not judgment, so that they can convince themselves that sin is no big deal. The Bible says that this is all due to the god of this world (Satan) blinding their eyes (II Corinthians 4:4). In other words, this is what is called "spiritual blindness," or the "Great Deception" led by the Great Deceiver, Satan himself.

God clearly tells Israel why He brings evil upon them, which is due to *"the multitude of your iniquity: because your sins were increased, I have done these things unto you"* (Jeremiah 30:15). But God lets them know that all the nations that have come against them will have their reckoning day as well. God said they that *"devour you shall be devoured"* (Jeremiah 30:16). But to the Jewish nation, God promises to heal their wounds! (Jeremiah 30:17). God will be faithful to His people in the end and why? Not because they are good, but because He is good, and He is a Promise Keeper. What He promised to Abraham a long time ago, He will fulfill in the end. But every nation that opposes Israel will be devoured, either now or later.

REBUILDING OF JERUSALEM

God will one day build the "palace" and it shall remain. This is speaking of the Millennial Temple of the Lord where He will rule in the Kingdom Age. Jerusalem will be the Capital City of the Lord's eternal reign. And out of Jerusalem shall proceed thanksgiving and the voice of merriment (Jeremiah 30:18-19). God said He would multiply the Jewish people and it will not be few. He will glorify them, and it won't be small. God has a great plan in the end for His people and for His city, Jerusalem, where Jesus died to set man free.

When the time of the Gentiles leading the world comes to an end, Israel, will be the nation that rules the world under Christ (Luke 21:24, Romans 11:25-29). God said in that day, *"You shall be My People, and I will be your God"* (Jeremiah 30:22). All of this is made possible because of the Cross of Christ.

But before that day, there will come the Great Tribulation. These will be the darkest days that the Jews and the world will ever face. The LORD spoke through Jeremiah, 2600 years before this time and said:

> *"Behold, the whirlwind of the LORD goes forth with fury, a continuing whirlwind: it shall fall with pain upon the head of the wicked. The fierce anger of the LORD shall not return, until*

He have done it, and until He have performed the intents of His heart: in the latter days you shall consider it"
(Jeremiah 30:23-24).

THE FALL IS COMING

One of the saddest chapters in all the book of Jeremiah is chapter 39. The prophesied judgment of Israel has now come. It is all so tragic and to think it could of all been avoided if only the King and the people had believed in the warnings of the prophet Jeremiah and repented.

There were three Babylonian sieges. The sieges lasted a total of two years. The army of Babylon came in and besieged Jerusalem. The city was broken up and all the princes of the King of Babylon came in and they sat in the middle gate. When King Zedekiah saw it, he fled. But the Chaldean army pursued him and captured him in the plains of Jericho (Jeremiah 39:6-7).

They brought the King of Israel to Nebuchadnezzar to have a meeting face-to-face; thus, fulfilling the prophecy God gave to Jeremiah (Jeremiah 32:4 and 34:3). Then the King of Babylon killed the sons of Zedekiah in Riblah right before his eyes and all the nobles of Judah were killed as well. Then he put out the eyes of Zedekiah so that he was now blind (Jeremiah 39:6-7). This is what the prophet Jeremiah pleaded with Zedekiah to avoid. How tragic and how very sad it all is.

JERUSALEM DESTROYED & THE PEOPLE DEPORTED

The Chaldeans burned the King's house and the houses of the people with fire and broke down the walls of Jerusalem. The anger of Nebuchadnezzar was incensed due to the failure of Jerusalem to surrender. This all sounds too familiar like the war between Russia and Ukraine that began in 2022.

This was the ending to the 500-year reign of Jerusalem as the premier city in the world. It would now be subject to gentile powers, as it is, at least in part, unto this very day. (JSESB, page 1317).

The captain of the Nebuchadnezzar's army Nebuzaradan would carry away the captive remnant to Babylon who were not killed in the slaughter. This was the third and final deportation. This all happened approximately in 586 B.C.

But Nebuzaradan left a remnant of the poor in the land. He gave them vineyards and fields. These people had been slaves of the nobles in Judah and now they were freed, and the nobles are dead or enslaved (Jeremiah 39:10).

The King of Babylon gave care for the prophet Jeremiah. No doubt, God put this favor in the heart of this wicked king. It's bad when the sinful world who knows not God treats the man of God better than the religious leaders of God's people.

The captain of the army, Nebuzaradan, set Jeremiah free and turned him over to his friend Gedaliah and he carried him home, so Jeremiah dwelt among the remnant people in the land of Israel (Jeremiah 39:14). Several months before Jeremiah was released from prison, he received a Word from God. The Lord told him that He would deliver him, and he would not fall by the sword, but his life would be spared because he had put his trust in the LORD (Jeremiah 39:15-18). God is always faithful and watching over His Word to perform it, and God always makes good on His promises. Jeremiah honored God in the midst of persecution, and now God would honor the prophet Jeremiah.

A GLORIOUS FUTURE

When the Lord comes back and sets up His Kingdom, He will be the God of all the families of Israel, and they shall be His people. What a glorious future God has for the Jewish people and the nation of Israel, (as well as all those who are in Christ; Jew and Gentile). There is coming a day when Israel will no longer be divided, but they will be one nation and all believing in Jesus as their Messiah.

God said that His people found grace in the wilderness and God established them in the Promise Land and gave them rest from their enemies. God said that He loves them with an everlasting love, and He will build them again into a great nation and she will be adorned with *"tabrets, and you shall go forth in the dances of them who make merry"* (Jeremiah 31:4). The word "tabrets" means a person who plays on his instrument. One day the people will be singing and dancing down the streets of Jerusalem as freedom will be finally found, as King Jesus rules and reigns from the capital city.

They are going to plant vineyards on the mountains and there is coming a day when the people shall cry and say, *"Arise you, and let us go up to Zion unto the LORD our God"* (Jeremiah 31:6). O Happy Day, O Happy Day,

When Jesus comes again and sets up His earthly Kingdom. It will be a day and time of great rejoicing and celebration.

God will bring His people from all over the world back to the Promise Land. They will come from the north, the south, the east, and the west. They will come blind, lame, and withered and God will heal them all. They will come weeping and with supplications. This weeping will be mixed with joy and sorrow. They will weep when they realize how long they were spiritually blind, and they will rejoice because they now see that Jesus is their One True Messiah.

REPENTANCE, THE ONLY WAY BACK

The Lord has redeemed Jacob and ransomed him from the hand of him who was stronger, which is speaking of the Antichrist who is filled with Satanic power. Therefore, they will come and sing in Zion and shall flow together in unity in the goodness of the LORD. They shall dance in celebration of their restoration and their victory, which was all wrought at the Cross of Christ. In the end, God will turn the Jewish mourning into joy.

He will comfort them and make them rejoice from all their past sorrows. Jeremiah said,

> *"Thus says the LORD; a voice was heard in Ramah, lamentation, and bitter weeping; Rachel weeping for her children refused to be comforted for her children, because they were not"* (Jeremiah 31:15).

Rachel was one of two wives of Jacob. She was the mother of Joseph and Benjamin; therefore, of the two kingdoms and the two people. She wept for her children figuratively speaking when they were carried captive to Babylon and again when they were slain by Herod in the time of Christ. Thus, to this extent, was the prophecy fulfilled as stated in Matthew 2:17-18. This verse also has meaning to the future as it pertains to the coming Great Tribulation (Zechariah 12:10-13; 1,9; Romans 11:25-29).

True repentance is the only way back to God. The word "repentance" means a changing of the mind, to turn from the way of sin and turn to God. If this is done, God will forgive and restore every time. The only question is, will sinful man return? Will God's backsliding daughter, return?

When one repents, their eyes are opened to the ways of God and why He does what He does. But as one continues in sin and rebellion, they cannot understand the ways of God as they should. But after one repents, they go from being a *"backsliding daughter"* to the "virgin of Israel." This is what is called in scripture as "justification by faith" (Romans 5:1).

After proper and sincere repentance comes blessing. Just as God has obligated Himself to judge sin, so He has obligated Himself to bless repentance. He will turn your backsliding ways into a habitation of justice and holiness. God will restore the sinner's weary sorrowful soul when one repents. As it has been said many times, God has never turned away one sinner who has truly repented.

God promises Israel that one day she will be a great nation again. And just as He has watched over them to remedy and discipline them as a nation; He will watch over them to build up and bless them again. We are already seeing the beginning of these scriptures being fulfilled as more and more Jews from all over the world are returning to their nation in these last days. Right now, the nation is growing at a rate that is faster than any other nation in the world. What is true physically right now will one day soon become true spiritually as well.

Jesus gave a prophecy about the nation of Israel that would take place in the last days just before He comes again. He said, *"Now learn a Parable of the fig tree; When his branch is yet tender, and putteth forth leaves, ye know that summer is near: So likewise ye, when you shall see those things know that it is near, even at the doors"* (Matthew 24:32-33).

In the Word of God, Israel is compared to a fig tree, as well as the vine, and the olive tree. Therefore, in this prophecy, Jesus teaches that when the nation is showing life again, that generation is going to see the coming of the Lord Jesus Christ. But take a closer look at the parable Jesus gave. He said the fig tree would be producing leaves, which means it is alive again; but He does not mention the tree producing fruit.

The nation of Israel, although alive and thriving after nearly 1900 years of being dead and desolate, is still not producing spiritual fruit. Why? Because they have not yet believed and received Jesus as their Messiah. This will begin to happen in the Great Tribulation with many Christian Jews being martyred. But then all of Israel will be saved at the Second Coming of Jesus Christ. Then and only then will the nation begin to produce spiritual fruit for the world to see again.

Jesus said,

> *"Abide in Me, and I in you. As the branch cannot bear fruit of itself, except it abide in the Vine; no more can you, except you abide in Me. I am the Vine, you are the branches: he who abides in Me,*

and I in him, the same brings forth much fruit: for without Me you can do nothing" (John 15:4-5).

One day soon the children of Israel will look at the One whom they pierced and rejected, and they will believe. And on that day, the Jewish people will receive their King, be reconnected to the Vine spiritually and from that point onward for all eternity, they will produce spiritual fruit that will remain forever.

NEW COVENANT

God said that He would make a "New Covenant" with the house of Israel and with the house of Judah. The Jews (most of them) have not accepted the New Covenant yet, but one day very soon they will, which will be at the beginning of the Kingdom Age. Israel did not keep the Old Covenant, which should have showed them, or at least it was intended to show them, that they were sinners and needed a Savior. The law of Moses was meant to be their tutor to lead them to Jesus and the Cross, as the Bible says: *"Wherefore the Law was our schoolmaster to bring us unto Christ, that we might be justified by faith"* (Galatians 3:24).

But now God said that He will write the New Covenant on their hearts, and He would be their God and they would be His people. They will no longer teach their neighbor with the words "Know the LORD" for they will all know Him. God promised that He will forgive their sin and remember their sins no more. What an amazing promise and what an amazing future the Jewish nation has, if only they would believe in God's Word right now (Jeremiah 31:33-34).

The city of Jerusalem will be built again, but this time it will be built for Jesus. This will all occur in the Kingdom Age. The whole land will be cleansed and will be holy unto the LORD; it shall not be plucked up, nor thrown down anymore, forever! (Jeremiah 31:40).

AMERICA IS IN IT'S FINAL HOUR

We have a nation right now that is mirroring ancient Israel. The same thing that happened to Israel in the days of Jeremiah is happening to our country today. Unfortunately, the United States of America is going down the same path as Israel did, and the Judgment that came for Israel was not good, friend. In fact, its destruction included slavery and death and I'm afraid that if America does not repent and turn back to God soon, our nation will suffer the same fate as ancient Israel did.

I know this is a sobering prediction but based on the Word of God, I cannot see any other outcome to this nation's rebellion and downright arrogance against God, the one Who founded this nation and blessed it as one of the greatest nation on earth.

The Bible says in Hebrews 13:8 that *"Jesus Christ the same yesterday and today, and forever."* Many people think that God has changed His ways under the New Covenant, and now He is less of a God of judgment and more of a God of love. No, my friend, God is a balanced God and He is unchanging. He is perfect in all His ways. It is us who are imbalanced both in our lifestyle and in how we view God. The bottom line is that He still judges sin, and He still judges nations who will not repent of their sin.

In this late hour, one might ask the question, "what can I personally do?" It is very simple; turn away from all deception and stop listening to voices of people who do not preach or teach the true gospel message. Don't attend churches that either water down the gospel message or add to the gospel message because God said both will be "accursed."

Come back to the Cross, preach Christ and Him crucified, give, and serve in a local church that presents the true Gospel message. Make it again all about Jesus. Die to self and everything that seeks to exalt self. Live out the Sermon on the Mount through the help and power of the Holy Spirit. Don't live for this world, but live for the Kingdom to come, pray as Jesus taught us to pray: *"Your Kingdom come, Your Will be done on earth, as it is in Heaven"* (Matthew 6:10). Understand we are living in the last days. Jesus said that the deception will be great in the last days, which I believe is the time we are living in right now. In fact, destruction is coming to this nation and the nations of the world very soon. The destruction will become so great that unless God shortened the days, no flesh would be saved (Matthew 24:22).

Jesus said that in that day, false Christs and false prophets will arise. This is, of course, speaking of the Antichrist and the False Prophet who are about to come on the scene very soon. They will possess the ability to show great signs and wonders that, if possible, shall deceive the very elect of God (Matthew 24:24).

The Greatest Deception the world has ever experienced is just ahead and it has already begun. So, come out from among the deception and do not get caught up in fighting for things that are temporal and not eternal. Do not allow a "Barabbas" spirit to come on you. This world is not your home and remember that you and I are just passing through. Remember that God has not called you to save society, but He called you and I to save souls out of society. As the scriptures says, *"Do the work of an evangelist"* (II Timothy 4:5).

TOTAL SOLAR ECLIPSE

On April 8, 2024, America experienced the second total solar eclipse which cut across the nation in the opposite direction of the total solar eclipse that occurred seven years prior in 2017. These two eclipses formed a giant **X** across our nation. The last time this exact thing happened in history was back in 1806 and 1811. After the second total eclipse that occurred in 1811, came a series of 3 giant earthquake that were all over 7.0 on the richer scale. These were the largest recorded earthquakes in America history. Now I ask you, could these two total eclipses happening again 200 years later be a warning sign from God that our nation is heading toward a great destruction due to our continual sinful ways? We will soon find out!

You may ask "What can we do in times like these? Our number one priority as believers in Christ is to do what Noah did with his generation before the flood came. You and I are to warn the world that a storm is coming and a flood that will destroy them, unlike anything this world has seen since the days of Noah's flood. It is called the Great Tribulation predicted in the Bible. The unfortunate news today is that just like in Noah's day most are not heeding the warnings of the coming judgment. Thank God Noah's wife, their three sons and wives did get on the boat, because through this one family, the whole human race was saved from complete annihilation. It is remarkable to think that no one else outside of Noah's family listened to his warnings. The Bible says that even the animals came two-by-two, and they got into the Ark. What a sad commentary to think that the animal kingdom had more spiritual sense then most of humanity.

But we are seeing the very same blindness right now in our nation and the world. People are so prideful and stubborn, and they do not want to listen or heed the warning of what is coming. How awful to remember when God closed the door to the Ark, and He was the One who closed it (Genesis 7:16). The entire population perished except for 8 people. What a horrendous sight to imagine.

Friend, if you have been reading this book entitled "The Great Deception" and you are not sure that you and your family are safe in God's Ark, then I want to encourage you right now to do something that will assure you of an Eternity with God and give you the peace of God that surpasses all understanding. Confess your sins to God, believe in what Jesus did for your on the Cross to save you from your sins, and surrender the rest of your life to following Him.

He will save you from the storm that is coming. That is what He came to do when He died on the Cross for your sins. He paid your debt of sin with His very life. It wasn't His sins that He died for; it was yours! He was perfect and He never sinned, not one time. But He shed His blood and died on that Cross for your sins and for the sins of the whole world.

Now let me encourage you to pray this simple prayer of faith and commitment to Christ. Pray this prayer and mean it with all your heart, and Jesus Christ by His Holy Spirit will come into your life right now and change it.

It is not the words of this pray that are so important, but it is the sincerity of your heart. If you mean these words, God will do a miracle for you right now. He will come into your heart and save your soul and change your life. You will be "Born Again!"

Pray to God right now and say these words out loud, so the devil can hear it.

SINNERS PRAYER

"Dear God in Heaven, I come to you in Jesus Name. I confess to You that I am a sinner and I need forgiveness. I am sorry for my sins, the things that I have done, the way that I have lived.

Please forgive me, please wash me, please cleanse me. Right now, I want to repent, turn from my sinful ways of Living and devote the rest of my life to following Jesus. Jesus, I believe you are the Son of God, God in the flesh.

I believe you shed your blood for me and died on the Cross. To save me. I believe you were buried and three days later You rose from the grave and You are Alive.

Right now, I open my heart and I invite you Jesus by the Power of the Holy Spirit, to come into my heart and Come into my life and change it. Please be alive in Me. And when my life is over, I ask you for a home in Heaven. In Jesus Name, Amen!"

If you just prayed that prayer and you meant it with all your heart, then you have become a new creation; old things have passed away and all things have become new (II Corinthians 5:17). You are now "born again" and Jesus by His Holy Spirit has come into your life. What an amazing spiritual transformation God has just done and will do in your life in the days ahead as you learn how to walk with Him.

I want to encourage you to find a true gospel-preaching church and commit yourself to it. Begin to spend time reading and studying God's Word (the Bible). Set time aside each day with Jesus, reading His Word and praying. Watch how this will become your favorite time of the day.

Tell others what God has done for you since you placed your faith in Jesus and what He did for you on the Cross. Let them know how they can be saved as well. Share with them the prayer that you prayed and invite them to pray it even as you have done. However, let them know that it is not a prayer that saves them, but its repentance and simple faith in Jesus Christ who died on the Cross, was buried, and three days later rose from the dead. Give them the good news, the gospel story!

I want to encourage you to call our ministry, Joshua Revolution, and let us know about your decision to follow Jesus Christ or your decision to come back to the Lord. We would like to send you a Bible and other resources to help you grow in your new faith. If you don't have a church and you live in the Greater Western New York area, we would love for you to come and visit our church, CrossRiver Tabernacle. Whatever we can do for you to help you grow in your knowledge of Christ, know that we are here to assist you.

I just want to conclude by saying that we love you. But even more importantly, Jesus loves you and He proved it when He died on the Cross for you! God Bless You!

JOSHUA REVOLUTION
PO Box 923
Grand Island, New York 14072
716.229.8000/1.888.444.2920
info@joshuarevolution.org

www.joshuarevolution.org

www.ingramcontent.com/pod-product-compliance
Lightning Source LLC
Chambersburg PA
CBHW070548160426
43199CB00014B/2419